VEILED
ATROCITIES

Additional Praise for *Veiled Atrocities*

"[K]nowing well how cruel Islamic laws are and that Saudi Arabia implements those laws strictly, I always thought I knew very well what kind of a cruel society Saudi Arabia would be. But after reading *Veiled Atrocities*, I realize that I knew far too little about the cruelty and brutality with which the heartland of Islam treats its own people as well as foreigners.... Alrabaa has documented these stories personally while teaching in Saudi Arabia, but I can guarantee that very few readers will be able to believe they are true."

—M. A. Khan, author of *Islamic Jihad: A Legacy of Forced Conversion, Imperialism and Slavery* and editor of Islam-watch.org

"Alrabaa gives the forgotten victims of the Saudi Arabian torture regime a face and a voice that deserves to be heard.... [He] is well acquainted with the exact wording of the hate message against Western societies and knows the way facts tend to be played down by the media, which would rather support the apologists and euphemists of the Shari'a than take a stand against the terror of this theocracy."

—Gunild Feigenwinter, German-Swiss author, feminist publisher

"*Veiled Atrocities* provides a chilling look at what happens when extreme religious observance and tribal culture merge to hold an entire nation hostage."

—Pam Meister, editor, FamilySecurityMatters.org

VEILED
ATROCITIES

TRUE STORIES OF OPPRESSION
IN SAUDI ARABIA

Sami Alrabaa

59 John Glenn Drive
Amherst, New York 14228-2119

Published 2010 by Prometheus Books

Inquiries should be addressed to
Prometheus Books
59 John Glenn Drive
Amherst, New York 14228–2119
VOICE: 716–691–0133
FAX: 716–691–0137
WWW.PROMETHEUSBOOKS.COM

14 13 12 11 10   5 4 3 2 1

Library of Congress Cataloging-in-Publication Data

Alrabaa, Sami.
    Veiled atrocities : true stories of oppression in Saudi Arabia / by Sami Alrabaa.
        p. cm.
    ISBN 978–1–61614–159–2 (pbk. : alk paper)
    1. Human rights—Saudi Arabia—Case studies. 2. Civil rights—Saudi Arabia—Case studies. 3. Islamic law—Saudi Arabia—Case studies. 4. Saudi Arabia—Social life and customs—Case studies. I. Title.

JC599.S33A37 2010
323.4'909538—dc22   2009047754

Printed in the United States of America

CONTENTS

6 CONTENTS

INTRODUCTION

"Human rights abuse" is a civilized euphemism for the barbaric ill-treatment of many innocent people in Saudi Arabia. No language in the world can fully describe the physical and mental suffering, the depths of injustice, and the inhumanity inflicted on those who are targeted for victimization. Their stories end abruptly with incarceration behind the walls of unknown prisons, mandatory deportation, murderous acts of arson, the executioner's blade, or a hailstorm of sharp stones aimed at a veiled human head. Their stories are silenced by coldhearted indifference and the complicity of the victimizer's family, petty officials, and the Saudi regime itself.

This book is not simply a general account of how repressive the Saudi regime is and how fanatic its religious establishment, Wahhabi Islam, is. Numerous books have been published about these issues. This book is a collection of true stories—stories of how people living in Saudi Arabia suffer under the Saudi regime and its Wahhabi fundamentalist establishment. These stories have not happened accidentally but represent a pattern—common practices that happen almost daily.

These stories document the practice of Shari'a law, which is a combination of edicts derived from the Qur'an and Hadith (a narrative record of the prophet Muhammad that Muslims are meant to imitate). Both the Saudi absolute regime and Wahhabis led by the "morality police," called *Mutawas*, who are notorious for their bestial brutality, use Shari'a and their whimsical tribal instincts to rule the richest oil country in the world. In Saudi Arabia there is no secular law and there are no modern courts. The Mutawas are the judges and the Saudi princes dictate the law.

The stories I tell here were first related to me in the 1990s and remain relevant today because the practices of the Saudi regime remain unchanged. I collected and documented these stories while I was teaching at King Saud University in Riyadh. They were narrated to me by the victims, their friends, or relatives. I cross-checked the stories by conducting multiple interviews. In some cases—amazingly—the actual victimizers themselves openly, often with condescending and smug contempt, corroborated the events.

The following stories and anecdotes appear in varying lengths and degrees of detail, and they may sound incredible, but they are not. The stories are real. They represent a pattern of social, political, and religious oppression found and continuously followed in Saudi Arabia. Only when you live in the country and speak Arabic do you get to hear such stories or to experience these veiled atrocities firsthand. Foreign reporters who are allowed into the kingdom are usually selected carefully and accompanied by Saudi intelligence agents. These reporters are allowed to interview and examine only what the agents approve of; these stories are different. They are true.

To protect both those who survived and those who dared to bear witness to the horrific details of the truth, I have used pseudonyms for those mentioned in the book. I have also altered identifying characteristics so as to protect the victims and their affiliates from persecution and maybe death, and to avoid prosecution filed by rich Saudi princes and Western courts infiltrated by Shari'a law.

Therefore, I have also changed to pseudonyms the names of all the princes and princesses mentioned in the book. Hundreds, if not thousands, in the Saudi royal family have names like Nayef, Mishel, Majid, Hissa, Truki, Migren, and Faisal. Their ages vary from one year to seventy, eighty, or more. Hence it would be impossible to tell who is who in the following stories. Very often, many Saudi princes do not know each other and have never met. Some of them have similar physical appearances. It is assumed that there are more than thirty thousand princes and princesses. Nobody knows the exact number. Saudi princes marry dozens of women and breed hundreds of children. Some of them do not even know how many sons and daughters they have. Besides, Saudis in general and princes in particular repeatedly use the names of their fathers, mothers, and grandparents when naming their sons and daughters.

While I was teaching at King Saud University, I was also asked to privately teach English and German to sons and daughters of some princes. Not because they could not afford native speakers of these languages. They simply wanted a bilingual teacher; someone who could speak both Arabic in addition to these foreign languages. Sometimes I told them that I was also teaching Prince so-and-so and Princess so-and-so, and I would ask, "Do you know him or her?" Very often the answer was "No."

Nevertheless, in order to avoid diluting *Veiled Atrocities* to fiction and maintain the authenticity of the these stories, I insist that the atrocities committed in Saudi Arabia are real and their perpetrators are Saudi princes, regardless of what their real names are.

The stories are narrated in a simple language that everybody understands because I want everybody to read the stories and learn how the "cradle of Islam" is ruled. Only when the world learns about what is really going on in Saudi Arabia will more public support rally and pressure increase on Western governments to force the Saudis to renounce religious intolerance and to respect human rights.

When I delivered the manuscript of this book to friends outside of Saudi Arabia and asked them to read it over, their response was uniform: they shook their heads in disbelief. Nobody in the civilized world seemed able to fathom the extent of the arbitrariness and the atrocities to which victims in Saudi Arabia are subjected. To them, the stories were incredible. Some remarked that I was telling stories about the actions of monsters from another planet. They could not believe that any human could act as does a Saudi corrupted by absolute power.

The Islamic terrorist attacks in New York, Bali, Madrid, and London were, in the main, carried out by Saudis or by Arabs who were brainwashed and trained in Saudi Arabia. The Taliban regime in Afghanistan was actually a replica of the Saudi regime. Saudi Arabia has financially supported, and is still supporting, fanatic Muslim organizations around the world. Therefore, it can hardly come as a surprise that at home, within the borders of this secretive country, the royal house behaves like a terrorist organization against its own inhabitants, both citizens and foreign workers. The house of al-Saud cultivates fanaticism, oppression, and arbitrariness. The process is systematic. While members of the al-Saud clan plunder Saudi Arabia's huge oil reserves, the so-called morality police— Mutawas—and the civilian police terrorize the population, in particular foreign workers, who are subject day in and day out to cruel, arbitrary victimization. They are picked up and arrested, jailed without trial, and barbarically tortured. Some are publicly and inhumanely slain after Friday prayer services.

In every one of their annual reports, international and regional human rights organizations have severely excoriated the Saudis' dismal human rights record. Yet Western governments read and then shelve these reports. They have decided, instead, to focus on the geopolitical advantages of Saudi Arabia; economic interests are more important than the victims of atrocious human rights abuse. It serves to mention that the religious intolerance and human rights violations depicted in the following collection of stories are not confined to the borders of Saudi Arabia. Saudi Arabia exports and funds Wahhabism (fanatic Islam) everywhere around the world. The fight against terror must begin in Saudi Arabia. Westerners cannot forget that fifteen of the criminals of 9/11 were Saudi. The West can no longer hide its ostrich head in the sand in return for petrodollars.

I have personally witnessed the purposeful silence of Western governments; while I was living in Riyadh, I translated for German politicians when they met with their Saudi counterparts. These politicians hushed up any reference to Saudi human rights abuse, nervous about damaging their economic interests. Back in Germany, the Free Democratic Party (FDP), for instance, accepted millions of dollars as a donation from the Saudis, which turned them into defenders of the Saudi regime. On one of his frequent visits to Saudi Arabia in the 1990s, a former leading FDP politician and chairman of the Arab-German Association was delighted to receive a donation of forty million dollars from an influential Saudi prince. The money was transferred to a secret account in Switzerland. Later, in 2003, the FDP politician committed suicide after this secret account was discovered by the German state prosecutor.

The majority of German politicians and mainstream media brazenly justify despotism in Saudi Arabia by referring to the country's historically deep-rooted traditions and economic strategic interests; hence, it will require time and patience to expect change in Saudi Arabia. Even Condoleeza Rice, the former US secretary of state, always included in her numerous press conferences apologies and euphemisms for the despotic Saudi regime, the foremost of which was that it was founded in "traditionalism."

The Saudis fully understand that the West, blinded as it is by oil, cash, and economic investment opportunities, is no threat at all. They demonstrate this with open contempt by daring to victimize Western professionals, not just third world workers. William Sampson, a Canadian-British biochemist, was snapped up by the Saudi police and jailed for two and half years on trumped-up charges. In his book, *The Confessions of an Innocent Man: Torture and Survival in a Saudi Prison*, he narrates how he was hellishly tortured and then forced, with four other Britons, to "confess" to a series of bombings in Riyadh and to espionage. The Saudis wanted scapegoats. They needed to "uphold their honor" by showing that no Saudi was capable of an act of terrorism against his own people. Neither the Canadian nor the British government was willing to show any muscle. They were willing to sacrifice their own citizens to keep the Saudi regime's feathers unruffled.

Barbaric torture, the slaying of innocents, and the elimination of others by flying them over the world's most forbidding desert—the "Empty Quarter"—and then tossing them out to be devoured by snakes and reptiles are not the fates of singular individuals. Numerous victims face these practices frequently when the Saudis administer fast-track "justice."

The purpose of this book, of these sad, true stories, is to rally more public support in the world to pressure Western governments into insisting that the Saudis stop the state-sanctioned terror within their borders. Similarly, the fascist regime in Saudi Arabia should be forced to stop cultivating fanatics who, after honing their skills on the ill-treatment of those trapped within the black hole of the kingdom, export their inhumanity to the world at large.

SAUDI SCHOOL TEXTBOOKS INCITE HATRED, VIOLENCE, AND DISCRIMINATION

O ne of the best ways to understand a culture is to examine how its children are reared and educated to instill within them the values, beliefs, traditions, and knowledge of their heritage and community. With this in mind, I went through school textbooks that are used regularly in Saudi Arabia. Here is an English translation of some passages from these books, which focus predominantly on monotheism and religion.

Fourth Grade:

- "Any other religion other than Islam is invalid (false)."
- "True faith" requires that one "hate (*yakrah*) the polytheists and the infidels."

Fifth Grade:

- "Every religion other than Islam is invalid."
- "It is not permitted to be a loyal to non-Muslims and to those who oppose God and His Prophet."
- "Whoever obeys the Prophet and accepts the oneness of God cannot be loyal to those who oppose God and His Prophet, even if they are his closest relatives."
- "A Muslim, even if he lives far away, is your brother in religion. Someone who opposes God, even if he is your brother by family tie, is your enemy in religion."
- "Just as Muslims were successful in the past when they came together in a sincere endeavor to evict the Christian crusaders from Palestine, so will the Arabs and Muslims emerge victorious, God willing, against the Jews and their allies if they stand together and fight a true jihad for God, for this is within God's power."
- "Jews are the people of the Sabbath, whose young people God turned into apes, and whose old people God turned into swine to punish them, as cited in Ibn Abbas: 'The apes are Jews, the keepers of the Sabbath; while the swine are the Christian infidels of the communion of Jesus.'"
- "The clash between our [Muslim] community (*umma*) and the Jews and Christians has endured, and it will continue as long as God wills. In this Hadith, Muhammad gives us an example of the battle between the Muslims and the Jews."
- "Narrated by Abu Hurayrah: The Prophet said, the hour [of judgment] will not come until the Muslims fight the Jews and kill them. [It will not come] until the Jew hides behind rocks and trees. [It will not come] until the rocks or the trees say, 'O Muslim! O servant of God! There is a Jew behind me. Come and kill him.'"
- "Muslims will triumph because they are right. He who is right is always victorious, even if most people are against him."
- "A woman who shows in public any part of her body except that of her eyes will be punished with hellfire by almighty Allah."

- "The infidels have established Christian hospitals and clinics and send medics all over the world. As one of the Christianizers said, 'Where you find people, you find pain. And where there's pain, there's a need for a doctor. And where there's a need for a doctor, there's an appropriate opportunity for missionary activity [Christianization].'"
- "The infidels have founded many schools and universities in the Muslim world at various educational levels. These include: the American Universities of Beirut and Cairo, the Jesuit University, Robert College in Istanbul, Gordon [Memorial] College in Khartoum, and others too numerous to mention."

Unfortunately, this kind of instruction pervades even the teachers' manuals.

Fifth Grade:

- Teach that after their death, non-Muslims will be sent to hell.
- Quiz: "Is it permissible to love the Jews and Christians? Of course not. Explain why."

Eighth Grade:

- Command Muslims to "hate" Christians, Jews, polytheists and other "unbelievers," including nondevout Muslims.
- Teach that the Crusades never ended and identify the American Universities in Beirut and in Cairo, other Western and Christian social service providers, media outlets, centers for academic studies of Orientalism, and campaigns for women's rights as part of the modern phase of the Crusades.
- Teach that "the Jews and the Christians are enemies of the [Muslim] believers" and that "the clash between the two realms" continues until the Day of Resurrection.
- Instruct students not to "greet," "befriend," "imitate," "show loyalty to," "be courteous to," or "respect" nonbelievers.

Ninth Grade:

- Define jihad to include "wrestling with the infidels by calling them to the faith and battling against them" and assert that the spread of Islam through jihad is a "religious obligation." [The word *qital*, translated here as "battle," is derived from the verb *qatala*, "to kill," and is virtually never used metaphorically.]
- Instruct that "the struggle between Muslims and Jews" will continue "until the hour [of judgment]" and that "Muslims will triumph because they are right" and "he who is right is always victorious."

Tenth Grade:

- Cite a selective teaching of violence against Jews, while in the same lesson ignoring the passages of the Qur'an and Hadith, narratives of the life of the Prophet, Peace be upon Him, that counsel tolerance.
- Teach the Protocols of the Elders of Zion as historical fact and relate modern events to it.
- Discuss Jews in violent terms, blaming them for virtually all the "subversion" and wars of the modern world.
- "Give examples of false religions, like Judaism, Christianity, paganism, etc."
- "Explain that when someone dies outside of Islam, hellfire is his fate."

By the way, over twenty Saudi schools, each chaired by the local ambassador from Saudi Arabia, are located throughout the world: Bonn, Berlin, Washington, Algiers, Ankara, Beijing, Djibouti, Islamabad, Istanbul, Jakarta, Karachi, Kuala Lumpur, London, Madrid, Moscow, Paris, Rabat, Rome, and Tunis. In fact, you can find some of the above lessons in many school textbooks in all the Arab Gulf countries: Egypt, Kuwait, United Arab Emirates, Qatar, and Jordan. Young boys' and girls' brains are stuffed with intolerance and animosity toward other religions and their followers. Then, as they grow up, they begin to act on what they have been taught: hatred, violence, and discrimination.

Wahhabism, Saudi Islam, is considered fundamentalist by many moderate Muslims. The truth of the matter is Wahhabism is a faithful inter-pretation of Islam. When you go through the Qur'an and Hadith, you find hundreds of passages in this legacy that incite hatred, violence, and dis-crimination. For further details, check out "Is Islam a Violent Faith?" (http://www.familysecuritymatters.org/publications/id.2287/pub_detail. asp) and "Woman in Hadith" (http://www.familysecuritymatters.org/ publications/id.2752/pub_detail.asp).

What does all that imply in terms of the war on terror?

The war on Islamic terror will remain futile unless the free world forces Saudi Arabia and the other Arab oil countries on the Persian Gulf to REMOVE hatred and violence from their school textbooks. The root causes of Islamic terror must be unearthed. This is not an internal issue and it has nothing to do with freedom of speech. The hatred that is taught in and around Saudi Arabia impacts all of us and world peace at large. The West must use all its leverage vis-à-vis these states to achieve this goal if it truly wants to win the war on terror.

I personally believe that the more Muslims around the world read the Qur'an thoroughly, the more they would turn their back to Islam. According to a recent unpublished survey by Berlin University, 13 percent of male Muslims have read the Qur'an, and among women it is only 7 percent.

Many Muslims around the globe, particularly non-Arabs, do not understand the Qur'an, which is written in an old, archaic Arabic. They learn about Islam from what their fanatic imams preach.

EDUCATION

Not only are the "morality police" and the "justice system"—if you could ever call them such—corrupt, but so is the education system. It is part of the Saudi effort to construct a "modern" façade. A former dissident colleague at King Saud University put it to me in private this way: "Saudi Arabia wants to show the world that it is a modern state. In addition to a national flag, modern cars, and modern highways, it has schools." The evolution theory of Darwin is banned from Saudi schools. Young students' brains are stuffed with Islamic fundamentalist tenets, as we examined in the previous chapter. Free research at Saudi universities is forbidden. What matters at the end of the day is a graduation "certificate." In a few words, the higher education system in Saudi Arabia is a diploma mill. All in all, the Saudi education system breeds fanatic Islamists rather than educated people.

A modern system of education was introduced into Saudi Arabia some forty years ago, with the discovery of oil. Before that, only the so-called "Qur'an schools" existed, where students memorized the Qur'an by heart. In addition to this, a little writing was taught. Only boys were educated; however, within the last twenty years, girls have been allowed to attend school, albeit principally in the larger cities. In the years when girls' schools were first opened—and even today—many Saudis believed female literacy is dangerous, since gullible young women might exchange love letters with unknown young men. It is generally believed that, if a woman falls in love, that in itself is a form of prostitution. Young people must enter into marriages arranged by their families, and they do not even meet their future spouse before the wedding. Getting to know each other, falling in love—both are foreign concepts. This philosophy is still supported by many Saudis, especially the elderly.

Therefore, the educational system in Saudi schools is totally different from anything in the West. Girls attend separate schools and have no contact with boys from kindergarten through university graduation. Boys are taught by male teachers, and girls are taught by female teachers.

When a large number of girls enroll at the Women's University in Riyadh, they must be taught by male instructors because of a shortage of female professors. However, male professors are not allowed to see the students. The university handles this situation in two ways: either he gives the lecture by video camera or he stands behind a specially treated glass screen that allows the students to see him but is opaque from his side. It is easy to hear the lecture because microphones and loudspeakers are used. However, Saudi girls do not ask questions of male teachers. According to Islamic belief, a woman's voice is sexually provocative.

The lack of contact can lead to bizarre situations. One day, a Western college lecturer was told to teach a girls' class. The lecture was delivered by video camera. He began with "Good morning," but wasn't too surprised not to hear a response, as that would have been immodest. He began the lecture. After half an hour, he asked for questions on any points that might have been unclear. He suggested that the girls send him their questions by fax, since he knew that hearing their voices would be considered a sexual stimulant. No questions were received, so he continued with the lesson. About an hour after his lecture, a Western female colleague who had happened to pass by the room while he was lecturing came to tell him: "You know, you really don't have to make such an effort. The girls were skipping out. There wasn't a single student in that lecture hall."

The girls, however, do like to turn up for their graduation ceremony. This is held annually in the main building, where the male students usually study. To divide the women from the male guests, a two-meter high fabric wall divides the parking lot into two sectors and snakes right up to the main entrance. The glass walls at the entrance to the building are plastered with sheets of blackout paper. The female students and lecturers arrive for the ceremony swathed in black from head to foot, even wearing black gloves. The male guests of honor are seated on a podium at the front—but behind a panel of tinted glass. This includes the governor of the city, the minister for scientific affairs, and the rector and the deans of the university. The women can see them, but the men can't see the women. During the distribution of diplomas, the prince passes the diploma to the young lady through a narrow slit in the glass wall. When she is called to receive it, it is not her name that is said aloud but rather an identifying number that she has received just before the ceremony. According to Saudi religious leaders, hearing a female name has an erotic effect on men.

In spite of the strict segregation of female students, the number of girls studying at Saudi universities has doubled. This is due to two reasons:

1. Some young fathers, who also got an education, respect learning and encourage their daughters to study. Why? Because an educated mother can help her children with their homework assignments.
2. A girl will campaign hard to continue her studies. Education will enable her to escape the isolation of life at home. In a technical college or university, she can chat and exchange experiences with other women.

Saudi women are generally allowed to take humanities courses at universities. After graduation, a few of them work at midlevel jobs. For the most part, they are employed as teachers or in child welfare positions. But, in order to work, a woman needs the written permission of her father, husband, or brother. Nowhere in the Islamic world is this so strongly enforced as in Saudi Arabia.

Saudi Arabia expects its children to attend school. Learning materials are presented quickly, and if a child falls behind, he or she is not assisted. Academic competitions and proficiency awards are few and far between. At the end of the year, all children are promoted to the next class. Similarly, all high school graduates are eligible for admittance to the country's three universities. If a student has low marks, "influence"—quietly requesting help from a high-ranking family friend—is used to guarantee university admission.

However, university studies are not much different from going to high school. University teaching methods follow a particular form. A narrow range of themes is explored in all subject areas. This information is presented to the students, who then memorize the material; this is called the "recorder method." There are almost no classroom discussions—for two particular reasons. First of all, in the interests of political censorship, all teaching materials, texts, and the opinions to be expressed by the professors are preauthorized by the Ministry of Education, so no "discussion" is needed. Second, the Egyptian professors, who are by far in the majority at Saudi universities, follow this system rigorously, semester after semester, so they won't have to create new lesson plans at any time. In effect, they never have to prepare for a lecture and are anxious to leave as soon as it's completed. At the beginning of each semester, students receive a packet of the subject matter that will be covered. Most students memorize the course material. They seldom do homework. It's either copied from homework that was submitted by students in previous semesters, or an outside person is paid to do the job. In any case, it's rarely assigned.

Students in both schools and universities are not motivated learners. In their home environments, one consistent fact is continually reinforced: their parents, relatives, and other men in the community get promoted, even if they are undereducated and performing poorly in the workplace. As long as a person has influential contacts, everything proceeds smoothly. And the teachers, especially the Saudi teachers, are just as unmotivated as their own students. They skip classes, which students then mimic. There is no chance of a Saudi teacher being fired. Also, Saudis are quickly promoted to the position of school administrator, which gets them out of the classroom and into an office. Their job performance is never reviewed, and they automatically take home a large annual bonus.

This is a typical dialogue that might take place between two recently graduated Saudi university students:

Mubarak: "My Dad got me a job in the Ministry for Electricity and Water. I'm going to be the director of a department. The Indian and Filipino workers will be going from house to house to read the meters. I'll be in my spacious air-conditioned office, reading the newspaper, drinking tea, telephoning friends, and cultivating contacts with useful individuals. Every once in a while, I'll disconnect the electricity and water supply of certain important clients. They'll come directly to me and ask for my help. By 'helping' them out, I'll have forged a relationship—something always useful against a 'rainy day.' Those kinds of connections you have to keep in place."

Mahmud: "My older brother got me a position in the Telecommunications Ministry. I'll be the director of services for a region. If telephone users find their line disconnected, they will contact me. I'll report it to the overseas provider, and they will fix it. Just like you, I'll get to sit in my office, drink tea, and chat with colleagues. What a nice job! I'll come and go as I like. Like you, I'll cultivate connections with leading citizens. If an important person doesn't have a telephone problem, I'll just disconnect his phone and wait to hear from him. My prompt and sympathetic actions will win me another influential friend. As for people whom I don't like, they'd better be ready for a long, long wait before their phone is reconnected. They'll know who the boss is."

Sarhan, a typical Saudi university student, can't wait to graduate. Almost every day of his childhood, his father's driver, a Filipino, dropped him off at school. His teachers, for the most part Egyptians, taught him a little reading, writing, and arithmetic. Sarhan usually skipped classes two days a week. It was boring to attend school every day. Why should he? His father didn't go to work every day, and certainly never on time.

In Saudi Arabia, parents are never informed of their child's absence from school.

Why bother? The school administrator's children also skip school. There are no parent-teacher meetings, and few parents know what grades their children are in. As for Sarhan, his report card often gave his results in classes in which he wasn't even enrolled.

Strict standards are in place in Islamic studies and art classes; therefore, children hate those two subjects. In the former, the Qur'an has to be memorized without any discussion of the meaning of the text. By the age of ten or twelve, a Saudi can recite scores of pages of their holy book like a cassette. In art classes, pupils are strictly forbidden to draw or paint images of people or animals, as it is forbidden by Islam; pictures create false gods, and Muslims believe that Allah is the only divine being.

However, publicity photos of the nation's political and business leaders can be found on billboards throughout the country. Their presence is tolerated by the religious leaders, of course, in the interests of political power and control. The children are left confused.

According to Islamic leaders, television images are acceptable because they can promote Islam to the masses. Foreign television series and movies show unveiled women, of course, which is debated by Islamic clerics. Some want television to show only images of Saudi Arabia's holy sites and to provide lectures on the Qur'an. Music and singing would also be forbidden. Others say that the images on TV are constantly moving, so they can't be worshipped. As for unveiled women, their images are "booty snatched from unbelievers, and therefore freely available for enjoyment by Muslim men."

Metro Canada reported on September 15, 2008, a "top Saudi judicial official says owners of satellite TV networks that air 'immoral content' should be prosecuted, punished and then given the death penalty if punishments don't deter them from corrupting people." Sheik Saleh al-Lihedan, the chief of the kingdom's highest tribunal, sought to explain an edict that he broadcasted in which he said it is permissible to kill the owners of satellite TV networks that broadcast indecent programs.

Academic freedom is limited widely in Saudi Arabia. Any discussion of the theory of evolution, Sigmund Freud, Karl Marx, Western systems of philosophy, and the history of art are strictly forbidden. Theological books or newspapers that have a critical or analytical stance are either forbidden or partly censored by the removal of the "offending" pages. Pictures of nude or seminude men and women in scientific or medical texts are blacked out with permanent markers.

Organized sport is popular the world over, and sports teams are the pride of most schools and universities. This is also true in Saudi Arabia. Saudi men and boys are allowed to play sports in public, but all women and girls are forbidden to do so—including foreign women. However, Saudi males have to wear shorts that reach their knees. This is also enforced in the matter of swimsuits. (A Saudi swimsuit consists of a long-sleeved shirt and pants that must cover the knees.) A Saudi man wears a short swimsuit only at foreign competitions, so he won't be laughed at.

In fact, the Saudi government does not like its traditions practiced by its citizens when they go abroad. For example, an announcement was made by the Ministry of the Interior informing Saudi citizens that they do not need to wear national dress when they leave the country, especially, one assumes, if they're off to celebrate the Carnival in Rio de Janeiro or Berlin.

In practice, Saudis wearing their national clothes outside Saudi Arabia draws much attention. They are stared at as weird, especially in the West. The Saudis also know that they are stigmatized outside their borders. They have fame for being financially rich but intellectually void, especially overseas. A study by Bielefeld University in Germany confirmed that attitude. The majority of Germans believe that a Saudi is rich but backward.

SMOKE AND DAGGERS

Work Ethics of Saudis in Academia

Clearly there are many issues with the educational system in Saudi Arabia—from the violence that is perpetuated via the course material provided to young Saudis to the corruption that has saturated the hallowed halls of higher education. To better understand the precarious situations facing foreign (and national) professors in Saudi Arabia, we examine the story of Tahmush, a professor who narrowly escaped the dangers of being an ambitious, hardworking, foreign university professor in Saudi Arabia.

"Do you really want to move to Saudi Arabia and work there? What if the Iraqis launch a rocket on Riyadh?" asked Klaus, with considerable anxiety.

"Relax," replied Tahmush. "The Iraqi army is weak. They've lost the war. It's peaceful down there now. Anyway, what am I going to do here in Germany? You know that I'm considered a foreign academic. The universities here have refused to give me a job. If I'm successful in Saudi Arabia, I'll stay there for life. Permanent unemployment in a country like this, as far as I'm concerned, is a kind of slow death."

Even the officials in the Saudi Embassy were surprised that Tahmush was willing to move to their country in 1991, shortly after the Gulf War ended.

Before the war had broken out, Tahmush had worked for five years as a lecturer at the University of Kuwait. Immediately before the war, he had left the country, sensing that the Iraqis would invade. It was getting dangerous, and the economy somehow anticipated the overnight invasion to come: the prices of food and goods were increasing daily, as well as becoming more and more scarce. Tahmush had flown to Germany, his second homeland, for the summer. He had a German passport, but his original and true nationality was Syrian.

His friend Klaus had given him the use of a small, wooden cottage in the forest—a cute and simple retreat suitable for lazy summer weekends. To save money, Tahmush lived there permanently. The Iraqi army invaded Kuwait in August 1990, and Tahmush ended up living in the cottage for over six months. In the winter it was very, very cold. He had to turn off the cold water; otherwise, the pipes would have frozen and burst. After that, he hauled his own water in an old car that he bought. His toilet was the forest. He heated the cottage with a little wood stove that he had brought up to Germany from Syria some time before. Although it wasn't luxurious, it was very romantic—especially when friends came to visit. They would all sit around the exotic little oven, drinking tea and smoking Middle Eastern water pipes and discussing the Gulf War. But it was an uncertain time, and, with no employment opportunities to be found in Germany or Syria, Tahmush had felt that maybe his future could only be found in the stars. After the liberation of Kuwait, the University of Kuwait did not recall him. It gave no reasons and the staff refused to answer his letters. His severance pay was cancelled and fifteen thousand dollars disappeared from his savings account with a Kuwaiti bank, which claimed that he'd never deposited any money with them. But he wasn't the only one to receive such treatment. The Kuwaitis were doing a profitable "housecleaning" of Arab nationals working in Kuwait, whose governments had not given them support in the Gulf War. Except for the Egyptians, Arab nationals were forced to leave—with no severance pay or compensation. Their savings accounts were wiped from the books of Kuwaiti banks.

Under these circumstances, Tahmush was pleased to get a job at King Saud University in Riyadh, the capital of Saudi Arabia. He quickly put himself through all the travel formalities and flew to his new home. For the first semester, he taught in the language center, giving classes in English and German. Abdullah, the director of personnel, was very pleased with Tahmush's Prussian work ethic. For his part, Tahmush was thrilled to be working again. His zeal bordered on self-exploitation. As a single man alone in the country, he allowed his work to be like a family and a hobby to him. He usually arrived at his office at six in the morning to drink an Arabic coffee laced with sweet-smelling cardamom. The lovely aroma wafted down the corridors. He worked until nine or ten at night. His job gave him pleasure, and in Riyadh there was little to do, so Tahmush worked long hours and spent most of his time at the university. Often, in the quiet of the evenings, Tahmush took a long walk around the beautifully landscaped university grounds. The security guards were suspicious of a pedestrian out alone for a stroll at that late hour. In Saudi Arabia, everyone travels by car, and no one walks for enjoyment and exercise.

Most of Tahmush's colleagues liked him. He was sociable, easy to get along with, and witty. They were amazed by his work ethic: no task was too much for him. For some colleagues, however, his behavior was unnerving; they derisively suggested that he slept in his office. Others said that he was married to the faculty. Their feelings about him were fueled by a bad conscience, as they did their allotted tasks and then immediately disappeared from the workplace, and had done so for years. At noon, they went home for lunch and a siesta. Tahmush used to lecture them, half-seriously and half-jokingly, "People, we are lucky to have jobs. There's nothing worse than being unemployed, believe me. Lack of work destroys the soul."

Mounir, a Lebanese colleague, whispered into Tahmush's ear: "It makes no difference to the Saudis whether we work hard, or we don't. They can fire us for the smallest mistake, or, indeed, for no mistake at all. That's why your colleagues exert minimal effort. This isn't the West, where good efforts are rewarded. And remember, if you have problems, they'll drop you like a hot potato. They have no loyalty."

Another colleague—a German who volunteered as the head of the German Academic Exchange Society but whose actual employment was with the German News Agency—told Tahmush: "Give it up. There's no point in doing solid academic work here in Saudi Arabia. The Saudis are only interested in quick money. And look at it from this perspective: if they stay backward, that favors Western countries. They'll keep depending on our experts and our products." Tahmush found his colleague's attitude cynical and demoralizing.

A Saudi colleague whispered to him, while his eyes darted around warily, that since the leaders of the country could rob the nation's wealth easily and with impunity, it was normal for an average citizen to have little enthusiasm for work and his own country's development. His voice then faded even softer. "This university is swimming in secret service agents. They work for the country's five secret service agencies. Under these circumstances, who is going to participate in open discussion and planning? It is possible, in this country, to disappear without a trace."

In spite of this advice, Tahmush continued to be annoyed by his colleagues' lack of work ethic. They were receiving salaries for doing almost nothing. The Saudi lecturers did the least, burdening the foreign employees with their uncompleted tasks.

This was complicated by the quasi-religious atmosphere of the university. All offices had to be locked up for a solid half hour at the times of the Muslim prayers. Every lecture and seminar was prefaced by prayers. The administration offices closed at around 11:30 a.m. daily, ostensibly so the workers could ritually wash before performing the noon prayers. However, most of the workers quietly disappeared and simply went home, even though their official working hours were from 8:00 a.m. to 2:00 p.m. Not that they would have done much of anything if they were Saudis; Saudi workers spent their time drinking tea and chattering while foreign employees did the actual work. No one dared to form an organization or give an unapproved seminar. Many topics were taboo: parliamentary democracy, women's emancipation, political parties, and Marxism. All religions, aside from Islam, were openly denigrated. Both Muslim students and professors tried to convert the foreign lecturers to their religion. They believed that everyone in the world was born Muslim but had been "deislamicized" as a child by the evil influence of other world religions.

King Saud University was a magnificent complex of buildings and a money-making investment for various Saudi princes. One owned the university's cafeterias and restaurants, another was in charge of maintenance and ran its colony of third world cleaning staff. These guest workers from India and the Philippines worked twelve to fourteen hours a day, every day, for ridiculously low salaries that were seldom paid regularly. They had no industrial safety of any kind and were at the mercy of their employers.

Although Tahmush found the Saudi society static, departments within the university itself could be subject to massive reorganization at breakneck speed at the whim of a single Saudi. For instance, Abdullah, the director of personnel, decided to expand the European-Language Learning Center into a full-fledged faculty. It would embrace Asiatic languages and even handle the translation of foreign books into Arabic. This kind of massive reorganization wouldn't be an easy task, and it was made even harder in an institution administered by Saudi employees who disliked work, which was surrounded in turn by a demoralized and cynical team of foreign lecturers who had relocated to Saudi Arabia only to enrich themselves.

Among the Saudis, the response was predictable. One lecturer, named Eid, was actually enthusiastic. None of the others were. Jasser was one of them. He had "bought" his doctorate from a small American university ten years before, and since then, he had done nothing but sign his name as the coauthor of books published in his field. But Jasser was a decision maker in his department, so others wanted to stay on his good side. Only 28 percent of the teaching faculty was Saudi nationals, and Jasser had good connections with those in positions of authority. He also cultivated the favor of students who came from influential families. For Jasser, the purpose of life was control and power, not loyalty and justice. He didn't understand friendship, and he didn't have any friends.

Qayed, another Saudi department member, had had his doctoral thesis written for him in Egypt and had probably received his PhD from Cairo in the mail, which was considered quite normal. He had majored in English but could barely speak it. He was a vice-dean for Administrative Development, but he wasn't sure of his job description and what he was supposed to do. Once in a while, he appeared in the Language Learning Center, occasionally in his office, and, from time to time, in a lecture hall. He also signed his name as the coauthor of new publications. Qayed was a deeply religious man who had decided to become a Mutawa, a defender of public morals. He worked for the secret service of a prince. William, an American who had converted to Islam, helped him in this. As a Westerner, William proselytized the Muslim religion, trying to gain new converts. He was well paid because he worked both for the same prince as Qayed and the CIA.

When Qayed was out of the university, he was busy with his own business enterprise: the importation of houseboys and maids from the Philippines. He actually kept housemaids imprisoned like the inmates of a work camp. About twenty girls were kept locked up like a herd of animals in a 180-square-foot basement room in his personal villa. When a client needed a housemaid immediately, Qayed just fetched one from the basement. The client didn't have to wait for the girl to be brought over from Manila.

Another of Tahmush's colleagues, Adnan, was a sixty-five-year-old Iraqi, a lazy and unscrupulous man with a history of dirty tricks. At one time, he had been a student in East Germany, where he had worked as an agent for the Stasi, the hated state secret police. His victims had been other Iraqi exchange students. Through his wife's connections with high-placed Saudis, Adnan had obtained his job as lecturer at King Saud University. There he had attempted to teach German, but now he was about to be fired. First of all, he was five years past the official retirement age. Second, he had a heart condition. And third, his teaching was terrible.

Adnan saw that Tahmush, with his bizarre and overmotivated work ethic, was working for Abdullah in the expansion of the language center. Adnan went to Tahmush and demanded the protection of his job, "or else things wouldn't go well for Tahmush." But Tahmush, as enthusiastic as always about hard work and dedication, shrugged off Adnan's request for "protection."

So Adnan started a campaign of rumors:

Tahmush was an Israeli spy. He had insulted the Muslim religion.

He was a Christian Arab from Syria.

The rumors circulated, but Tahmush's colleagues told him to ignore the nonsense and travel back to Germany for his summer vacation.

So he left.

Three weeks later, Tahmush received an urgent and hurried phone call from Riyadh. He had been fired, but the speaker didn't dare to say more. When Tahmush reached Abdullah by phone, everything was confirmed. Adnan was a friend of the chief of a secret service agency. Tahmush had been reported (by Adnan, of course) as a Mossad agent—an Israeli spy. Also, Adnan claimed that he had criticized the Muslim religion. The governor of Riyadh had had Tahmush dismissed; otherwise, he would have appeared not to have confidence in his own agents.

Tahmush, based once again in the cute cottage in the German forest, restarted his job search, feeling ambiguous about his situation. On the one hand, he was upset to have lost his employment again, especially after all of his hard work. On the other, he was grateful that he had followed his friends' advice to leave Saudi Arabia for the summer.

Tahmush's story could have had an alternate outcome: the death sentence. Many people are executed in Saudi Arabia because of false accusations that are dealt by those who have power—or those who want power. Public prosecutions take place every Friday. So Tahmush was happy, very happy, that the bad news reached him while he was in Germany. Because the punishment for criticizing the Muslim religion is beheading.

THE DEAN

Saudi universities infested with corruption are quite modest in terms of quality and performance, as Tahmush's story in the previous chapter demonstrated. The Saudi teaching staff still constitutes a minority. Most of the staff come from Arab universities. The majority of Saudi lecturers and professors graduate from Egyptian universities with little work and diligence. For Egyptian professors in Egypt, Saudi students and professors are a valuable asset. The majority of Saudi students get their degrees for little work and Saudi lecturers are promoted to professors without much merit and effort; their "publications" for promotion are largely written by Arab colleagues. The driving force behind all this is very clear. Egyptian professors dream of working in Saudi Arabia because there they earn much, much more money than they do in Egypt, and hence the Saudi would-be professors are of great help in that respect.

Dr. Faisal, a forty-two-year-old Saudi, is a lecturer at King Saud University in Riyadh. He also serves as dean of the faculty of humanities. The number of Saudi faculty members, however, is modest—only 30 percent. The rest of the teaching staff, for the most part, is from Egypt because there are well-established academic ties between Saudi and Egyptian universities. After all, the first modern universities in Saudi Arabia were founded by Egyptians. The rector of Dr. Faisal's university is, in fact, Egyptian.

A cultural agreement between Saudi Arabia and Egypt provides a framework whereby Egyptian universities provide their Saudi counterparts with technicians, administrative personnel, and instructors. Egyptian assistant professors and lecturers are very keen on getting positions in

Saudi Arabia. By Egyptian standards, the salaries offered there are fabulously high: one month's pay in Saudi Arabia is the equivalent of a year's earnings at an Egyptian university.

Due to their large numbers, Egyptian academics working at Saudi universities control a majority of the votes cast at promotion committee meetings. Therefore, their support is important in determining whether or not a Saudi lecturer or assistant professor is promoted. The promotion system used in both countries is based on the American model; that is, a candidate is promoted after he has published a specified number of research articles that are ratified by a panel of the committee members. The Egyptians make good use of their power. They create a situation whereby the Saudi academics are dependent on them. But, in reality, they are dependent on each other.

Naturally, Dr. Faisal, a lecturer and a Saudi national, would like to be promoted. He uses the following method to ensure his success. First of all, he has foreign colleagues write for him scholarly articles that are published under his name. When his published papers near the requisite number, he attempts to recruit Egyptian professors to participate in his promotion meeting. These professors confidentially assure him of their full support. In Egypt, the battle to get a university position in Saudi Arabia is hard fought, as the economic situation in Egypt is worsening day by day. And Saudi Arabia, which lies right next door, is a veritable gold mine.

Dr. Faisal then flies to Egypt to recruit support. Before his departure, he has researched which contacts will provide him the most influence. The vice-rector of one of Egypt's largest universities has shown a strong interest in being approached. And, as vice-rector, he is acquainted with nearly all the humanities professors and academic experts in Egypt. Dr. Faisal knows that he can enlist the support of those individuals by enticing them with a great offer: the chance, in the future, to be asked to assess the worth of scholarly papers written by Saudi academics. Their endorsement would mean that a Saudi owed them a favor. It would be a win-win situation.

Upon his arrival in Cairo, Dr. Faisal is received at the university by Professor Ali, the vice-rector of the university. Professor Ali is surrounded by an actual entourage—a carefully assembled and hierarchically assembled delegation. It includes his brothers, an advisor to the minister of science, the dean of the humanities faculty, the department head for social sciences, and two assistant professors. Dr Faisal's reception isn't just cordial; it is positively exuberant. But, to tell the truth, Egyptians are well known for their charm and good humor.

Dr. Faisal is then invited to dinner in his hotel restaurant. During the journey, those members of the delegation who share his taxi heap him with flowery praise. For example, Professor Ali informs Dr. Faisal that his presence has brightened the skies of the entire country. Dr. Faisal happens to note that the streets are quite crowded. Answer: All Egypt is celebrating the visit of Dr. Faisal!

After their dinner, Professor Ali and the others bid farewell to Dr. Faisal, who returns to his hotel room. But shortly afterward there is a knock at the door. He opens it to discover a young woman in her midtwenties standing before him with several books in her arms.

"May I help you?" he asks, totally surprised.

"Are you Dr. Faisal?"

"Yes."

"I am so sorry for appearing like this out of nowhere. I'm a student at al-Shams University, and I study social sciences. I happened to be sitting at the next table to yours in the restaurant, and I learned from your conversation that you're a professor in Saudi Arabia. I'm writing a research project on the educational system in your country. Please, may I come in? I know that it's a little late, but I won't stay long."

Dr. Faisal is confused. He is a religious man, but rather liberal. True enough, he prays five times a day—but if he can't get around to it, he'll settle for one long prayer in the evening. As for sex outside of marriage, it certainly wouldn't be proper, of course.

"I'll stay. But not for long, I assure you," she says, and walks in with a smile.

According to Dr. Faisal, all they did was discuss social structures in Saudi Arabia's schools. According to Professor Ali, the lady seduced him, and they ended up in his hotel bed. She was a student who also worked part-time as a call girl. Professor Ali had given her the job of entertaining his guest, and had, in exchange, guaranteed her good graduation marks. Dr. Faisal should enjoy his visit to Cairo! He should come back often!

The next morning, Dr. Faisal and Professor Ali meet for breakfast. Dr. Faisal gives Ali the names of three Saudi students who are currently writing their doctoral theses at the University of Cairo. They need help.

"No problem," says Ali. "Help is what they'll get." It might be useful to mention at this point that many Saudi students at Egyptian universities need "help" because they are too busy with girlfriends to focus on their studies. By Egyptian standards, they are incredibly rich, so they can certainly enjoy a fine lifestyle. For this reason, there are plenty of Egyptian women intent on monopolizing their time.

Dr. Faisal then pulls two files out of his briefcase and says: "Here is an article written by me, and one written by a colleague. Can you arrange for their publication? I'm aiming for an assistant professorship."

"Not a problem," replies Professor Ali. "As good as done. The editor of the journal is a friend of mine."

In fact, Ali knows all the publishers and editors of Egypt's academic journals. He also knows the key members of the advisory boards of publishing houses, which, if they are large, are undoubtedly state owned.

Professor Ali and his colleagues are skilled at making money from job-related activities. For instance, they earn a lot from the sale of textbooks. Almost every Egyptian professor obliges his students to buy his own published book as a course requirement.

Since a professor often has over a thousand students attending his lectures each semester, this can easily double his income.

The textbook itself is usually created in a particular way. An Egyptian professor translates selected chapters from foreign-language textbooks into Arabic. Alternatively, he can have his assistants do the translation for free. Usually, a professor has two or three assistants; they are dependent on him for promotion and need to curry his support.

As in any business, academics have to take full advantage of opportunities as they arise. For instance, Ali's friend and colleague Professor Guhari was awarded a visiting professorship at a German university for three months, which also employed two of his doctoral candidates. They were employed as short-term lecturers. Professor Guhari arrived with his family, quickly contacted the two candidates, and visited the university library with them. They checked out several textbooks from the category "Sociology in Folklore." Then the work was divided and assigned. Each candidate was to loosely translate a few chapters from various books into Arabic.

Three months later, the "new book" was ready. It contained no references to the original sources. It was titled *An Introduction to the Sociology of Folklore*, by Professor Mohammed al-Guhari, PhD, and released by Dar al-Maref Publishing House, Cairo. Getting it published in Egypt had not been a problem. He himself, after all, was a professional advisor to the state publishing company. As for the translators? Their efforts were as unacknowledged as if they had been ghosts.

And now back to Dr. Faisal, who has left Egypt and returned to Saudi Arabia. He has successfully recruited Professor Ali. In exchange, he arrives in Saudi Arabia with a list of names: Egyptian lecturers and professors, from various disciplines, who would like to be invited to work at Saudi universities. The mutual dependency of the two men is now perfectly balanced.

However, Dr. Faisal knows what Professor Ali really wants, and he knows its benefits, too. Consequently, the year brings exciting changes for Ali. He moves to Riyadh to work at Dr. Faisal's university. After being met at the airport with warm words of welcome, he moves into university housing—a large apartment—and receives a light timetable with few lectures and seminars. He is appointed a representative on the University Academic Council for the Faculty of Humanities. Eighty percent of its members are Egyptian.

That year, Dr. Faisal submits his application to the council for promotion to a professorship. With the help of other Egyptian council members, Dr. Ali identifies sympathetic experts in Dr. Faisal's field who support the worthiness of his publications. Dr. Faisal becomes a full professor.

Dr. Faisal has many other Saudi colleagues who also know how to personally benefit from their employment with a university. First of all, there is Rabi, the director of the English Language Training Center. He dismisses five to ten language instructors from Western countries each year.

He is then obliged to visit England for two to three months to recruit new teachers, which conveniently allows him to get away from his wife, and also pass his free hours in interesting ways in fascinating, distinctly liberal London.

And then there is Abdulrahman, who is in charge of assigning housing to foreign faculty. Only recently was he able to obtain an undergraduate university degree. It simply wasn't possible until he was put in control of matching professors to appropriate apartments. The university apartments are coveted: they are fully serviced, attractive, and in short supply. Abdulrahman had carefully matched professors to the most desirable units based exclusively on their willingness to help him get his degree. He is now pursuing postgraduate studies by distance learning through the University of Cairo.

Abdulrahman's brother, Khalid, is an office manager at King Saud University.

He also earned his university degree while holding that position, although it's strange to say. As a dedicated employee, Khalid also consented to assume the onerous task of dealing with the university's ongoing renovation and purchasing needs. Since then he has mysteriously become rich. The contracting firms that he "pays" are fictional. As for major university purchases, they are undertaken by Khalid personally, who simply pockets the money and forgets to go shopping. For many years, the university library has gone without receiving new books, as Khalid controls the library budget. He is even in charge of the offices and toilets. The offices can't access paper and other stationery supplies. As for the bathrooms, they haven't seen toilet paper or soap in years.

THE "MORALITY" POLICE

In addition to the corruption that has contaminated the educational system of Saudi Arabia, there also is much immorality to be found within the country's so-called "morality" police. Here we examine stories about some of Saudi Arabia's Mutawas (a kind of religious police, also called morality police), who are not few in number, especially in the larger cities. Mutawas are pseudoreligious Muslims who function as guardians of public morality. In some cases, they are appointed by official Saudi authorities, in others, by independent organizations of religious fanatics.

The Mutawas believe that they have a mandate to act on behalf of Allah and his prophet Muhammad, and they are certain that their efforts will win them a place in paradise.

They patrol the streets to ensure that Islamic customs—in accordance with Saudi tradition—are adhered to by everyone. Their particular interest is to make sure that all women, both Muslim and non-Muslim, are completely veiled from head to foot. They also make sure that all activity ceases during the five daily prayer times. Sometimes they also force non-Muslims to attend prayers. Anyone who does not observe the country's strict customs—whether deliberately or out of ignorance—is arrested.

For instance, if a person is out walking on a public street during prayer time, he will be quickly scooped up into a patrol van by the Mutawas, if need be, with violence, and taken to one of their holding stations. There he will face religious lectures for a couple of hours, or perhaps a couple of days, depending on their mood.

A mother in the parking lot of a shopping center lifts her crying child into the backseat of a sports utility wagon as she attempts to comfort and calm him down. In doing so, her abaya—a black, concealing outer garment that reaches right to the ground—gets twisted, so that her ankles become visible. A passing Mutawa notices this and screams at her rudely to tend to her offensive appearance. Her husband, who is approaching the car, asks what is going on, and, as a response, is arrested, bundled into a police van, and taken to a police station. There, an angry lecture is shouted at him about the proper way a Muslim woman should dress when she is in public, and how she should move to avoid exposing her body in any way. He is told that he is completely responsible for his wife's actions and behavior. His role is to keep her constantly under surveillance, so if she ever accidentally exposes any of her skin, he can immediately correct the shocking situation.

After a busy afternoon of shopping, a family is relaxing on the lawn in a designated green area. The father goes to a nearby ice cream shop to buy cones for everybody. As they are enjoying their treat, a Mutawa passes by. He yells at the woman to get her behavior in line. The baffled husband asks the Mutawa what the problem is, and is informed that she is showing her tongue while licking the ice cream. In his opinion, women should lick ice cream cones in private.

Seldom does a husband escape an encounter with the Mutawas with one lecture or one trip to the police station. The man whose wife has demonstrated unprincipled behavior is often summoned back several more times. The subsequent lectures are actually small, theological seminars.

However, the arrogant and ever-vigilant Mutawas are well known for hypocritical self-righteousness, and this can be seen in many examples of unprincipled abuse.

One Mutawa brought his luxury American car—manufactured by "unbelievers," by "infidels"—to an exclusive repair shop. Eight Indian mechanics were employed there: five Hindus and three Muslims. The business belonged to a Saudi, a semiliterate police officer who had purchased the building and all the tools and equipment. The ordering of new tools and the knowledge of how to repair all the latest models were in the hands of the Indian employees. These workers had to pay the owner eight thousand Saudi riyals each month, whether they collected it from customers or not. If they didn't hand it over, they would be deported back to India with the return flight tickets that they had had to purchase before being allowed into Saudi Arabia. In consequence, they often worked fifteen to eighteen hours a day. Any repairs to the vehicles of the owner and all his relatives had to be done for free. And yet the Saudi shop owner was a devout Muslim who prayed five times a day without fail.

This Mutawa returned to the shop two days later to pick up his car. The repairs cost 1,700 Saudi riyals (453 US dollars), including parts and labor. The Mutawa inspected his vehicle; everything was in order. Suddenly the call to noon prayer wafted on the air from the local mosque. He gruffly summoned all eight workers, as though he were calling a herd of cattle, ordering them to participate in the prayers. The Hindus immediately started to make a silent and discreet beeline toward their lodging—a makeshift barracks about as comfortable as a goats' stable, which leaned against the garage wall. The eight Indians slept, cooked, ate, washed, and answered the calls of nature in that single room.

But the Mutawa commanded them to return: "Come back here! We are all going to pray together." They cast nervous, sideways glances at each other, and then one of them hesitantly ventured the meek reply, "Sir, we are not Muslims." The Mutawa responded in a loud and aggressive tone, "That doesn't matter at all! Prayer will cleanse your souls of the filth of your religion! Line up behind me, and don't talk back!" Realizing that they had no choice, all eight Indians lined up behind him as he led the prayers. Alarmed and insecure, they attempted to follow ritual bows and prostrations. Afterward, the Mutawa said that he wanted to take his vehicle for a test drive. He drove off without paying, disappeared, and was never seen again.

Many Saudi Muslims believe that Islam is vastly superior to all of the world's other religions. They believe that as a reward for their fidelity, God forgives a Muslim's every mistake if that person prays and fasts. However, God forgives only Muslims. Many Saudi Muslims also believe that Muhammad allegedly stated that on the Day of the Last Judgment, no matter what, all Muslims will be admitted to paradise. With this idea as the basis of his religious philosophy, our dishonest Mutawa's line of reasoning is as follows: God forgives a Muslim if he cheats or defrauds another person, just as long as the victim isn't a fellow Muslim.

Omar, a Syrian university lecturer working in Saudi Arabia, also encountered the heartless Mutawas on their rounds. He had recently married and was now responsible for the daily grind of getting his wife to her workplace, since women aren't allowed to drive. She was a medical doctor and worked in a hospital. Her making the trip by bus was problematic: the buses were usually dirty, unreliable, and hopelessly overfilled with male commuters. A taxi was also out of the question; according to the Mutawas, a single woman traveling by taxi is a religious offense. Omar was left to the task of ferrying his wife back and forth. He drove her to work in the morning, brought her home at noon for the three-hour break, and then drove her again for the afternoon shift.

On Wednesday evening, Omar picked up his wife as usual. They were driving along the public road, listening to music on the car radio, swapping jokes, and anticipating a stress-free, enjoyable weekend together. Suddenly a morality police van swerved in front of Omar, and, through a loudspeaker, he was ordered to pull over. Four Mutawas scrambled out of the van. As they approached, one of them loudly jeered a question: Who was the woman in his car? "My wife!" replied Omar indignantly.

"Anybody can come up with that story!"

Omar was new to Saudi Arabia and didn't know that the Mutawas have the authority to flag down motorists and ask personal questions. He leaned out of the car window and asked the four men who they were. "Is that any of your concern?" retorted one Mutawa angrily, and then added, "It looks like it's come to the point where foreigners don't know our role." With that, he dealt Omar a hefty slap across the face. "You must submit to the dictates of Islam, rather than questioning who points you toward religious behavior. In this country, all must respect the moral principles of Islam, even unbelievers like you. This is a sacred country, a Muslim country!"

Omar got out of his car and punched the man.

The other three Mutawas rushed to their colleague's assistance; they pushed Omar against the side of his car, restrained him, and beat him until his blood dripped onto the pavement. His wife screamed for help and shouted at them, "Stop! This is my husband! Leave him alone!"

"If he were your husband, he wouldn't have been laughing with you. A husband never laughs with his wife in a public place!" replied one of them.

The doctor pulled an English-language copy of their marriage certificate from her purse and showed it to the Mutawas. They had been legally married in the United States.

Omar and his wife were arrested on the spot and detained for deportation. Later, they were forced onto a plane and summarily deported.

Ibrahim is a liberal-minded Saudi. He is married to a Canadian of Chinese heritage. They have three daughters, ranging from six to seventeen years of age. The children have Saudi nationality, but the wife doesn't; she only has a residency visa.

One day, Ibrahim's wife received an invitation to the official opening of an art show in downtown Riyadh. The reception was, of course, only for women. Ibrahim drove her and their daughters to the event. At the gate of the exhibition hall, the woman and the three girls were stopped by two Mutawas and asked to produce their identity documents. The woman showed her residency visa and was admitted. The daughters showed their Saudi identity cards and were refused. The Mutawas explained that the event had been organized by foreigners and would be patronized by foreigners. It wasn't advisable that young Saudi females be admitted to such an event, where their pure attitudes would be contaminated and defiled by viewing the pictures and hearing the opinions of foreign women.

Saudi television is dominated by religious programs that seem to bring the Mutawas right into Saudi living rooms. Most programs are built around letters submitted by viewers, which are read aloud and then receive a response by a religious authority. The letters often repeat themselves and are mostly bogus.

In response to the question whether Saudi children should be allowed to have Christian playmates, a scholar who was the president of the Agency for Islamic Legislation responded: "Adult Muslims should avoid coming into contact with Christians, Hindus, Buddhists, or people of any other religion,

so under no circumstances should Muslim children be exposed to nonbelievers. Muslims should spend time only with others who share their faith.
Muslim children should only have Muslim playmates, because they are
easily influenced by impure religious customs and traditions. A Muslim
family should do everything in its power to ensure that its neighbors are
fellow-Muslims. Non-Muslim neighbors and coworkers should be avoided;
if possible, try to get them removed. Saudi Arabia is a holy land and should
not be defiled by the filthy presence of unbelievers. We have enough cultural
and social contamination from Western countries, from the Judeo-Christian
world, as it is. They are all damned," lectured Dr. Abdullah al-Lhedan. Then
he added, "We must follow the example of our Prophet, peace be upon Him,
who fought against the Christians and Jews in Mecca and Medina. He
refused to have them as neighbors, and he refused to trade with them. Saudi
Arabia must not just boycott Israel, but also the entire Western world!" However, Dr. al-Lhedan has a home filled with every modern convenience—
electrical and electronic—and drives an American luxury car . . . all of which
were invented and then manufactured by "unbelievers."

Later in the same program, an Indian Muslim voiced concerns about
his job. "I am a practicing Muslim, and work in a shoe store. Sometimes
women come into the shop without a male chaperone to purchase shoes. I
have to serve them. Can I continue with this job? I haven't found another
position, and when I do, I'll have to pay a sponsorship transfer penalty of
two thousand riyals (534 US dollars). My income is only five hundred
riyals ($133) per month."

"Brother Nur al-Hak, you must not continue with this job," answered
the academic. "A good Muslim lives and works without any contact with
unknown women. He should not look at them, and certainly not serve
them. Brother Nur, you must change your job immediately. What you are
doing is a sin and an insult to Islam. If you don't find another job, then
follow the example of the animals on God's earth. They do not work, yet
they manage not to starve."

(Here it might be useful to point out that the animals on God's earth
don't practice sexual segregation and none are shrouded in black veils.)

A Saudi girl wrote to the program complaining that her father was forcing her to marry an old man. She had just turned fifteen, and her husband-to-be was almost sixty. The man was very rich and intended to shower their family with money. Could she refuse this marriage?

Sheikh Abdullah intoned: "Praise be to Allah! You must accept this marriage for two reasons. First of all, you must respect all of your parents' decisions. If you are making your parents happy, then you are also pleasing Allah. A father's decision must only be rejected if he turns his back on Muslim teachings or wants his children to renounce the faith. Secondly, it is a good idea to marry this man in spite of his age to rescue him from the temptation to marry a foreigner or a non-Muslim. A good Saudi Muslim woman will sacrifice her own personal happiness to help her society by propagating racially pure Arab offspring. We must populate our holy land!"

(Here it is worth commenting that almost all Islamic teachers in Saudi Arabia apply an arbitrary and narrow interpretation of their religion by consistently reinforcing and insisting upon the dominance of men over women.)

Sheikh al-Lhedan was asked by one viewer if he could be allowed to use his left hand to eat and drink, since his right arm had been amputated after an auto accident.

His answer: "No, definitely not, even if your only hand is your left hand. First of all, you know that the prophet Muhammad, Allah bless his soul, ordered us to wipe our backsides with our left hand and to pour water with our right hand to cleanse the left after it has done its job. Nowadays we don't have to pour water with our right hand—it comes out of the tap. However, that doesn't allow us to spurn Muhammad's teachings. Over the left side of a person's body, devils are leering at him, while on his right side he is accompanied by angels. Therefore, the left hand is always unclean; it is problematic. Therefore I request our viewer, who does not have a right hand, to allow himself to be fed by someone else. He is free to work with his left hand, that's not a problem, but using it for drinking or eating is strictly forbidden."

During the same broadcast Sheikh al-Lhedan had to grapple with a similar question. It concerns feet. Should one step into a mosque with the right or the left foot?

His answer: "First, let us remember that only Muslims are allowed to enter a mosque. Non-Muslims are never to be admitted, because their dirty souls frighten away the angels from the building. Allah and his prophet Muhammad, peace be upon Him, have declared that the presence of Jews and Christians will render a mosque unclean. As for your question about feet, well, they are judged exactly like hands. The left foot is less clean. It is believed that our Prophet said that the angel Gabriel kicks unbelievers into hell with his left foot. Therefore it is advisable to enter a mosque with the right foot. First the right, and then the left."

Another television viewer had an interesting question. When a man hears the word "woman" mentioned in conversation, is he allowed to say "May God keep you far from their uncleanness" to his companion? His wife gets angry when she hears this expression used and claims that it is not Islamic.

Sheikh al-Lhedan replies, "Please inform your wife that it is indeed Islamic, as it was introduced by our Prophet himself. Each time the word 'woman' was mentioned, Muhammad told all those assembled "May God keep you far from their uncleanness." The meaning of this sentence is straightforward. Women menstruate regularly, during which time they are ritually unclean. A Muslim man must never touch a menstruating woman, and should, indeed, stay far away from her at that time. This is the origin and meaning of that saying."

Another query came from a viewer who had heard that watching television and listening to the radio were un-Islamic.

"Yes, that's true, but distinctions have to be made," explained Sheikh al-Lhedan. "Religious programs like this one are certainly advisable. Listening to the Qur'an being chanted is the best, if that is possible for you. Documentary films about Islam are recommended, but a man should not look at any television show if a woman will appear on the screen. It is also forbidden to listen to women on the radio. Remember that a Muslim man is not allowed to hear the voice of an unknown woman. That has an uncontrollably erotic effect on him. It is always seductive and will tempt him away from his prayers." He then added, "This leads me to another theme that I simply must discuss: music, singing, and dancing at weddings. All of these are signs of decadence. In the early years of our religion, they did not exist in our culture. These are influences from the Christian Arab populations of Lebanon, Syria, and Egypt. And, of course, they are exported by modern Western society. These regrettable practices are beamed into our very houses by satellite TV stations. They invade our homes and infect out wives and children. These TV stations must be blocked. In our daily lives and at our weddings only the chanting of the Qur'an, our holy book, should be heard."

Sheikh al-Lhedan made a habit of terrorizing Saudi radio and television stations. On television, men and women could not be shown together. During interviews, men and women sat in segregated groups in what was actually the same studio, but a "split screen" was used by the cameras. On both radio and TV, a man was never allowed to interview a woman, and a woman was not allowed to interview a man.

Najat, a young Saudi woman who was almost twenty, had been born deaf and dumb. One day she went out to one of Riyadh's largest shopping centers with one of her younger brothers, Taleb. He dropped her off and went to do an errand; he planned to return in an hour to fetch her.

Najat was able to make her purchases in less than an hour, so she went outside and stood in front of a large shop window so her brother could see her. To pass the time, she examined the beautifully decorated display.

A "morality" police car cruised slowly past. The Mutawas drive large, late-model, air-conditioned vehicles. They are equipped with a fridge for refreshments, radio equipment, binoculars, and handcuffs. A sheet of tinted glass divides the interior into two compartments; in the rear section, women are transported. The Mutawas drive around high-traffic streets and open city squares, watching every move made by both men and women. In this case, they took notice of Najat. The binoculars were removed from the glove compartment, they parked, and she was closely observed.

"Look at that. There's a whore waiting for her lover," said one of them with a smile, beginning to smell prey, and he handed the binoculars to another Mutawa.

"She's acting innocent. How cute. Just wait, little whore, we're going to snap you up."

Then Taleb pulled up in his car. Because she was engrossed in examining a pretty dress in the window, and because she was deaf, he got out of the car and went to her side. A light tap on her shoulder signaled that he was there and ready to take her home.

The Mutawas were sure that their suspicions had just been confirmed. She simply had to be a whore. Quickly, they scrambled out of their car and ran at full speed up to Taleb and Najat. Without saying anything, without even a question, both of them were seized and dragged toward the detention vehicle. Najat couldn't scream, but she was holding her purse in her right hand and managed to use it to hit a Mutawa in the face. In revenge, he kicked her in the backside. Taleb defended himself as well, shouting, "What is this? Who are you? Leave me and my sister alone!"

Taleb was punched two times in the stomach. He passed out. The Mutawas tossed him into the men's detention compartment. Najat was pushed violently into the women's section, and the door was slammed shut. She beat her hands against the door and drummed her feet on the floor. The Mutawas relaxed in the speeding car and laughed, saying that she sounded like a wild animal that had just been ensnared.

The Mutawas drove their booty to a holding station. Taleb was a diabetic, and when he became angry or upset, he often lapsed into unconsciousness. Since he remained unconscious at the police station, they transferred him to a hospital.

Najat was interrogated . . . but how? She could neither hear nor speak. Furthermore, she had no understanding of the situation. It was completely puzzling to her. One of the Mutawas ripped off her black veil and demanded her name. When she didn't reply, he punched her in the face. She simply punched him back. He simply concluded that any woman who was disrespectful enough to hit a man had to be a whore. She should be stoned to death. Another Mutawa took her handbag. She lunged at him to get it back, and, seething with anger, managed to scratch his face with her nails. The Mutawa overpowered her, pinned her hands behind her back, and hustled her off to a darkened cell. His colleague rummaged through her purse and found her Saudi identity card.

The morality police chief quickly passed sentence on Najat. He wrote, among other things: "Najat was working as a prostitute and was caught in the very act of picking up a client. We advise that she be stoned to death . . ." Two Mutawas delivered the document to the governor of Riyadh, an al-Saud prince. He jotted down a verdict to match the suggestion, then signed it. Najat was to be publicly stoned to death the following Friday.

The parents of Najat and Taleb had searched for their children for a week when they received the horrifying news: their daughter had already been stoned to death, and their son had been secretly hospitalized. They rushed to his bedside only to discover that he was also in police detention, as he was being guarded by two armed officers. The parents were despondent. The father drove quickly to the governor's office and demanded an immediate interview.

Overwhelmed with fury, Taleb's father demanded the reason why his daughter had been stoned to death and his son was in the hospital. The governor staunchly replied that he should look at his own children for the answer; his daughter had been working the streets as a prostitute, and her brother had been assisting her. His children had been caught due to the good detective skills of his Mutawas. Taleb's father should be thanking them for catching his children early on in the game, before they infected other Saudi sons and daughters with the same debauched carryings-on. In fact, Taleb's father should be proud and relieved that the honor of his family name had been saved.

Because Taleb's father knew that his country had neither laws nor a real justice system, he decided to deal with the matter personally. He bought a large spray canister of inflammable DDT and went to see the Mutawa chief who had written the recommendation for the stoning of his deaf and dumb daughter. He sprayed the man with the substance and quickly lit and tossed a match. Other Mutawas were nearby. When they heard the agonized screams for help, they rushed into the office, put out the fire, and arrested Taleb's father. The Mutawa chief managed to survive his extensive injuries.

Taleb's father was publicly beheaded.

After his release from the hospital, Taleb received two hundred lashes.

One of the Mutawas who arrested Najat told me her tragic story. Taleb, who was a former student of mine, then confirmed it.

THE BORDER

Amputated for a Crime He Never Committed

Despite public statements to the contrary, it seems that corruption, human rights abuse, fanaticism, and violence pervade much of the Saudi lifestyle, from one border to the next. Mohammed's story, as provided here, demonstrates just how ubiquitous this corruption has become and just how life-altering, or life-ending, it can be.

Mohammed is a truck driver. He transports perishable food—fruits and vegetables—in his air-conditioned trailer, shuttling between Syria, Lebanon, Jordan, Kuwait, Saudi Arabia, the United Arab Emirates, and Oman. But his usual run is between Lebanon and Saudi Arabia. He goes to Lebanon to the fruit and vegetable wholesalers, where he takes his place in a long line of trucks waiting to be loaded. The pressure and stress are tangible. He purchases large quantities, makes sure that his trailer is completely packed, and then immediately drives off in the direction of Saudi Arabia. That's where most of the produce will go to market.

Mohammed is functionally illiterate—he can barely read and write. However, he understands trucking and does his job well. He's thirty-eight years old, married, the father of four children, and a practicing Muslim. He prays five times a day, is a decent man, and is always ready to help others in need. He is also a traditionalist. Every time he returns from a trip, he kisses the hands of his father and mother. He provides for his wife and children, for his aged parents who receive no pension money, and for those of his siblings who are unemployed. In effect, he is the source of both income and unemployment insurance for his extended family. Not surprisingly, he tends to be authoritarian; he expects his opinions to be respected and unchallenged. He believes that a wife belongs at home, in the kitchen. She should never shake hands with a man in greeting, for two specific reasons. First, she might be having her monthly period, and thus be ritually impure. Second, shaking hands with a woman could arouse impure thoughts in a man and distract him from his dedication to God.

Mohammed's trip from Lebanon to the Syrian-Jordanian border was quiet and uneventful. He listened to the radio—music and recitations from the Qur'an. However, the closer he came to the border, the more nervous and tense he became. When he got there, he parked on the right shoulder, got out of the truck, and walked over to Passport Control with his papers. This was in an old hall that had received its last coat of paint probably twenty years before; it was impossible to determine the color of the room. The sweat from the shirt backs of many men forced to wait there had bleached its walls. Right now, the room was hot, dark, loud, and very crowded. Long lines that snaked back and forth had been formed. Which one should Mohammed choose? The scene was totally familiar to him. It had been this way for many years. He chose a line, and waited patiently for five hours.

The passports of the waiting men were collected. After a few hours, they were redistributed by being tossed into the air. The hall was so full that not a single passport reached the ground. Every man scrambled to retrieve his own. Those who had the wrong passport yelled out the name under the photograph. This was a tricky process: yelling out a name and listening for your own. Suddenly a police official shouted out the name of a woman: "Fatima Saleh! Fatima Saleh!"

"Here!" replied a woman who was covered in black from head to toe. It was impossible to even see her eyes. The police officer told her to uncover her face. She lifted her veil for a moment, then quickly dropped it.

Mohammed commented to the man waiting beside him: "Hey, that's a prostitute from Syria. Did you know that Saudis recruit prostitutes in Syria and get them past the border controls by veiling them and claiming they are married? After all, a Saudi often has four wives." What he didn't realize, perhaps, were the larger philosophical dimensions. The veiling of women's faces in Saudi Arabia is approved of by men for two principal reasons: first, they find veiled women sexually provocative; and second, under a veil a prostitute can move freely to meet with her "clients."

However, a veiled woman in Saudi Arabia is not openly suspected of being a prostitute, due to the unpleasant consequences of an incorrect judgment. Once, in Riyadh, a police officer stopped a car driver and asked him where he had picked up the fully veiled "sweetie" who was with him in the vehicle. The man pulled a pistol out of the glove compartment and shot the officer dead. The woman was his wife.

To return to Mohammed's story, after five hours he got his passport back. He was almost free to continue his journey. Now he had to get the contents of his truck cleared by customs. He ran from one office to another, paying charges in hard currency. Some of them had to be paid at the border crossing's bank. "What's the exchange rate today? How much money will the customs officer ask for?" he asked the teller. "Ask them yourself," came the reply.

Once again, Mohammed took his place in a long line. When he reached the customs officer, the man told Mohammed, "I don't know how much you should pay!" So back he went into the line to see the bank teller. "The customs officer doesn't know how much to charge."

"So? Is that my problem?" said the teller.

Mohammed said to himself, I could stand in line for days trying to solve this in an honorable way. So he stood in line to see the customs officer and offered him a bribe. "Everything in order," said the man on duty. "Now, give me this amount of money in fees." Mohammed passed over the money and got his paper stamped "Charges paid," with the man's signature scrawled across it.

Now it was on to the next step. "This picture in your driver's license doesn't look like you."

"I assure you, that's my photo."

"Well, I don't believe it. Go to Damascus and get it authenticated there."

"Sir, please believe me, that's my photo. I've been traveling this route for years using this driver's license. Not only that, but I have perishable goods in my truck. Please don't do this to me."

"Forget it. Follow the rules. Next!"

Mohammed had to comply. But he would arrive too late; all the doors would be closed. The distance was almost ninety-five miles.

Mohammed got in his truck and drove home. His house was in a suburb of Damascus, so at least that was in his favor.

The next day, Mohammed found himself standing in a long line in Damascus. During his wait, he chatted with another truck driver, who gave him some advice. "You'll have to use a bribe; otherwise, he'll tell you to get a new driver's license. That means a road test and all the paperwork. It'll cost you five thousand lira—two months' salary. You see, this is a mafia setup. Every time a border crossing official sends a driver here, he gets a kickback. They settle with each other every two weeks. You're lucky you didn't run into it before. So take my advice. Pass the guy a thousand lira."

Mohammed placed the bill between his paperwork and driver's license. His driver's license photo was declared valid.

He got into his truck and resumed his trip to Saudi Arabia, his papers now fully approved. Just before he reached the Jordanian border, two Syrian border policemen flagged him to a stop. He had to tip them five hundred lira to obtain their permission to continue. But he was able to cross the Jordanian border without a hitch.

Shortly before reaching the Saudi border, Mohammed heard a strange noise coming from the truck's engine. He parked, raised the hood, and listened closely. Amazingly, two soldiers appeared and asked him why he was stopping in a military zone. Mohammed explained his situation politely and told them that he had no idea that stopping was forbidden. "I'll drive away right now; I'm sorry," he said, shutting the hood and moving to the truck's door.

"Stop now!" snapped one of the soldiers. "You're coming with me to the barracks. If what you say is the truth, tell it to the commander."

"All right, no problem," said Mohammed as he showed that he was prepared to walk with them.

"No, not on foot. Bring your truck. God only knows what you've got in it."

Mohammed drove with one of the soldiers beside him. The other trotted along beside the truck.

"Where to?" asked Mohammed. "I don't see anything around here."

"Straight ahead."

Mohammed drove, and he couldn't spot a barracks, a house, not even a tree. Everything was a desolate steppe of sand and stones. After two kilometers, they approached a pair of earth-colored tents. Mohammed found that the commander was inside one of them, bored, and playing absently with his prayer beads. The two soldiers made their report. "Sir, we discovered a spy, and we have arrested him." Mohammed was left speechless and fought to pull himself together.

"That's not true! I only stopped to check the engine of my truck!"

"Then why did you choose to stop in front of a military camp?"

"What military camp? I didn't even know that one existed around here! I swear to you, I'm a truck driver. I've got nothing to do with politics."

"Take him out," said the officer. "You know where."

Mohammed was placed in an excavated room that was an underground hole. He was given a piece of bread and a little water. Feeling himself in hell, he broke down and cried. He thought of his wife, children, parents, sisters, and brothers. Who would provide for them? And what would become of the fruits and vegetables in his truck? No, no—getting back home to his family, that was the only important thing.

He was kept there for two days and two nights. Two days without seeing the sun, without light. He didn't sleep. Then, in the darkness of the night, he was suddenly pulled out and released. "Well, you're getting away easily this time. We've decided to believe you. However, next time you're caught, you'll be punished to the full extent—probably life in prison. Don't ever be seen around here again. And one other thing: if you talk about this to others, you'll be inviting pure hell. Do you understand? Now, get lost!" said the military commander as he slammed shut the driver's side door of Mohammed's truck.

Mohammed started the truck. He drove off into the darkness, tired, bitter, and yet happy to be free. "Me . . . a spy! Me . . . a spy! And for whom? The Israelis? The Jordanians and Israelis have made peace. King Hussein and Yitzhak Rabin signed a peace accord. Who else is there? Syria, Saudi Arabia, Iraq. They aren't fighting, they're all Arab nations. They're brothers. I don't understand politics. I've never been able to get it."

Mohammed drove toward Saudi Arabia. At the next highway rest stop he planned to pick up gas, buy some food, and get a few hours' sleep. As soon as he arrived, he filled up his tank and bought some breakfast. Dawn had broken, so he went to the back of his truck to check on his goods. He opened the doors and his face drained of color: the truck was empty.

What now? If he turned back, the Jordanian border police at the Syrian border would ask him why he hadn't crossed into Saudi Arabia to offload his goods. The paperwork clearly stated that the produce was to be sold in that country. If they believed that he had illegally sold the goods here in Jordan, he would be prosecuted. So Mohammed decided to continue and enter Saudi Arabia. "What if the border police there catch me with an empty truck?" he wondered. "Well, I'll be in trouble either way. And if I make it across the border, I can return with a truckload of goods to sell in Syria."

Mohammed prayed ceaselessly as he drove. He begged God not to have the inspection agents tell him to open up the truck.

At the border between Jordan and Saudi Arabia, he stopped for the Jordanian border crossing control. The Jordanian official, looking at his paperwork, asked him for some fruit. He had a craving for something fresh. Mohammed gave him a confidential smile and turned on the charm. "Look . . . it's no problem, but wait until my next trip through. Just between you and me, this shipment is half-rotten. I promise to bring you a top-quality selection next time through." No, no—the man wanted apples. He had a craving for apples. He opened the storage doors and found an empty truck.

"What's going on? Where are the goods?"

"I can't tell you," replied Mohammed. "It's a promise."

Mohammed followed the man into an office. This was unheard of. Where had he sold the goods?

He was handled like a criminal of major importance. He was interrogated. Undoubtedly, he was a smuggler. But—in what? Guns? Drugs?

"Talk, Mohammed," his interrogators repeated. And, at last, he broke down and told them all about what had happened while crossing the Jordanian desert. The officials then traveled by police car with Mohammed to the place where he had been kidnapped. As they approached the tents two miles off the highway, they were fired upon. The police arranged for reinforcements. After a one-hour gun battle, the so-called "soldiers" in the desert were overcome. They proved to be highway robbers in stolen military outfits. And they had robbed more than one truck.

Mohammed was returned to his truck at the border crossing. He requested an official letter explaining that his shipment had been stolen. "Oh! That's out of the question! We can't have the Saudis and the Syrians believing that Jordanians are thieves. That would shame us, and also ruin our reputation as a transit country and trading partner."

Mohammed traveled on. He reached the Saudi border crossing at noon on a Wednesday, during the time for prayer. Everything was closed down until four or five o'clock and he couldn't get through. And now it was the Muslim weekend—Thursday and Friday. Trucks were not inspected and not allowed to cross. So Mohammed spent two and a half days waiting in the open beside his truck, in no man's land, in 113-degree heat.

On Saturday, Mohammed made sure that he was the first in the line. His passport and other papers were properly stamped. Everything went fine, and he returned to his truck in relief and pulled away, knowing that now he would face his last hurdle. Sometimes trucks were inspected at the last guard station where the railing was lifted for open passage. He smiled at the man in the booth, greeted him, and said, "Fine weather today."

The man replied: "Open the back of your truck."

Mohammed began to shake. He got out, protesting that he'd already been cleared by the man's colleagues. "I have fruits and vegetables here for my Saudi brothers," he declared, acting insulted by their request.

But the official was waiting impatiently. Mohammed opened the doors. "Fruits and vegetables for your Saudi brothers, well, look at this!" sneered the inspector. "Where's the shipment? Disappeared, correct? What's your trick?"

He called in the police dogs—two huge German shepherds—but they couldn't detect anything. Then two Filipinos were brought over. They drove the truck off to the side and proceeded to dismantle it, inspecting every part of its assemblage. In the meantime, Mohammed was placed in a holding cell at the border. He spent the night there and was called in the next day.

"Where's your shipment?"

Mohammed explained the whole story.

"Where's your proof?"

Mohammed swore before Allah and the Qur'an that his story was true.

A border guard punched him in the stomach, and then in the face. They demanded that Mohammed tell the truth. But then the call to prayer was sounded by the mosque, so they had to stop.

"Get ready to pray, dog," said one of the Saudis.

After ten minutes, they came back to get him. He was forced to stand behind them and pray. Then he was returned to his cell.

The interrogators kept it up for a week. Shortly before prayer time, he was beaten to force a confession from him; then he was forced to pray with his torturers.

Finally, he was called in for a special meeting.

"Mohammed, who owns your truck?" he was asked.

"A Syrian named Kassem Abdrabbo. It's registered in Damascus."

"Are you aware that your truck was stolen?"

"No, no. I swear that I didn't know that."

"Do you know an Iraqi truck driver named Rashid?"

"No, I don't."

"Were you present when the truck was sold?"

"To whom? When? I don't understand."

Mohammed was punched again and told to confess that he had been involved in the robbery and sale of his vehicle.

Reduced to tears, Mohammed cried, "Ask Kassem! Speak to Kassem! I know nothing about the truck being stolen! I'm just a simple driver!"

After a few days, the border police received information that Mohammed's air-conditioned truck had originally belonged to a Saudi and was stolen during the Gulf War in 1991. The truck had been registered in Saudi Arabia and given a Saudi license number. A previous driver, an Iraqi, had sold the truck, using false papers, to Kassem in Damascus.

Mohammed was taken to Riyadh. There he received a legal judgment by the court of the governor of Riyadh. Mohammed was to be punished publicly. He was to have both his arms amputated.

According to Muslim law, robbery is punished by cutting off the hands or arms of the offender.

After his arms were cut off, Mohammed was taken to a prison hospital for treatment. His stumps were attended to and bandaged. After his condition stabilized, he was deported to Syria.

When Mohammed's father saw him, he exclaimed, "No animal on earth would do to my son what the Saudis have done. The Saudis are not humans. They are devils living on God's earth."

One week later, a court bailiff appeared at Mohammed's home with a court order. He reminded Mohammed that when he had taken on his job as a trucker, he had signed a form that stated that, if the truck was stolen while it was under his responsibility, everything owned by Mohammed and his family would be passed over to Kassem Abdrabbo in payment. Even their house and land.

Mohammed, who was almost illiterate, had signed the agreement without understanding it.

ACCIDENTS WILL HAPPEN

Not only do professional truck drivers like Mohammed face danger on Saudi roads, but so does everyone who gets behind the wheel; and, as we will again see, it is often the innocent bystander and the foreigner who pays the price for the consequences of such danger and corruption.

In Saudi Arabia, the range of available leisure activities is quite limited. Most people spend their free time in malls, shopping or window-shopping. At home, they prepare special dinners and invite their relatives or friends over. There are no cinemas, theater performances, or art exhibitions—they are forbidden by the religious authorities. Young people don't have youth clubs where they can socialize and learn new skills. Riyadh has a couple of small parks, but they are restricted to family groups; single men aren't allowed in. Illogically, the parks close at 10 p.m., exactly the time when the weather starts to cool down and people decide to go out. The temperature during the day can easily reach 115 degrees Fahrenheit in summer, but the nights cool down to between the upper sixties and seventies.

Young people—only the boys—get behind the wheel of a car and drive aimlessly around the city. They can't think of anything else to do. Most of them don't have driver's licenses.

Women aren't allowed to drive in Saudi Arabia. During the Gulf War, they rebelled against this restriction that kept them constantly, day by day, dependent on the availability and willingness of male family members to act as chauffeurs. A number of well-educated women, mostly teachers at schools and the university, got into their family cars and drove in a protest convoy around Riyadh. They had lived abroad and obtained foreign driver's licenses. All of them were arrested and lost their jobs. A number of them are still being detained in Saudi jails.

Atiya, a thirty-eight-year-old Egyptian architect, was driving through Riyadh one evening with his wife and three children. At that time a Saudi boy was out on the streets, driving his BMW at speeds well over sixty miles per hour through the city. At one intersection, he paid no attention to the red light and roared right through. There was an enormous crash as he hit Atiya's car. The mother and her three children were killed. Atiya was severely injured. The fifteen-year-old Saudi driver was only slightly hurt.

An ambulance sped Atiya and the corpses of his family members to the nearest hospital as the police interviewed eyewitnesses at the scene of the accident and established that the boy was at fault. He protested. "The light was green!" he insisted.

"How old are you?" asked a policeman.

"Fifteen."

"Then you don't have a driver's license."

"I've got my father's!" announced the boy proudly.

One week later the police came to interview Atiya in the hospital. He was in terrible shape. His left arm had been broken in several places. Both his legs were broken, and he had head injuries. He had been crying incessantly since he had learned that his family had perished.

The policeman began his interview.

"Are you Atiya Alawi?"

"Yes," he answered, with tears in his eyes.

"You should have driven more carefully."

"I did drive carefully! The light turned green, and I entered the intersection slowly."

"That's not true. We have eyewitnesses who have testified that you drove through a red light."

Atiya was overcome by panic and incomprehension. "I swear to you, the light was green! This is impossible!" he shouted, and suffered a heart attack as he spoke. He began to cry again.

"Relax. You have to recover. We'll talk about this later. But please, tell me, where do you work?"

"I work for al-Nafjan Construction Company."

When a car accident occurs that involves a Saudi and a foreign worker, witnesses are usually invented who "testify" that the foreigner was at fault. Courtroom trials and lawyers are nonexistent, so the foreigner is almost always declared guilty.

Two months later, Atiya returned to work. He was called in to meet with his boss.

"I'm so happy to see you here with us again. I certainly hope that you're fully recovered." And in the same breath he told him, "I'm sorry to have to tell you this, but we had to send two months' worth of your paychecks to the Police Department to cover the costs of repairing the other car involved in your accident. The repairs to the BMW cost seven thousand riyals," almost two thousand US dollars.

Atiya was left speechless.

Many foreign workers in Saudi Arabia have to pay for their own entry visas, so Atiya already had debts because he still had to pay three thousand riyals (eight hundred US dollars) for the entry visas of his now deceased family members. Furthermore, Atiya was considered the breadwinner for his extended family back in Egypt: his parents, six underage or unemployed siblings, and two divorced sisters along with their children.

An Afghan taxi driver was involved in a car accident with a Saudi in Riyadh. Both of them were driving too quickly. The Saudi driver, a seventy-year-old man who wasn't wearing his seatbelt, applied his breaks with full force and lurched forward into the windshield of his car. He died instantly. The Afghani, realizing that the Saudi man was crumpled without any sign of life over the steering wheel, panicked and fled the scene.

In Saudi Arabia it is highly advisable to do exactly that—disappear as quickly as possible—because the relatives of the dead man might kill the other driver as recompense. It is called "blood vengeance" and is completely acceptable under Saudi law. The police searched for the taxi driver, Hafis, and found him; he was arrested and jailed. As far as the relatives of the Saudi man were concerned, the accident was a clear-cut case of murder.

According to Bedouin custom, anyone who causes a death—no matter what the circumstances—must either pay "blood money," which can be very expensive, or be beheaded. Hafis was given a choice: pay the equivalent of fifty thousand US dollars to the bereaved family, or die. He had no money since he was under contract to turn over to his employer three hundred riyals (eighty US dollars) in income each day. Just to meet this obligation alone he was on the road fifteen hours a day. If he was lucky, he earned an extra fifty riyals (thirteen US dollars) for himself. From that, he had to live and send support money back home to his family in Afghanistan.

One week later, Hafis was found dead from multiple stab wounds in his jail cell. A son of the deceased man had secretly arranged to be admitted and had murdered him. The police did not make a serious effort at finding him; it was simply a case of blood revenge, which was tolerated as long as the perpetrator was a Saudi. Any foreigner who tried to do it would be arrested and charged.

Automobile liability insurance is not sold in Saudi Arabia. However, anyone who wants to can choose to insure his vehicle. But this is also problematic. Local insurance companies usually don't pay out if their client has an accident, and foreign insurance companies don't like to deal in automobile insurance because of the unprofitable number of claims due to the high accident rate. At any rate, many Islamic scholars insist that insurance

contravenes the teachings of Islam. Profits from the sale of insurance policies are invested, which generates interest, and accepting income from
interest is a sin. Good Muslims do not take profits generated by interest.
This is *riba* ("usury"), and according to Islam, it is sinful.

The history of this rule against interest stems from the time of
Muhammad. During his lifetime, the richest citizens of Mecca and
Medina, the cradle of the Islamic religion, were Jews. As moneylenders,
they ruled the economic life of the region. Because the Jews refused to
convert to Islam, Muhammad punished them by declaring that charging
interest for financial loans was illegal.

PRINCE MAJID AND PORNOGRAPHY

On a first visit to Saudi Arabia, walking out on the public streets, it's easy to believe that this is a country where people only eat, sleep, and pray. No cocktail lounges, no bars, no night life, no brothels, no strolling prostitutes, and no "peep" shows. After some time, you come to understand that all these things are available—not openly, but behind high, thick walls.

Prince Majid discovered some time ago a lucrative marketing opportunity: the establishment of a company that would sell pornographic movies and books in Saudi Arabia. And because he is a prince, he can do what he likes without any interference. To begin, he imported the books and movies from Germany, Sweden, the United States, and even Israel, albeit indirectly. Gradually, he found this increasingly cumbersome—not only that, but the prices kept going up. Obviously it would be cheaper to produce the materials in Saudi Arabia, luring charming, pretty, local women into the enterprise. And, to be sure, local men would love to see Arab women featured in sex films. He would please his clientele and cut costs at the same time.

Behind the high, thick walls of Prince Majid's palace, major renovations were begun. Film and photography studios were built, cameras and editing equipment were imported from Japan, and sets were put into place, which included lavish décor, saunas, bars, extensive green lawns, and—of course—beds.

Majid had top-level contacts in the region's underworld, especially in Cairo, Casablanca, Dubai, Bahrain, and Beirut. Since he regularly held weekend orgies in his palace using women from these cities, it was easy for him to engage them in pornographic productions. In fact, some of them lived in his palace indefinitely, waiting to be summoned to the next orgy. However, the prince established a large recruitment department, consisting of both men and women, to enlist new girls. His guests at the weekly orgies didn't want the same girl twice, and now he was developing this hobby into a business. The film directors and cameramen were brought in from Cairo.

With nothing standing in his way, production of the pornographic films and books moved ahead, and the materials were marketed on the Saudi black market for reasonable prices. Prince Majid was even able to export to other Arab countries, Sweden, Germany, Denmark, and Russia. Business was booming.

But Prince Majid wanted to expand into child pornography, making use of underage girls and boys, because of customer demand. The only question was how to get the children. One of his recruiters mentioned the many poor boys who worked in the traffic intersections, trying to sell boxes of Kleenex to car drivers while they were stopped for red lights. They could be easily lured into such a venture if they were paid. But Prince Majid had no idea how they could obtain little girls for sex roles. A female recruiter told him, "No problem. I've got the answer. But first, go ahead and start with the boys."

Prince Majid sent out two employees, a man and a woman, to travel to that part of the city where young boys sold Kleenex boxes. They were in luck. A seven-year-old sprinted from car window to car window the second the lights turned red. Exhaust fumes seemed to wreathe his relentless efforts. He was wearing what must have once been a white, handmade robe, but now ingrained dirt had rendered its color indescribable. When he jumped to the window of their car, seemingly appearing from nowhere, the memorized, essentially hopeless patter was quick: one box cost two riyals (fifty US cents), a package of six cost ten.

"We'll buy all of your packages. How many do you have?" said the woman.

The boy was overjoyed. "Five. You want all of them? I'll go get them." Then he ran to a nearby laneway where the boxes were hidden under a covering. The recruiters pulled their car off the road and parked.

"Put them in the car trunk," said the woman. He did so, and then came to her window for his payment. "You know, why don't you come for a ride with us? I'll need you to unload those boxes, and I'll pay you extra." She waved a hundred-riyal bill in his face and then gave it to him. The boy's face gleamed, and he got in immediately. He gawked at the car's interior and began to gently stroke the leather seats.

"I've never been in a car like this. Such a nice car," he enthused. "My dad doesn't have a car. When I grow up, I'll buy one like this. How much is it?" His voice was lively and cheerful.

"Two hundred thousand riyals," replied the male recruiter.

"Oh. . . . Oh. I'll never have that much money."

"Come on, now," said the woman. "If you are obedient and do what others tell you, you will earn a lot of money."

The car approached the palace, and a huge gate was opened for them. They traveled down a boulevard lined with green trees for almost half a mile before reaching the house. Finally they reached an enormous, round, paved courtyard with a fountain in the middle. The man and woman got out, but the child didn't want to leave the leather seat.

"Get out!" shouted the woman.

The boy did as he was told, but he didn't know which way to look— there was too much to take in.

"Everything here is so beautiful," he said.

"Do you want to live here?" asked the woman.

"Oh, yes!"

"By the way, what's your name?"

"Salim."

"Okay, let's go in." The woman preceded him up the palace stairs.

"The Kleenex," said Salim.

"Salim, forget about it. Follow me." She kept walking, and at one of the side entrances shouted, "Maria!"

Maria, a Filipino housemaid, appeared. "Yes, Madam?"

"Clean the boy up, feed him, and then bring him to me. Is that clear?"

"Yes, Madam."

"Salim, go with Maria and get something to eat." Then she disappeared into an adjoining room, where preparations were under way for a porno film involving the child.

Within an hour, Salim was back, almost unrecognizable now that he was clean and dressed in new clothes. The boy was both curious and adventuresome, which pleased Prince Majid, who was present.

In a room with a hidden movie camera, Salim was offered a number of toys, including a shiny wind-up train set placed on miniature tracks. He immediately got down on the floor to play with it. Then a woman entered the room, wearing a sleeveless, low-cut summer dress. She sat beside Salim and also began to play with the train. When the train had wound down, she removed its key and placed it in her cleavage. Salim was forced to retrieve the key from between her breasts, while she laughed and laughed at him. After renewing his confidence in her with some chatter about the toy, she suddenly detached a train car and placed it between her legs. Salim, confused, was laughing as he tried to snatch the toy away. When he did so, she simulated erotic movements and then flashed her naked crotch at him and the filming camera. Salim took no notice. She kissed him on the mouth, and Salim pushed her away. Then she groped at his clothing. "You saw between my legs; now I want to see your penis."

"Why?" was his response. "Mine isn't all hairy like yours."

But she grabbed at his penis. "You're hurting me. Go away. I want to play."

The woman then became aggressive and acted as though she intended to rape him. She slowly took off her clothes and told Salim to do the same. He escaped her grasp, but all the room's doors had been locked from the outside. In the next room, the proceedings were being followed on the camera monitor, and the prince liked the way things were progressing. Salim thought it was odd when the woman undressed him.

They then continued to play with the train.

The little boy suddenly was overcome with exhaustion. He simply fell asleep on the floor.

The woman gently rolled Salim onto his back and simulated sexual intercourse with him. Astraddle over him, she writhed like a snake, bent down to kiss his mouth, and held the seven-year-old's penis close to her vagina. She moaned and cried out dramatically, finally screaming out in an erotic climax: "I have come!"

Everyone was pleased with the woman's performance—even the prince. But he was especially happy with Salim's naïve behavior in the movie. "Well," said the director, "we have to hope that he'll do well with the man, too."

Salim was deeply asleep, and he was put to bed while another room was prepared for a pornographic film with a man. After a one-hour nap, he was given a glass of juice spiked with gin, and a piece of chocolate. Then he was brought into a room that contained a miniature BMW convertible, a child's toy complete with all the options of a real car. When Salim got in to drive the electric car, the slightly built porn actor sat beside him on the narrow seat and initiated sexual contact, as the woman had earlier. But Salim was embarrassed, so he was taken out of the room to drink more juice laced with gin. Upon his return, the man simulated sex with the child. This was a real cruelty for Salim, whose attention was torn in two directions: by the puzzling body movements of the strange man, and by his desire to play with the amazing, shiny electric car parked beside them.

Prince Majid needed a little girl. They were difficult to come by in Saudi Arabia but easy enough in the Philippines, where young girls thronged the streets with their friends. Child prostitution was well established in Manila, so Hasan, one of the prince's recruiters, was told to travel to Manila and bring back a couple of attractive, underage girls.

"Wait a minute!" said Hasan. "Prince Talal has a Foreign Labor Recruitment Agency. Maybe he can get you a couple of girls."

"Stuff it," replied the prince. "Then what? That guy will be blackmailing me at the next opportunity. No way. You are going to fly to Manila and recruit them yourself."

Hasan, who was Lebanese, made inquiries at a couple of nightclubs when he arrived in Manila.

"I need three small girls for Saudi Arabia," he told a bartender.

The man glanced vacantly around the room, as though he hadn't heard, while he considered his response. "For you or for a prince? If it's for a prince, forget it. Those guys are nothing but problems. Recently one of them killed a Filipino girl while he was having sex with her, and then he dumped her body. Her family wants it returned for burial. Not a chance of that happening."

"Look, these girls are going to a prince, but he's a decent, upstanding person. They'll be well treated. We intend to use them in porn films. They'll probably become famous."

"Well, it *is* a problem. Our girls are ready and willing to travel abroad, but not to Saudi Arabia."

"I'll pay well," said Hasan. There was a pause.

"How much?"

"I don't know."

"These girls and their parents will expect a lot of money."

"Money isn't an issue. Finding the right girls is."

"How do you intend to smuggle them?" asked the bartender.

"No problem," replied Hasan.

The bartender then opened a drawer and pulled out a homemade catalog. It contained photos of girls from all age groups. He flipped through it and said, "Well, here we are. Look at these girls. They might be good, and they're between eight and twelve years old."

"Yeah, you're right. This one is pretty. And how about this one here, and that one there."

"Wait," said the bartender. Photo album in hand, he got on the phone for a lengthy conversation in Tagalog, a language Hasan didn't understand.

"Okay," he said after hanging up. "Meet me here early tomorrow evening. We'll go together and meet two of them, for a start. By the way, they're sisters."

The next day, as agreed, the two men made the trip. The girls lived in Manila's slums, in a district of houses made of discarded boards and tin.

Hasan and the bartender, whose name was Jim, made their way along narrow laneways littered with anything and everything unwanted: garbage, sewer water, flies, insects, and people.

The girls lived with their family, and Jim knew them all: a mother, grandmother, stepfather, four small children, and the two girls. The girls, of course, were also children: Julie was eight years old, and Carmen was twelve.

Jim negotiated with the mother and stepfather in Tagalog. Then he turned to Hasan and announced, "They want three thousand American for each girl. And you are responsible for all their expenses—including the air tickets, of course."

Hasan replied that the girls were cute and that his prince would be very pleased.

On their way back to the bar, Jim told Hasan, "Tomorrow I'll get you a third girl. And, by the way, right now all three of these girls are out of work. Because of that advantage, and because I'll have associated expenses in getting them passports, I'll need ten thousand US dollars from you."

Within a few days, illegal passports were ready. They stated that Hasan was the father of the girls and that their mother was a Filipino. The girls were instructed to call Hasan "Papa" while they were traveling.

They left Manila without a hitch, and upon arrival in Saudi Arabia, were inspected by immigration officers who had been specially planted by the prince. The children were granted entry without comment.

On the very next day, the girls had makeup applied to their faces and were put to work.

At first, the children were very shy and refused to cooperate with the adult "actors." Finally, Carmen, the oldest girl, spoke up. "We need drugs," she announced.

The girls were addicts and worked willingly as prostitutes when "under the influence." Prince Majid ordered in the drugs, the girls took them, and, now quite uninhibited, they willingly agreed to anything asked of them—all possible sex roles, in any position, with either a man or a woman, alone or in orgy settings.

Prince Majid's in-house enterprise was a great success. He was able to market his films on satellite television channels. Also, his business was further protected when he obtained incontrovertible property rights to his products by getting bar codes assigned to them. This was arranged by an Italian pornography distribution network and was valid for all the Gulf countries.

WALEED AND MISHEL

Hunting Women à la Saudi

Waleed, a son of one of an important Saudi prince, is well known for being the most spoiled of the prince's thirty-four sons. He gets to do whatever he wants, and, like Prince Majid and his pornography business—and every other Saudi prince, for that matter—he gets away with it. For instance, he collects luxury automobiles like toys. He owns palaces in some of the world's most beautiful travel destinations: Hawaii, Bali, the Azores, and Marbella. He likes women and treats them as sexual objects, just like almost all the men of the al-Saud family. But he doesn't like to get his women easily and without effort. He prefers to conquer them.

Prince Waleed has developed an interesting and unique taste: a love of Damascus, the Arabic dialect spoken in the Syrian capital. He considers it very sexy—especially when it comes from the mouth of a woman. He thinks it is a real treat, a total delight, if two things can be found in the same woman: a beautiful body and the Damascene dialect. For that, he is willing to pay any sum of money. He has no interest in prostitutes; she has to be an ordinary person for Waleed to take notice. And she has to be someone who needs to be conquered. To do this, he uses all the technical skills of the Ministry of the Interior.

As the son of a government minister, Prince Waleed has access to a wide range of information and engineering expertise. He uses a technical infrastructure that was created by a large German electronics firm, which, in turn, employs a skilled, imported workforce to keep it running smoothly. Gert, an electronics engineer for this German company, explains: "The engineering we have put in place consists of bugs planted in everyone's telephone. However, it's not the usual matter of eavesdropping on people's phone calls. We can actually listen to everything being said in any apartment—within a certain range of the telephone, of course. Conversations are tracked in a special room of Prince Waleed's palace, but there is also a special hook-up to Prince Waleed's private monitoring room.

"Prince Waleed likes to hear what women say in the privacy of their own homes—and especially in their bedrooms. From this he can discern whether or not the woman appeals to him. He has a lot of experience in doing this. For instance, if a woman's voice sounds young and sexy, he puts in an order for her to be delivered. That puts into action a huge group of employees, most of them men and women from Syria, to manipulate her either into his palace or into one of his gorgeous apartments in Riyadh."

According to Gert, Prince Waleed himself proudly explained to Gert, personally, how he lures women into his palaces. As Gert retells the story, this is what Prince Waleed had to say: "My monitoring staff is assigned to listen in on telephone conversations in progress. The discussions that match what I'm interested in are retained for analysis. That means finding out names, events, dates and times, acquaintances, friends, experiences, habits, and so on. Would you like to listen to one? This is an excerpt of a conversation between two female friends, Kaukab and Maysun. The latter has just gotten married. I find this conversation absolutely charming."

Kaukab: Hello, Maysun. How's it going?
Maysun: Just fine. And you?
Kaukab: So how have been your honeymoon nights with Maher?
Maysun: Oh, really lovely. But I do have to admit that the first experience wasn't so good. Maher was really excited, and he threw himself on me like a wild animal. It really hurt, and the next day I kept getting pains. The second night was better. I actually enjoyed it, although I didn't show

it, of course. . . . You know very well that our men really dislike it when a woman moans and shows that she's enjoying sex. Maher was hot almost all the time, so I didn't even need to put on my sexy underwear! I'm so glad that he likes my body. He constantly kisses me—especially my breasts and thighs. He says they're beautiful. My breasts are already hurting. I think he's bruised them.

Kaukab: My husband acted the same way during our first nights together. Afterward he really cooled down. Now I have to do everything possible to tempt him: perfume, sexy lingerie . . . I position my body in a provocative position in bed, just to turn him on. Sometimes I succeed, and sometimes I don't. Sometimes when he's really turned on I deliberately act uninterested. That really gets him going. You know, we've got to make a business of selling ourselves. Otherwise, our husbands are going to find their happiness elsewhere, or even divorce us. Let me give you my advice: don't give him too much, but always tease and tempt him. When he gets interested, laugh and run away. Keep him a little confused. In the end, you'll have your husband like a pet on a leash, and *you'll* be the one jerking *him* around.

Maysun: Aren't you slick and foxy!

Kaukab: You said it! Only with sex can a husband be lured home. . . . That's the truth of it. . . . You know, your wedding was very nice. The reception hall was full. It was impressive.

Maysun: Yes, our two families invited a lot of guests. A lot of them I didn't even know.

"After I heard this conversation," explained the prince, "I had a Syrian employee named Samira phone Maysun and engage her in conversation. To do this successfully, she used some information from the recording. She phoned during the morning, when husbands are at work. Samira is very clever and voluble. Listen to the taped excerpt . . ."

Samira: Hi, Maysun. This is Samira. How are you?

Maysun: Hello. Which Samira?

Samira: Don't you remember me? My husband and I were at your wedding! It was a lovely wedding, I must say.

Maysun is not sure if she really knows this caller, but it doesn't matter. She is aware that she didn't know many of the guests who attended her wedding; she'd never seen them before. Anyway, she realizes that it's kind of this woman to give her a call. Riyadh is a bleak and boring city, and having another girlfriend is never a bad idea. Out of politeness, boredom, and curiosity, Maysun continues with the conversation.

> **Maysun:** You know, there were simply so many people there, and as the bride I was feeling shy and nervous. I'm so sorry, but I simply can't remember all the names and faces. Maybe when I see you, I'll remember your face.
> **Samira:** I'm sure of that. And it will be lovely to see you again, Maysun.

Maysun and Samira spoke on the phone a few more times. Through their conversations a friendship developed—as much as that's possible without meeting face to face. When Samira felt that she had fully gained Maysun's trust, she invited her over for a morning coffee party at one of Prince Waleed's apartments. A number of other employees of Prince Waleed pretended to be Samira's lady friends. They discussed and chattered, mainly about men. To assess Maysun's reaction, a few of the women recounted occasions when they had had sex with strangers.

"It gives you a chance to enjoy life and earn money, too. And not a little money," one of the women commented saucily.

Sometimes Maysun reacted to these racy stories with embarrassment, at other times with nervous laughter. Samira and the others told her that she was young and really still quite inexperienced, but she should "try a different man" sometime. "It's just great," one of them enthused.

To make an assessment of Maysun, Prince Waleed was hiding behind a glass wall and watched the party's proceedings in the living room. Of course, Maysun and the others couldn't see him. As the women chatted, Samira slipped out, went to Prince Waleed, and asked if he was interested. He replied that he wanted to see more of Maysun's body. So the air-conditioning was turned down, and the room heated up. The women began to groan, grumble, and complain. They called servants and told them to get the cold air pumping again. The conversation was too entertaining to be abandoned, so no one made a move to leave. As no men were present, they unbuttoned their blouses and jacked up their skirts. Giggling and laughing, they flapped them like fans. Maysun imitated them. Prince Waleed decided that she was cute and that, yes, he absolutely wanted her.

Maysun was invited to Samira's again, and this time they were alone. Once again the theme of sex with strange men was raised. Samira plunged her hand into her handbag and pulled out an expensive and dazzlingly beautiful necklace. She waved it in Maysun's face. "Look at this. Isn't it magnificent?"

"Oh, how amazing! I've never seen anything so gorgeous!"

"Do you have any idea how I got this?"

Samira put it into Maysun's hand and carefully assessed her facial expressions.

"Well, from your husband, I assume."

"Nonsense!" said Samira. "From a prince!"

"From a prince?" Maysun parroted, astonished.

"Yes, it was a gift from a Saudi prince."

"How? And why did he give it to you?" Maysun asked, with even more amazement and curiosity.

"I'll tell you if you promise to *never* tell anyone else. . . . I slept with him. Then he gave me this necklace. Isn't it lovely?" She looked at it admiringly with no trace of regret.

"How could you have done that? And what will your husband say when he finds this necklace?" Maysun lectured in a tone of moral authority, looking demandingly into her new girlfriend's eyes.

"Relax! He'll never find out about it! I'm going to sell this necklace in the gold market and deposit the money into my bank account in Damascus. That's private, and he'll never discover anything. Maysun, my dear, little innocent, we can never trust our own husbands. Many of them abandon us for another wife. Wake up, sweetheart! Go to bed with a prince a couple of times, and you'll put enough money in the bank for two or three years. The prince I sleep with is simply fantastic. He's very nice and very tender. To say it openly—in contrast to my husband, he actually understands how to make love. Sooner or later, you'll have this experience, too. Only the first nights of your honeymoon are enjoyable with your own husband. Later, everything starts going downhill, and the woman ends up the loser. Remember—you promised to keep this a secret. But think about it . . . what's so bad about getting both love and gold, without having to actually work for it? If you want, I can arrange something like this for you. What do you say? Take it. It's a good opportunity," she forcefully suggested.

"Oh Samira, I could never cheat on my husband. I just couldn't do it."

"And how do you know that your husband isn't cheating on you?" Samira acidly retorted.

"I can feel it. I just know it. And even if he did, I wouldn't just go out and sleep with other men. And I certainly wouldn't do it for money."

Prince Waleed was listening to this from behind the glass wall. He was thrilled to hear that Maysun had no intention of cheating on her husband. Pleased and very excited, he slipped off his clothes. Laughing insanely, he stalked into the living room stark naked.

Samira quickly moved to tape the young woman's mouth. Overcome by panic and shock, hardly able to believe this was happening, Maysun nevertheless gathered her wits and attempted to fight back. Samira helped the prince restrain her. Her clothes were deftly removed, and she was raped by this complete stranger in the presence of her so-called "girlfriend."

Afterward, Maysun was delivered a formal lecture as if she were guilty of a criminal act. The information was clear and precise. If she spoke to anyone about the "incident," something terrible would happen. The lowest level of punishment would be the deportation of her family from the kingdom. The maximum would be their collective murder.

Maysun was returned to her home and her marriage—shocked, humiliated, traumatized, and spiraling downward into mental depression. She didn't have the strength of character to challenge the prince.

Another woman who was entrapped the same way actually had the audacity to register a complaint with the governor of Riyadh. He listened to her testimony and then pretended to conduct an investigation of the matter. His conclusion was that all women lie, and their testimony can't be trusted; her accusation was bogus. As a punishment, she received one hundred lashes in public and her husband was sentenced to a month in jail. In the end, the woman and her family were summarily deported.

Other princes employ different methods that are faster, but no less brutal. For example, Prince Mishel, a half brother of Prince Waleed, and two of his cousins hit the road at sundown in a huge American limousine with tinted windows. It's "fully loaded" with everything and anything—a telephone, refrigerator, music system, television, and cameras, to name a few of its amenities. They cruise the city of Riyadh, up and down and through any district, looking for an adventure with women.

In Saudi Arabia, women aren't allowed to drive cars, and they are seldom seen strolling on the streets or walking to the shops. It's rare to find a woman walking alone or even on foot with a group of female friends. Women don't venture out to shop alone because they are afraid of being accused of "trying to pick up a man." A woman walking alone is either followed by strange men or is hassled by the Mutawas, the morality police. Middle-class and upper-class women move around easily, as they are driven by a chauffeur—either a male family member, or a hired driver from the Philippines or India.

Most Saudi women don't work, especially if they belong to a rich family. They sit at home and try to cope with boredom. A phone call from a strange man brings a dash of excitement into the monotony of their lives. For many such women, a male stranger's phone number means hot, steamy, and pornographic phone sex. All they talk about is sex: how often do you have sex, what positions have you tried, does your husband sexually satisfy you, and so forth. Occasionally, this leads to a clandestine meeting between the two. In light of the fact that a large number of Saudi men are married to more than one woman and usually see each wife once a week or less, the women seek revenge by sleeping with strangers.

A popular story that circulates in Riyadh concerns a woman whose husband had eight wives. He very seldom saw her or spoke to her. She got the phone number of a strange man through her girlfriend, and it led to a lot of sexually charged conversations. Finally, she agreed to meet him in an apartment that he had discreetly rented for any illicit rendezvous that came his way. Veiled in black from head to toe, she slipped into the building. As she stepped into the apartment, she discovered that the man was her own husband.

Many Saudi men take advantage of the low status of Saudi women and hunt them down like animals. The princes of the country are above the law—they can do whatever they want and employ any level of violence to get it. The following story was told to me by a close relative of Ghada, the mother of two girls who were hunted by a prince.

Prince Mishel and his companions, out cruising the streets of Riyadh at sundown, notice two sisters in a middle-class car: twenty-year-old Amal and seventeen-year-old Nura. A Sri Lankan driver is chauffeuring them. The prince tails their vehicle. To ascertain that the girls don't come from an important family, they call the Traffic Ministry and report the vehicle's license plate number. Prince Mishel wants to know the name of the owner of the car: "This is Prince Mishel speaking. Give me the name of the owner of the car with license plate number 1381995."

"Certainly, Your Highness. One moment, please." The on-duty clerk wouldn't dream of asking for reasons why he should release confidential information—not unless he wanted to face indefinite detention in a very unpleasant jail in a southern region of the country.

The owner of the vehicle is no one important, so the prince hits the gas pedal. Under no circumstances is this car going to get out of sight.

Amal and Nura get out at a shopping center, and the prince and his cousins begin to trail them on foot. Finally, he confronts them and tries to make direct contact. In the busy aisles of a large store, he tries to give them his phone number, written on a small piece of paper. The girls refuse to accept it. The prince quickly tosses it into their shopping cart. Amal picks up the number just to get the men to leave them alone. Unfortunately, that encourages the prince to plan his next move.

Women who accept his phone number almost always call, driven by boredom and curiosity. Some women simply phone to experience what men outside their narrow family circle do for a living, to find out their opinions, to discover their interests and hobbies. If the prince is really interested in a strange woman, and she insistently refuses his advances, he gets even more provoked and excited. Such women become the focus of a determined and incessant hunt.

Amal and Nura leave the shopping center and get into their waiting car. The prince and his cousins follow while calling home for "reinforcements"—another vehicle to join in the pursuit. Now there are two strong, menacing luxury vehicles following the girls. The second car is driven by one of the prince's chauffeurs, and two personal servants accompany him. The prince gets in contact with those in the second car by phone, so the chauffeur will know when and where to collide with the girls' car.

At exactly the right moment, when there is little traffic on the road, the prince's chauffeur stages a traffic accident. The two servants quickly scramble out and bundle the two young women into Prince Mishel's vehicle. The prince careens off with the women. They are forced to inhale anesthetic fumes. He drives to one of the apartments that he maintains for the triumphant conclusion of his "woman hunts." The disoriented and half-doped girls are carried in. Prince Mishel rapes them and photographs them in the nude.

Now fully conscious, they are driven to the suburbs, to the edge of the desert, and set free. The prince shows them the photos and tells them that he will circulate them openly if they tell anyone about their abduction. "Talk to anyone about this, and I will see that both of you get your throats slit. So keep your mouths shut. Understood?"

Nura spits into Prince Mishel's face. Furious, he knocks her to the ground and mercilessly stomps on her body. The two sisters scream and shout for help, but no one hears them. "Whores, this will show you who rules in this country!" Mishel yells and then speeds off in his car with his cousins.

As Prince Mishel was in the process of abducting and raping the daughters, the chauffeur and the mother of the girls both had to deal with troubles of their own. The Sri Lankan chauffeur of the girls' car had gotten into a fistfight with the prince's servants at the scene of the accident. He was overwhelmed and they punched him until the blood ran. As he lay knocked unconscious beside the road, a passing taxi driver stopped and took him to the nearest hospital. Meanwhile, the girls' mother had become concerned and worried about her two daughters. She reproached herself for letting them go out shopping alone. Phone calls were made to everyone: family, friends, the police. Their father wasn't available; he was with his other wife.

Amal and Nura pulled the shreds of their ripped clothing together and covered themselves in their black abayas. After a while, they were able to flag down a taxi and make their way home. The two young women were shaking with fear and constantly crying during the entire trip. Their mother was impatiently waiting in the garden of their home. When the gate swung open and the girls appeared, she sighed with relief and ran to embrace them both. The three women found themselves crying as though they were at a funeral. "What is it? What's happened?" demanded the mother through her tears.

"Something terrible . . . " sobbed Amal.

"A car accident?"

"No . . . no . . . much worse. Let's go inside."

In the living room, Amal and Nura told their mother everything. Amal gave her mother the license plate number of the prince's car. Overcome by fury, she called her husband.

"Just a moment; he'll be right with you," announced the maid who picked up.

The mother of the girls, Ghada, told him that a prince and his cousins had raped their daughters.

"Well, that's what happens when you give girls a liberal upbringing. I told you that they should always be kept at home. But you—"

Ghada slammed down the phone. "Idiot," she hissed. "What's the use of talking to him?!"

The next day, a policeman came to the door, accompanied by two Mutawas, the fanatical "religious police" of Saudi Arabia. They wanted to speak to the head of the house.

"He's not here," said the maid.

"Is the mother at home?"

"Yes. Just a moment." She went and summoned Ghada.

After Ghada arrived, the policeman said, "We would like you and your two daughters, who arrived home very late yesterday evening, to report to police headquarters. Is that possible?"

At first, Ghada hesitated. Then she thought, this will be a chance to bring the prince to justice. She dressed, put on her abaya, and accompanied the men with her two daughters.

In a private office, Ghada was shown a couple of photos that showed her two daughters sprawled naked on a bed. She showed no reaction, but her blood was boiling with anger as she asked who had taken the pictures.

"You don't need to know that. We are simply showing you these to prove that your daughters are working as prostitutes," replied the police officer with a triumphant sneer.

"Enough. Enough," said Ghada. She ripped the photos into shreds and burst into loud weeping. "You are pigs! My daughters are more honorable than your wives!" she screamed.

Amal and Nura were bundled into a dark cell. Their mother was sent home in a taxi.

The following Friday, the two girls were stoned to death.

Ghada resolutely decided to get revenge on the prince who had destroyed her children. She borrowed a chauffeured car from a girlfriend since her own vehicle was in the shop for repairs and her Sri Lankan driver was still in the hospital. As dusk descended on the city of Riyadh, she had herself driven through the streets, alone in the backseat and veiled from head to foot. She was looking for Prince Mishel's cruising, predatory car. Ghada was armed. Tucked in her handbag was her husband's pistol—he was an army officer.

She struck gold. Prince Mishel was out on the streets in his luxury vehicle, hunting for women. He sat behind the wheel, beside another man in the passenger seat who was probably also a member of the royal family. They ogled the passengers of each passing car. Ghada told her driver to pass Mishel's car very, very slowly. Mishel's eyes caught Ghada, and his car latched onto theirs. Like all Saudis, he assumed that under the mysterious black veil was a beautiful, young woman.

To entice Mishel, Ghada told her driver to now turn on the cassette player very loudly. She had given him a tape set to a particular song at the beginning of the evening. Ghada had chosen a love song with the words, "Please, come to me . . . I need your love . . ." She rolled down her window and turned to look directly at Mishel. He immediately understood that she was on the hunt just as much as he was. This would be easy and fun.

Ghada instructed her driver to head toward the open desert. Mishel followed their car. Out in the desert, with no one to be seen in any direction, Ghada's vehicle came to a stop, and Mishel parked alongside. Ghada simply got out and stepped into his car.

"Well, sweetheart, shall we start with a little foreplay?" asked Mishel, his eyes glowing with lust.

"Yes. Let's do it. But first, make this seat into a bed," she sweetly urged in an enticing, seductive voice.

Mishel and the other man quickly folded down the backseat.

"Get undressed, both of you. I want to sleep with both of you at the same time," she demanded with a provocative and very feminine self-assurance.

"This is our lucky night!" laughed the two men. They took off their clothes and stretched out on the makeshift bed.

Ghada pulled the loaded and cocked pistol out of her handbag and shot the two men dead.

Then she riddled Prince Mishel's body with bullets.

POLYGAMY AS HEROISM

G hanima, a thirty-eight-year-old Saudi woman, is unmarried. She can barely read and write. She doesn't have a job—she doesn't need one. She lives with her mother and her brothers, both married and single, in a huge house. They are well off; all seven brothers either run their own businesses or have a good position in a private enterprise. Four of her sisters are married and have moved out to live elsewhere in Riyadh with their husbands. Two of her sisters are children who still live at home. Approximately half of Saudi Arabia's marriageable women are over thirty years of age, and their chances of finding a lifelong husband are slim. Saudi men are not interested in marrying older women, and such women are usually not allowed to marry foreigners. As we saw with how Prince Nayef and Prince Mishel treat women, all Saudi women stand the chance of being victimized because they are of such inferior status; in particular, single women are the victims of fierce social stigmatization—they are contemptuously treated as inferior.

In Saudi Arabia, neither men nor women participate in political or social organizations. In spite of this, Ghanima decided to secretly assist older, unmarried Saudi women in their search for husbands. Fortunately, she personally knew a good number of women who were considered too old for marriage.

Most Saudi men marry for the first time between the age of twenty and twenty-five. The bride is expected to be much younger. It's still not unusual for her to be thirteen years old or even younger. When a Saudi man is older and looking for a second, third, or fourth wife, he still tends to pick a very young girl. They prefer girls with little education. Grade school is fine, but serious academic training is out of the question. Educated women are generally described as arrogant, self-confident, and emancipated. Saudi society is patriarchal and an uneducated girl is easier to domineer and order around.

Ghanima didn't undertake her clandestine business to rebel against the system, but instead on religious grounds: the prophet Muhammad had ordered his wives to seek out husbands for unmarried women. Ghanima wanted to find husbands for Saudi spinsters over the age of twenty-five.

First of all, she invited two acquaintances—both single women over the age of thirty—to a meeting. She wanted to establish a steering committee. The three of them decided to compile a database of all single, older women in the entire country: their phone numbers, addresses, appearance, assets, and so on. Fired with ambition, they also decided to create a similar list of men who didn't have four wives. These gentlemen would be contacted and cajoled into accepting their full quota of spouses.

Word got around the big cities that Ghanima had founded a marriage agency. Soon, women started coming to visit her to request a husband for a daughter or sister. A lot of money was collected to help Ghanima's campaign. Photo albums of available single females were assembled. Ghanima organized groups of women who went from house to house with the albums, trying to interest the men of the house in the charming ladies.

Saudi men were quite receptive but most of their wives were not. They didn't like the idea of sharing their husband with another woman. Their resistance was Ghanima's greatest hurdle.

When Ghanima visited a house and was able to speak to an annoyed and unreceptive wife, she always argued, "Good Muslim wives should be willing to make sacrifices for their Muslim sisters. In our society, we must share both unhappiness and joy. Show solidarity and be generous! Our prophet Muhammad recommended this to us through his own example. In his time, many men were killed in battle. The surviving men married the widows of their fallen comrades."

Some women welcomed Ghanima's idea, but for very different reasons than she had envisaged. One of them openly told her that her husband was a brutal wife-beater. He showed her absolutely no affection and often beat their children, as well. It would be no great loss if he married another woman; his attention would be diverted away from her for a time. She was, however, afraid that he might divorce her and leave her with no financial support. The government didn't make it mandatory for ex-husbands to pay child support. Who would look after her and the children? She couldn't get a job—she had no skills and had never worked outside her home. Become a cleaning lady? She couldn't support a family on that income. She could go onto the streets and beg, but it was against the law in Saudi Arabia. The government wouldn't help her. Her only alternative would be to ask her parents or brothers for financial support.

Prince Ahmed supported Ghanima's campaign. He made a public pronouncement that, if any Saudi man accepted an older woman as one of his wives, he would get an automatic award of ten thousand Saudi riyals (about 2,600 US dollars). If the single, older women had children, he would receive three thousand riyals (800 US dollars) for each of them. Many men took up the prince's offer. It was a welcome, fully funded adventure for them. Many Saudi men who live in cities maintain an apartment for their sexual escapades—an undisturbed place to bring their booty: prostitutes or women for one-night stands. Well, now it could be legal. Nasty tongues pointed out that the use of certain apartment buildings in certain city districts was turning Riyadh into Bangkok. Defenders pointed out that Saudi money, previously spent on the prostitutes of Bangkok, would now stay domiciled. The transaction that Ghanima's marriage service offered, backed by the prince, would benefit both Saudi men and Saudi women. It would be legal, Islamic, and clean.

Prince Ahmed had personally spoken by phone to Sister Ghanima (as he addressed her) to congratulate her and wish her further success. He also promised further financial support for her organization. The prince was nearly illiterate, but he had big dreams for the Saudi people. He wanted the population to explode so that they would become a demographic power in the Gulf, with a population larger than Iran or Iraq, Saudi Arabia's ancient enemies.

Most of the men who responded to Ghanima's campaign collected their ten thousand riyals and slept with their new wives only a couple of times. They didn't want to father children, and some even used condoms to assure that. Most Saudi women don't even know what a condom is. A number of men divorced the older woman after a few days. That was easy enough to do, according to Saudi law; the man had only to say the words "I divorce you" three times in the presence of male witnesses. Most of the women provided by Ghanima became second wives, and often the first wife had no idea that a new lady had entered the family circle. Ghanima had to factor this into her assessment of her success. A few marriages à la Ghanima were, indeed, successful.

A few of the brides were clever and protected themselves. They insisted that the bridegroom buy them gold jewelry worth twenty thousand riyals (over five thousand US dollars) as wedding presents. Several self-confident women amassed wealth in the form of a villa or other real estate, stocks and bonds, and so on. For a number of wealthy men, the marriage was worth the expense: they paid and they gave gifts.

In mosques across Saudi Arabia, the imams' Friday prayers praised Ghanima's actions and example; she was venerated and held in high esteem. All Muslim men were to support her work with open praise and active participation. Every one of them was urged to contact Ghanima with information about any unmarried older daughters or sisters in his family. Furthermore, they were not to expect a high bride price, as this was an undertaking inspired by the dictates of their religion.

One of the sheikhs preached the following sermon in a mosque: "Our daughters and sisters are the purest women in the world. Even if they are older, they should be able to live normal lives and enjoy life's pleasures legally. We must follow the example of our Prophet. He and his friends married every single woman and widow who was available. We must show solidarity in this. Ghanima has executed an act of heroism: she is protecting our men from infection with venereal diseases and AIDS. A Muslim's semen is sacred. It must be given, as a special gift, only to a Muslim woman . . ."

THE PRINCE

One of the evils of our world is the arrogance of power, absolute power, in either the material or political sense. The powerful encapsulate themselves in an awareness of their own strength, and as a consequence become blind and highhanded. One such individual is a Saudi Arabian prince. He was born into power and then grew into the possession of unlimited power. Therefore he practices absolute rule, both materially and politically, without a second thought. He also believes that his incredible wealth and power validate any extreme of unlicensed behavior. Again, women are no exception. For him, they are objects of lust, salable items that can be used in any way, and he expects them to unquestioningly comply with his every whim . . . and every perversion.

Over twenty thousand princes and princesses of the ruling al-Saud family live in Saudi Arabia. At the beginning of the twentieth century, King Abdulaziz al-Saud, the founder of Saudi Arabia, left as his family legacy over eighty sons and an undeclared number of daughters. He is said to have married over one hundred times. The male members of the al-Saud family consider Arabia to be the private asset and wealth base of a family business. It is not without good reason that the country is called Saudi Arabia.

The women of the al-Saud family, however, play a minor part in Saudi society. Their only contribution is the bearing of children. But they are protected by an unwritten, tacitly understood al-Saud family law; only women who are actually members of the al-Saud family, or those from a tribe of very high standing, can be retained as permanent wives. This law is strongly applied to keep the wealth and power of the al-Saud family firmly consolidated. Therefore, a prince can marry a woman from outside the family, but only for a certain length of time; such marriages must end in divorce.

Some princes conform to the dictates of the prophet Muhammad, who stated that a Muslim man can be married to up to four women. But, to enjoy more than four, they stay married for only a short period of time and then divorce. Not every prince conforms to this pattern. Some powerful ones marry very often and don't bother to get divorced. Some have lost track of how many women are legally their wives. And marriages to foreigners from outside the pale of the Arab world are never registered.

When she is divorced, the wife can ask for nothing. She leaves with nothing more than her wedding gifts from the prince: gold and jewelry. Many princes regard marriage to non-Saudi women as a legal and more elegant form of acquiring the services of a prostitute.

Immediately after the discovery of oil, the al-Saud family was extremely rich, but comparatively small in numbers. Over the course of forty years, the family grew exponentially. This is hardly surprising, since each prince could marry an almost unimaginable number of women and from those sexual unions produce an enormous number of children and grandchildren. Of course, not every prince has equal power and wealth. The more distant a prince's link to the sons of King Abdulaziz, the weaker his position and influence.

The remaining sons of King Abdulaziz consolidated power at the center of the clan: The current king, King Abdullah, his brothers, and their sons and grandsons run the country with absolute centralized authority and enjoy endless wealth. Saudi Arabia is practically run by King Abdullah, Crown Prince Sultan; Prince Nayef, the home minister; and Prince Bandar, a son of Prince Sultan and head of the intelligence service.

Prince Faisal is one from the center of the al-Saud clan. He is over seventy years of age, just over five feet tall, and extremely fat. His skin color is very fair, and he has a round, wide face with high cheekbones and brown, saucer-shaped eyes that seem to emanate a reproachful scowl. In public he likes to speak about Islam. In almost every interview he thanks God for the gift of Islam, which the Almighty conferred on Saudi Arabia.

Thanks to Islam, Saudi Arabia is a land of justice and mercy that is free of exploitation, prostitution, alcohol and drugs, he says.

Prince Faisal usually marries about every two weeks and divorces after a couple days or so. Depending on the prince's mood, the ex-wife might leave with valuable gifts, a car, and a villa. She also gets a financial settlement, but sometimes it isn't a large amount. She is not allowed to remarry. This is one of the strictest conditions of her divorce.

Sometimes the prince keeps a wife for months or even years—usually this is only the case if she becomes pregnant with a son. Sons demonstrate a man's virility and create family strength. "A society needs men," is one of Prince Faisal's favorite sayings. As one of the most powerful men in the country, he doesn't restrict himself to four wives. He located a religious teacher somewhere within the country who found a Qur'anic commentary, a Surra, which, in that scholar's opinion, can be interpreted to mean that a Muslim can have more than four wives.

An entire organization exists simply to help Prince Faisal tie the knot. Officials are sent out far and wide to search the country for girls with certain qualities particularly appealing to the prince. She must be a light-skinned virgin. She has to have a round face and be a bit plump, with heavy thighs, nice curves, and wide hips. Her school reports are of no interest.

Of course, he owns many palaces all over the country and abroad. In the winter, he gets married in Saudi Arabia, because the weather is pleasant. In the summer, he gets married abroad. His favorite overseas locales include Austria, Switzerland, Morocco, and California.

He only marries Arab women so that he can communicate better with them in bed. Before the bride enters his bedroom, she is lectured by a marriage committee about how to behave, what the prince expects, and what he enjoys most. He likes it very much, in bed, when women say obscene words and when they refer to their own sexual organs, as well as his, using the correct terms.

Prince Faisal first married at the age of seventeen. Since then, he has produced an estimated four hundred sons and daughters. He has more daughters than sons. No one knows the exact number, including the prince.

One of his ex-wives, Muna, a Moroccan, lives with her daughter,

Karima, in Casablanca. Muna is in now her late thirties but looks younger. She has fair skin and light green eyes. Her marriage to Faisal, if it can be described as a marriage, lasted one week. She didn't receive a financial settlement or support payments for their daughter. Karima has never met her father and often asks about him. Muna attempted in vain to organize a meeting of the father and daughter, so he could at least exchange a few words with her. Prince Faisal's marriage bureau always rejected her requests—sometimes with politeness, and sometimes quite brusquely. In the short space of her one-week marriage, Muna had many painful experiences. She explained her own story.

In 1990 I was working as a secretary to Saudi Crown Prince Abdullah's chief of staff in Casablanca. At that time I was a pretty, young girl. One day my boss, a fatherly type but nevertheless a ruthless businessman, asked me if I would be willing to marry Prince Faisal, an important Saudi prince. Of course, I thought it was a joke. "No, really," he insisted. "Some of his people took notice of you when they were here in Casablanca, and they know you'd be just perfect for him." My boss described the prince, painting a delightful picture in my imagination. He was superrich, super nice, and I would live the rest of my life as a princess. Well, I was young—nineteen years old—and inexperienced.

I came from a humble home. I had seven sisters and brothers, all younger than me. My father, a sincere and modest person, was the doorman at the government tax offices. My mother, who was kind and sweet, had worked not only at home but also as a cleaning lady up until recently. We had to get by with little money. I had worked as a secretary for six months in that office, and my salary went directly to my mother, who was now frequently ill.

I told my boss that I would think about it. Then I went home and consulted my parents. They reacted with mixed feelings. To begin, of course, they didn't believe it. Then they thought that maybe it was some kind of trap.

Every day my boss would ask me for my reply. "Well, did you think it through? I hope you come to a positive decision, because you only meet up with a chance like this once in a lifetime. Seize the opportunity. This is a golden chance—your only chance. Only once in a lifetime . . ."

"But I don't even know him!" I replied.

"C'mon, he's a prince. What do you need to know about him? You'll be swimming in money. If only I had you for a daughter. I could tell you immediately to go ahead and marry him. You'll really regret it if you reject this offer."

"Regret" turned out to be the right word. I regret that I ever consented. I regret that I accepted his advice.

After further consideration, I decided to accept the offer of marriage. I was actually afraid that, if I refused, I would lose my job because my boss was so intent on my agreement. It also seemed to me that he wanted to do a favor for the prince. And anyway, who knows, maybe he was a good prince. Maybe my family would be able to live better in the future. But in spite of everything, I still wasn't able to envision an offer of marriage from one of Saudi Arabia's most important princes as reality. I was more or less rubbing my eyes to find out if this was a dream.

When I told my boss, a couple days later, that I consented to the marriage, he was as overjoyed as if I had agreed to marry his own son. Very excited, he immediately telephoned someone; I think he phoned the prince's marriage bureau.

That afternoon, a man who was accompanied by a woman came to our office. He was tall and slim, with dark skin and black eyes that he fixed on me aggressively. The woman wore a headscarf and was comparatively short; she was also overweight and had a small, pointed face. She had applied her makeup thickly, and the heavy rouge on her cheeks couldn't conceal her dark, coarse skin. She observed me with inexpressive eyes and a cold-hearted manner. To my mind, she behaved like the headmistress of some English boarding school. From their accents I realized that they were Saudis. My boss greeted them effusively and introduced me.

The woman addressed me. "As you probably have already learned from your employer, Director Bu Zayed, His Highness Prince Faisal wishes to marry you. His Highness has commanded me to present you with this gift."

She then handed me a large, dark red, velvet box. When I opened it, it seemed to be dripping and flashing with fine gold. I was looking at an amazing, astounding matched jewelry set: a necklace, earrings, a bracelet, and a wristwatch.

She then continued, "His Majesty wants the marriage to be kept strictly secret. No one is to know about it except the members of your immediate family—your parents, sisters, and brothers. They must, under no circumstances, tell anyone else."

It was a carrot-and-stick situation: first she presented gold, and then demanded secrecy. I found that odd.

Then the man pulled a sealed business envelope from his inside suit pocket and handed it to me. "Open it." I did so, and what did I pull out? Money. A lot of money. More money than I had ever, in my entire lifetime, held in my hands. ". . . So much! Oh, my God!" I exclaimed. Later I was to learn that I shouldn't have reacted so enthusiastically.

The woman said, "We would like you to go home now, with as little fuss as possible. Don't attract attention to yourself. Tell your family, in a discreet way, that you have to take a trip and that you'll be away for two weeks. We will wait for you here. And don't forget—this must remain a secret."

I was overwhelmed. It was simply too much for me; everything was happening so fast. I didn't have the strength to sort things through and consider them. I was stupefied.

Excited, I made my way home. I tried to calm myself down and gather the courage I would need to tell my parents that a prince would be marrying me, and that was why I had to travel abroad for two weeks. I considered, back and forth, what would be the best way to make the announcement, and how to ensure that they would keep it secret. What would they think? Their daughter is going to secretly marry an unknown prince. Well, no parent in his or her right mind would accept that. I would have to lie.

Before long, I was home. Luckily, both my parents were there, and they were alone. Agitated, I announced, "Dear Mother, dear Father, please sit down. Let's drink a coffee together. I need to have a confidential discussion with you about something amazing."

My parents gaped with surprise, and they exchanged sideways glances with each other, as no one had ever spoken to them like this before. In our house, amazing things didn't happen. They sat down and stared at me expectantly.

I quickly prepared coffee, presented it to them, and announced in a quavering voice, "Imagine, I am going to marry a prince. A powerful Saudi Arabian prince." I hadn't expected them to believe me, and they didn't. They stared at me like stone statues and obviously couldn't take it in. Finally, my father picked up his coffee, took a noisy sip, and said, "Don't talk nonsense to us." My mother rubbed both her eyes as though she had just woken up, and said, with kindness and sympathy, "My dear Muna, speak seriously, and leave us to cope with life's bitter realities." She then tried to change the subject.

"Mother, I'm telling the truth. At first, just like you, I didn't believe it. Let me tell you what happened." I explained everything, including my boss's involvement and encouragement. Then I added in a serious and determined tone, "I am obliged to take a one-week marriage preparation course. During it I will be instructed in how the wife of a prince should behave, and if I pass it, the prince will marry me. Then there will be a huge marriage celebration, and, of course, you will attend."

My parents just stared at me. They simply didn't know what to say. They were so confused, they couldn't even comment on my story. They had never experienced such a thing, never even heard of it, and I had never lied to them in my lifetime. Their reaction filled me with fear and uncertainty. But, because I had accepted the prince's proposal, I didn't want to be plagued by doubts or hear any contradictions. I interpreted their silence as tacit agreement, as though they wanted to say, "If this is the truth, then do as you wish. We can't advise you."

To avoid any complications, I got to my feet and decided to leave. I didn't know if I should take clothing and personal belongings on the trip. I didn't even own a suitcase because I had never traveled in my life. So I decided to take nothing. Anyway, the neighbors would notice if I dragged my chic clothes out of the house, even if they were stuffed in a garbage bag. No—better to simply disappear. I now had a lot of money. I'd be able to buy clothes on the way. Then I wondered if I should at least offer my parents part of the money? I'd better not. They'd wonder, "What are you doing with so much money?" Did you have to do something? Some of the women in our neighborhood worked as prostitutes, and my parents had always denounced this. No, better not to leave any money. And it would be smart to leave quickly, before my sisters and brothers came home.

I returned to the office. My boss and the two Saudis had already grown impatient and unsettled, so when they saw me, smiles lit up their faces. I was told that we would now travel to the prince's palace. Outside, an incredible, huge limousine pulled up—I had no idea of the manufacturer, since I hardly knew about such things—but certainly I had never seen a car like that in my entire life. I got inside with the two Saudis. We drove and drove, but not a word was said. Then we entered a hilly district of exclusive residences. The uneven, intensely green landscape was dotted with impressive villas, charming bungalows, and magnificent palaces. Suddenly the woman said, "We're almost there." A few minutes later the limousine pulled up to a magnificent home—a small palace.

Once inside, the woman informed me that the preparatory period for my wedding would last up to four days. In the meantime, I was to consider myself at home and to remember that all of the prince's residences were equally mine. I was given a set of rooms exclusively for my own use, including a temporary bedroom. If I needed anything at all, I was to dial "96" on the telephone. His Majesty had informed the staff that my every wish was to be fulfilled.

I was then invited to have dinner. I was conducted into a dining room and seated at the table, which was over thirty feet long and covered with delicacies of every kind. Although I was in fact hungry, I could barely eat. At home, I ate with my family, and here I was sitting alone like some dictator. Afterward, I was taken to another room for coffee. The walls were covered with Gobelin tapestries and paintings, and a spacious balcony looked out over a beautiful and secluded landscape: there was nothing to see except grass, trees, and the distant line of the horizon. However, in spite of all the magnificence, I found the house eerily cold, and I was touched by an indescribable sense of fear.

I spent the night in my assigned bedroom, sleeping in a wide, dream bed—the lilac-colored sheets and pillowcases were silk. The yellow disc of the full moon, set against an inky sky, shone straight in through the window. Normally, I adore the full moon, but that night it was like a threatening monster from outer space. It seemed to be laughing at me. I lay on my back, so I could keep a watch over the room's two doors—one leading into the house, and the other to the balcony. I imagined that I heard noises. I thought someone was approaching to enter the room. Overcome by paranoia, I didn't sleep all night. When the moon disappeared, I got up. I felt chained. I decided to go home.

In the morning I gathered my few belongings and opened the bedroom door. Who was sitting there? The Saudi woman. She was waiting for me. Breakfast was ready, and afterward I would have to try on my wedding dress and other gowns. I didn't find the courage to tell her that I wanted to return to my parents. The woman intimidated me so much that I found myself simply following her.

After a hurried meal, I was taken to another room. Three women were busy at work cutting fabric and sewing. My wedding gown stood in the middle, on a dress form, atop a pedestal. I was asked to try it on. It was a traditional Moroccan-style dress embroidered with gold thread. I examined myself in the full-length mirror. It was absolutely magnificent, and I looked gorgeous in it; the color and style suited me perfectly. The seamstresses took note of some small alterations. Then I was fitted for a number of other outfits as well. Finally, I was asked to take a seat and flip through ready-to-wear catalogues, pointing out anything that appealed to me.

To give me something to do and drive away boredom, the Saudi woman—who I now realized was the manager of this residence—took me to a room with a television and a stereo system, so I could watch a movie or listen to music. There were a lot of magazines on the coffee table. Most of them were in English.

While watching a movie, I drifted off and fell into a sound sleep; I was dead tired. Suddenly, I woke up. Checking the time on the gold watch that the prince had given me, I noticed that it was five o'clock in the afternoon. I went to my bedroom, changed out of my clothes, and went back to sleep.

I didn't wake up until nine o'clock the next morning. A handwritten note lay on my bedside table, which read:

> Good morning, dear Muna,
> When you wake up, look inside the clothes closets.
> Yours,
> Manal

I immediately went to the closets and opened them. They were completely full of clothes—among them, the items I had pointed out from the magazines. Two gorgeous negligee housecoats were draped over a nearby chair. The vanity table was covered with a tastefully arranged array of cosmetics from leading French companies, as well as expensive perfumes. The sight of so many beautiful gifts, and so much generosity, calmed my fears and jittery nerves.

Right away I took a shower and slipped into an absolutely charming dress that fit perfectly. I felt better, a little more certain about my decision, and a little more self-confident. I dialed 96 on the telephone. Manal, the Saudi woman, picked up. I told her that I was dressed and ready for breakfast. She replied in a friendly voice, "You learn fast! That's very good! Because this is how it has to be. Breakfast is ready, Muna. It's waiting for you."

After I ate, Manal informed me that we would be traveling to Riyadh, the capital of Saudi Arabia, the very next day. The marriage would take place there, and my groom was waiting for me. The suspense was growing, and I was happy that the uncertainty and ongoing surprises were now coming to an end. Manal told me not to worry about anything; the servants would arrange for the transport of all my new belongings. However, we absolutely had to be ready to leave the villa at 9 a.m. tomorrow morning; the plane would take off at 10 a.m., sharp.

We arrived at the Casablanca Airport at 9:45 a.m. A private jet, part of the Saudi Royal Airlines fleet, was waiting for us. Our limousine drove right up to the airplane's access stairs. The captain and crew were lined up on the tarmac to greet us. Inside, I was given a special, very wide, and comfortable seat near the front of the plane. Manal sat directly behind me. The flight attendants offered me everything possible: drinks, food, newspapers, and games. I could even fully recline the seat, so I decided to try that, and actually napped for half an hour. The only people on the flight were Manal, seven maidservants, a number of men whom I assumed were bodyguards, and me. I had seen the men briefly at the airport. On the flight, they were hidden from my view; I was completely surrounded by women.

Before we landed, Manal came to me and told me that I'd have to put on an abaya—a black, loose robe of light material. My abaya was pure silk. I also had to put on a headscarf and veil my face. The facial veil had already been tied for me, I just had to lower it down over my head. It looked like some strange kind of hat. Manal dressed similarly. "These are mandatory local customs," she explained, and then added jokingly that this was a "women's uniform" here in Saudi Arabia, to protect us from the sharp, lustful gazes of men. "Poor men!" she said. Both of us had a good laugh, which helped to dispel the tension. It made me feel so much better; I hadn't laughed in days.

The plane landed in the private, royal landing area of King Khaled Airport in Riyadh, which serves only the personal airplanes of the Saudi princes. Not surprisingly, there were no passport and immigration formalities; we were escorted from the steps of the plane into several waiting limousines. Our vehicles were preceded by a police car, which drove very fast, lights flashing, while we followed closely. After half an hour, we drove through a huge gate in the high walls surrounding a palace. It was simply enormous, and floodlights illuminated it on all sides. Everything gleamed in their light: the facades, the walls, the hanging lamps and lampposts. Directly in front of the building, a pond contained a large, gushing fountain whose cascading water was illuminated in many colors by spotlights. The garden beds were thickly planted with flowers of every type and color. The palace reminded me of *One Thousand and One Nights*. On top, a seemingly endless range of Japanese-style roofs receded before our gaze.

No one greeted me at the door. Manal said to me, "A person is not greeted when she walks into her own home." That was a hint that I should relax and feel in charge. Once inside, we walked up the staircase and entered the hall of the palace. Enormous crystal and gold chandeliers, in absolutely zany artistic designs, were suspended from its ceiling. The walls were covered in marble. It looked like photos I had seen of palaces in Paris or Vienna built in the heyday of their aristocracies. Manal then showed me through the palace, room by room, and each of them was more magnificent than the one previous. I was even led through the master bedroom and bathroom. The bathroom was certainly over four hundred square feet in size, and in the middle was a round bathtub the size of a small swimming pool. Above this, there were holes in the ceiling through which the shower water was directed, so that anyone taking a shower would have the impression of standing in a pleasant rain. On one side of the bathroom stood a large screen decorated with photos of the most beautiful landscapes of the world, such as Norway and Upper Austria. One would have the sensation of bathing in the open air, surrounded by landscapes of snow, lakes and rivers, and greenery.

I still felt wary of Manal; I didn't know her well enough to fully trust her. She spoke little and behaved very formally. She had disclosed hardly anything about the wedding, and I didn't dare to approach the topic.

After our palace tour, Manal said that it would be a good idea if I withdrew to my own room and made sure I got a lot of rest, because my marriage would take place the next day. If I needed anything, once again I was to dial 96 on the phone. "Everyone here is at your service." Then she guided me back to my bedroom—the palace was so huge, I couldn't remember where it was.

I was, in fact, quite tired, but now I couldn't get to sleep. I was excited. Lately I had felt very lonely; time had dragged and my life had had no focus. I had wanted to be with my family, to confide in someone close to me. Surrounded as I was by every kind of material thing, my heart felt sick. I couldn't enjoy such finery, thinking that I might end up unhappy and emotionally deprived. But hopefully, all would go well, and I would see my parents and sisters and brothers again soon.

I went to bed and tried to sleep, but I couldn't unwind. I didn't want to get up and read or watch television. I was afraid again. I shut my eyes tight and tried to trick myself into falling asleep. Perhaps I did nod off, but every once in a while I would open my eyes and glance nervously at the door. Maybe a witch would enter with a candelabra in her gnarled hand, some former wife of the prince whom he had locked in the attic, intent on killing me, like in some English thriller.

I honestly believe that I didn't properly fall asleep until daylight, subconsciously dominated by the idea that monsters can only walk in the dark. It was noon when I woke up. Physically, I felt weak; I would have liked to stay in bed all day long. But mentally, I was now driven by curiosity. I wanted to know what would come next. I wanted an end to the fears and uncertainty that had come to dominate my life second by second.

I was bathing when the telephone rang. It was Manal inquiring when I'd be ready. Of course, I could take as long as I wanted, she then mentioned deferentially. But I moved fast. By doing so, I wanted to show the palace that I could make my own decisions.

Outside my room, Manal was waiting for me, seated with two other women who said they were sisters of the prince. I was very happy to finally meet some family members. After exchanging polite greetings and some appropriate small talk, we went to eat together. Afterward they asked me some standard conversational questions about my tastes: what were my favorite colors, foods, and countries I would love to visit . . . and then, suddenly, they jumped to intimate topics. One of them described how her husband liked to have sex with her, in extreme detail. I was shocked. She calmed me down by counseling that I was young and inexperienced but advised that every woman has to know her husband's sexual preferences to keep his love and attention.

She then narrated to me, in exact detail, that her brother preferred this and that when he was making love. She had collected this information from his ex-wives. He was a tender lover, of course, but one had to know how to handle him in sexual matters. In some respects, I was absolutely disgusted by the prince's sexual tastes. But I suppressed my reaction. Everything was becoming very uncomfortable. The one thing that was clear to me was that they wanted, somehow or other, to teach me about their brother. I felt like a whore being lectured about how to sexually satisfy a client. As the conversation drew to a close, the women became cheerful and very upbeat. They had apparently noticed that I was reacting negatively to the last part of our "getting-to-know-you" session. They announced that they were going to go to their brother immediately, just to tell him how charming I was. They got to their feet and took their leave with a flurry of cheek kisses.

Manal seated herself opposite me and informed me that the marriage would take place that evening. Then she abruptly got up and left. I sat there alone, lost, in a huge palace reception room. Everything, everywhere, looked cold. I tried to repress my thoughts and feelings. But how? And why? I went back into my bedroom and burst into tears. Then, suddenly, I was filled with anger. I pulled myself together and decided to go to the Moroccan Embassy. I picked up my purse and headed out the door. I would go out onto the street and hail a taxi. As I descended the stairs, I found Manal sitting in an alcove. "Where to, Muna?" she asked.

"I'm going to the Moroccan Embassy."

"What's this?" she asked, deeply concerned.

"I'm not going through with this. I'm going home."

"Calm down, calm down. Tell me what's happened. Did the prince's sisters make you angry?"

"No. But I'm going to the Moroccan Embassy," I replied insistently.

Manal came to me and tried to embrace me. But I pushed her away and strode to the door.

"Muna, the embassy is closed today. This is the weekend. But you needn't be concerned, the ambassador himself is coming here. He's going to be a guest at the wedding." When I heard that, my resolve melted. I sank onto a couch and blubbered like a baby. Manal drew near. She slowly sat down. Then she laid her hands on my head, my shoulders. She began to stroke me. "I understand, I understand. It's hard for a young woman like you to be so far away from your home and family. You're not used to it. But I assure you, Muna, everything is going to be just fine. So many women dream about this—the chance to marry a real prince. We're going to pull this off; believe me."

The telephone rang. Manal went and picked it up, but all she said was "Yes ... yes ... yes." Then she asked the speaker to hold and turned to me. She announced that a diplomat from my embassy would come—perhaps the ambassador himself—and that it was certain that he'd come by before the wedding. She quickly finished the call and hung up. Then she said, "The ceremony will be at eight o'clock this evening, and the Moroccan ambassador is on the guest list, Muna." I had four hours to get ready. Manal told me that the hairdresser and cosmetician were waiting for me. "Let's go upstairs," she gently suggested.

When Manal told me that I had four hours left, my ambivalent feelings strengthened. On the one hand, I wanted to marry, and most certainly with a prince whose wealth could improve the lifestyle of all my family members. But I didn't want to marry a prince who intended to lock me into a golden cage.

My minder accompanied me to the palace's beauty salon. It was fully equipped and staffed, of course, only by women, who treated me discreetly and kindly. When they did my hair, they seemed to know exactly what to do, while at the same time inquiring about my personal preferences and responding to them. They treated every inch of my skin with a range of creams and oils. One worker commented during the process that the prince preferred soft and firm skin. It was almost three hours before I was finished. Manal took me back to my room, where the seamstresses carefully slipped my wedding dress over my head. Then I was conducted toward a large reception room from which the sound of Arabic music and singing was emanating. Inside were women, strangely enough, in Western clothing, and all of them were singing. In the middle, one of them was performing a belly dance. A few ladies sat in a corner, playing musical instruments. The room was gorgeous and exotic. The floors were covered with beautiful, expensive carpets and edged with long, narrow, firm mattresses with silk bolsters that formed low-lying seats. The chairs for the married couple were somewhat elevated to show respect. As I was slowly paraded toward them, the women entertained me with a song in my praise, which referred to me by name. It was very exciting. Then I took my place in the bride's seat of honor.

As the guests entertained themselves, Manal approached and quietly informed me that the Moroccan ambassador was waiting to speak with me in an adjacent chamber. She accompanied me and then disappeared. An older gentleman got to his feet and politely greeted me. I had the impression that he was uncomfortable, and that he wanted to share something with me and then promptly leave. We sat opposite each other.

The ambassador said, "I will not keep you long. First of all, may I congratulate you on the occasion of your marriage, and wish you all the best. Please ... you don't need to thank me. I want to tell you that you are marrying one of the best princes of Saudi Arabia—a man with a fine personality. He is also one of the country's most important politicians; he is a minister and is also responsible for numerous other administrative offices. You are going to enjoy a wonderful life at his side." He then asked me if I had any questions.

"How old is he?" I asked.

"In all honesty, maybe sixty, but he looks forty. Furthermore, he has a lot of vitality."

"How many wives does he have?"

"I don't know exactly. But he keeps a woman if she pleases him. He finds happiness with only a few of his wives. The others, he divorces."

"Why does he want to keep our marriage a secret?"

"He does this with all new marriages. If the relationship doesn't work out, the disappointment and the scandal are kept behind the palace walls. In a while, when he sees that his marriage to you is a success, he will most certainly want to meet your parents and the rest of your family." There was a little pause, so he concluded, "If you have no further questions, allow me to accompany you to the door, so you can continue your celebrations."

Manal was waiting for me there. Without saying a word, we stepped back into the festivities.

After a few minutes, the arrival of the prince was announced. A song was also sung in his honor. He was highly praised: he was the most handsome, the most generous, the manliest man among men. Then he appeared, wearing his Saudi robes under a flowing golden cloak. The prince was about five feet, four inches tall, and he was fat; he must have weighed over two hundred and fifty pounds. He looked like he was in his late forties. He sat down beside me. I made it appear that I was staring at the floor, but from under my transparent veil I could observe everything. As he had not greeted me, our relationship began with silence.

His behavior was not correct for a Middle Eastern wedding: the groom is expected to give the guests the impression that he is anxious to check out his wife's physical attributes, since the human body and sexuality are inseparable in Arab and Islamic culture. But my new husband just sat there, casually looking around like he was waiting in an airport. My duty as the bride was to appear as bashful as a little girl. This would please both the guests and my husband, who would take it as a sign that I was a virginal, inexperienced woman.

The prince was served coffee and dates. Incense had already wafted through the room, but since the prince's arrival it had become much stronger. Some kind of intoxicant had been added, which smelled like perfume. It lowered our inhibitions and sexually aroused us. The music and singing became louder. Suddenly, the prince stood up. All the women in the room promptly stood up, and so did I. He took me by the left hand and slowly walked toward the door, with me by his side. All of the guests followed, continuing to sing, and they followed us right to the door of our bedroom. The prince and I entered alone, and the door was shut behind us.

We could still hear the singing, but it slowly faded as the guests returned to the hall. I sat down in an armchair and stared at the floor. The prince removed his festive cloak and his headdress; then he approached me. He slowly raised the veil from my face and exclaimed, "My God, you are beautiful!" Then he took me by my upper arms and lifted me to my feet. I didn't resist, but I felt very shy and very frightened. He directed me toward our marriage bed. And I have to say that he was indeed a very tender and caring lover. However, he was so sexually excited that everything seemed to be over in five minutes. Then he suggested that we return to our guests.

I had hoped for and anticipated his wanting to get to know me as a person. I thought that he would ask me questions about myself, my life. And I wanted to get to know him, too. But no. Suddenly I felt like a prostitute; I didn't feel like the bride of a fairy tale prince.

Back in the reception hall, the women were still singing. When we entered, the volume increased. The fumes of the intoxicating incense were renewed and once again wafted through the room. Under the spell of the perfumed drug, several guests sank to the floor and gazed with unfocussed eyes into the distance. Two women began to kiss each other passionately. Later, I was to learn that all these women had been engaged to function as "wedding guests." They had been brought from various Arab countries, and they lived in the palace. They sang, they danced, they performed on musical instruments, and they enjoyed the party.

Next, we were served a Lebanese dinner accompanied by alcoholic drinks. The prince likes to drink Lebanese Raki when he eats Lebanese food. Before him was placed a huge copper tray on which over a hundred small plates displayed different types of dishes. He invited me to eat and drink.

"I don't drink Raki," I replied. I ate very little and tried not to show my fury. He gobbled and drank with great enjoyment, and took no notice of me whatsoever.

In the meantime, a number of the women had removed their clothes so that they sat half-naked, in a stupor, in the warm reception hall. Others were engaging in uninhibited sexual acts. After the prince had finished eating and drinking, he got to his feet and began to clumsily dance with some of the women. Everyone was laughing. I found it shockingly inappropriate. Later I learned that His Majesty encouraged this kind of behavior at his marriages because he believed it stimulated his appetite.

Eventually, he collapsed onto his seat, dead tired from all the fun and flirting. When he fell asleep, the wedding celebrations promptly ended. Manal entered with two very strong servant men who bodily carried the prince to his "nuptial" bed. The entire wedding, if it could be called that, had been the height of impropriety and shamelessness.

My husband, Prince Faisal, lay in bed like a dead body. The only sign of life was his endless snoring. The quieter the palace became, the more fear took hold of me. I was filled with revulsion at the idea of lying down by his side. I curled up in an armchair with a coverlet and imagined how lucky I would be if he never woke up. I was filled with panic that he could wake at any moment and summon me to the bed for sex. Finally, I fell asleep and was only woken by the predawn call to prayer from the nearby mosque. The prince also woke—with a start—and looked around. I stood up and made it look as if I were searching for something. When he saw me, he mumbled, "What are you doing there?" I was certain that he had no idea what my name was. I replied, "I'm looking for . . . for . . ." but he interrupted and summoned me back to his bed. Instead, I went into the bathroom, hoping that he would drift off and fall back asleep. Suddenly I heard, "Where are you? Come here immediately!" I thought I'd better get back before he got really angry.

He was lying on one side of the bed, and he reached his arms into the air, saying "Come to me!" I headed for the free side of the bed, but when I came within arm's reach he forcefully grabbed me and pulled me onto him. This time he treated me crudely and with brutality. It was rape. I was afraid of what might happen if I didn't cooperate. I did whatever he ordered, and I allowed him to do whatever he pleased to me. Finally he stood up, dialed someone on the telephone, and announced, "I'm on my way right now." He put on his housecoat and left the room without a word or even a glance. I believe that he went to his wing of the palace.

At noon, Manal came into the bedroom and informed me that I was moving. "Why? Where?" I asked.

"His Highness's orders. I myself don't have the details. Get ready."

Two servants came into the room and began packing my belongings. They were taken out to a waiting vehicle. Manal came back and announced that a car was waiting for me. She was in a hurry and left without saying good-bye. I assumed that this was a short trip. A limousine was waiting, and the driver opened the rear door for me. He drove away, and a second limo followed. I asked who was in it, and he replied tersely that they were security guards. I didn't dare ask where he was going. I was just happy to get away from the palace.

Half an hour later, we arrived in front of a two-story house—a Saudi villa. I got out. The chauffeur and the security guards carried my suitcases of clothes into the house. Then I was beckoned into the villa. Once inside, the head security agent told me that I would be living in this villa until His Highness decided otherwise. He gave me a telephone number and told me that if I needed anything, I should dial it. He also told me that a soldier had the house under surveillance. Then he and the other men left.

I was left inside, completely alone.

First I made an inspection of the place. It was luxurious, with beautiful furniture. Then I asked myself, "What now?" I considered phoning my former boss at his office and asking for help, but I couldn't find the country code for Morocco. There was no telephone book in the house. I went outside to ask for assistance. I went to the soldier in his little guardhouse at the front gate. He said that he didn't know but advised me to use the telephone number I had been given. When I dialed it, a man answered. "I would like the country code so I can call Morocco, please," I stated.

"One moment," he replied. After a few seconds, he informed me that he didn't have it.

"May I speak to Manal?"

"Manal? I don't know anyone named Manal," he said, and hung up.

I was furious and called back. This time I said, "This is Princess Muna speaking. I was speaking to you just now, and you hung up on me. Who do you think you are? Find me the dialing code for Morocco and call me back immediately. Wait—I don't know the telephone number of the line I am using just now. Please tell me what it is."

"Dear lady, I don't know either your phone number or the dialing code for Morocco," he replied, and hung up.

I was so upset, I could have killed myself. I wept, I wailed. I needed help. I had to get out of there. But how? Now I was filled with self-reproach. Why hadn't I asked the Moroccan ambassador for his phone number, his business card?

Two hours later, I was visited by the head security agent who had accompanied me in my move to the villa. He was polite and respectful. "I understand that you would like the country code so you can make a phone call to Morocco. I have brought the number for you, and also two servants—a housemaid and a chauffeur. They are sitting in the backseat of my car. May I bring them in? Here is the number." As soon as he went out to his vehicle, I ran to the phone. I dialed the country code and my boss's office number in Casablanca. A recorded voice announced: "No connection to this number." I kept dialing and redialing, even after the security agent reentered. He said, "Let me try it." Then he announced, "No wonder you're having difficulty. This phone line isn't connected to an international service. I'll look into it—you'll have to be provided with the 'zero' number service. Don't worry about it. It's easy to arrange." Then he pulled a white envelope from his pocket and handed it to me. "From His Highness," he said. There were two thousand Saudi riyals (over five hundred US dollars) inside.

The security agent introduced me to the housemaid and driver. Then he said, "My name is Ajlan, and I will drop by from time to time to see how you are." And he left.

The housemaid, Julia, and the driver, Ron, were immediately very likeable. Both of them were Filipinos in their midtwenties. They always gave me friendly smiles, and I had the impression that they actually cared about me. Maybe they already knew that I was just a victim of the prince's lust. Julia asked me what my favorite dishes were, and Ron asked me if I needed anything from the store. I immediately began to beg him to drive me to a place from where I could phone Morocco. "Oh, Madam, I'm so sorry, but I'm not allowed to do that. I have mandatory instructions that you are not to leave this house."

"Who told you this?"

"Prince Faisal's staff members."

"Okay—tell you what. Can *you* phone Morocco for me? This is the number—"

Ron interrupted me. "Madam, I'd like to tell you a secret. Can you promise me that you'll keep it to yourself?"

My heart beat faster. "Certainly."

"Madam, all three of us are being watched twenty-four hours a day. Maybe I can call when the level of surveillance slackens. But not from your house phone. It's bugged."

My legs could no longer hold me up; I sank onto a couch. Julia sat beside me and tried to offer comfort. Later, she went into the kitchen and brought me something to drink. In her I found solace and human warmth—qualities I had yet to encounter in any Saudi. She gave me courage. Talking to her cheered me up.

Later, at ten o'clock at night, Ajlan, the head security agent, returned.

He was a tall, strong Saudi with an uncombed beard and a thick belly bulging beneath his long, Arab gown. But in other respects, his appearance and demeanor had transformed. His eyes had the glassy stare of a madman or someone on drugs. He smelled terrible. His black eyes were glowering as they fixed on me, and he mumbled excitedly, "I have to come by to see if you need anything."

I suppressed my fear and replied, "How nice of you."

Then he said, "I've brought you something nice. Come here into the next room, and I'll show you." I wavered and then followed him. When we were inside, I noticed that he was carrying a bag under his arm. He opened it up and pulled out a bottle of whisky.

Alarmed, I loudly announced, "I don't drink alcohol," and turned to go out. But he reached the door before me and blocked it. Then he shut and locked it, removed the key, and hid it in his clothing. I warned him to leave me alone, or I would let loose with screams that would be heard everywhere.

"Nobody's going to hear you except for my staff, and they're waiting for me," he laughed. He scooped me off my feet and pushed me down onto the floor. I screamed, and he clapped his right hand over my mouth so that I could barely breathe. He raped me. When he was finished, he returned the unopened whisky bottle to its bag and disappeared.

Julia came in and took me in her arms. She said nothing, but just cried. She took me to a bathroom and helped me to wash.

Later, in the living room, she whispered to me, "That pig has raped me too, Madam."

As we were sitting there, Ron entered. "Is everything all right, Madam? I was outside, and I heard you screaming. That pig raped you, didn't he?" Later Ron told us that he had been standing with Ajlan's fellow officers when I began to scream, and that they had laughed and commented, "Listen to that! Sounds like she's really enjoying it!"

The day after the rape, I felt weak and abject. The walls seemed to be closing in on me. I was sinking into depression. Toward noon, Julia entered my room and said in concern, "Madam isn't feeling well?"

"I feel terrible. Life is awful. I didn't sleep all night."

"Shall we take you to a hospital? We know Filipino staff members who could help you. I'll call."

When she returned, she said, "An ambulance is waiting outside. Let me help you dress." She also packed a small bag with a few items in case I had to stay overnight.

The soldier at the gate argued with the ambulance personnel. He told them that I was not allowed even to go to a hospital for emergency treatment without official permission. The Sudanese doctor who was with the team assured the guard that he would personally shoulder the blame. The guard wanted to attack the doctor, but a passing Saudi man intervened. "Imagine if your wife or son was ill. Would you prevent your own family members from going to a hospital? Leave the doctor alone, and let the ambulance people do their job." The guard backed off reluctantly, and the ambulance sped away.

In the hospital I received a full examination, and it was determined that I was in an overall weak condition. An Indian doctor examined me. He believed my physical problems had been caused by the onset of mental depression. He prescribed medicines for me, counseled total rest, and had me taken to a private room. I found that the medicines relieved my body of pain, but they didn't remove my intense sadness. I felt abandoned by every chance to live a happy life and cried almost incessantly during my three days in the hospital. After what seemed like an eternity, Ron appeared. I was released and driven back to the villa.

As we drove toward home, I begged Ron to take me to a place where I could telephone Morocco. Ron said it was dangerous—he might lose his job. He promised that he'd do something for me when the time was right. Then he suggested that I write letters, both to Morocco and to the Moroccan ambassador in Riyadh. He would take the letters from me, and he could be sure of getting the ambassador's letter directly into his hands. I agreed.

Back at home—although I certainly didn't see it as such—I sat on my bed and wrote two long letters: one to my former boss in Casablanca, and one to the ambassador. I described my miserable condition and begged for their help. I immediately took them to Ron and begged him to smuggle them out. Because the security guard kept a tight watch on him, Ron waited until after dark and then went out to make a few purchases. In the grocery store he handed the letter for Morocco over to another Filipino, who promised to convey it forward. But Ron kept the ambassador's letter; he planned to handle that himself.

While Ron was out, I received a phone call from the prince's secretary. His Highness, Prince Faisal, wanted to see me. I replied, "I am sick," but the secretary took no notice. He said that a car would come by at 9 p.m. to pick me up. I became furious. "I just finished telling you, I am sick!" He sarcastically commented that my voice sounded quite healthy. I snapped back, "Do I have to be dead for you to realize that I'm sick? I told you that I'm sick, and no one even cares about it!" I began to wail and cry, and simply hung up.

At about 9 p.m. Manal suddenly appeared in my bedroom. "What's going on? Well, you actually do look sick. What's the matter?" She had come to fetch me to see the prince, not to see if I was all right.

"I've been sick for days, and none of you care about it! But when he wants sex, he has me called for, and you treat me like goods to be delivered!"

"Who is 'he'?" asked Manal.

"His Highness. Who else?"

"Don't talk like this, or you'll get into big trouble. Right now, the prince wants to see you. We can discuss what's bothering you later. Hurry up. If you make him wait, he's going to get angry."

Then I told her, "An apparent chief of security for this villa has raped me. Nobody would intervene. Two other security guards were standing outside while it happened. They could hear me screaming. They laughed and said that I was enjoying it. Those aren't security guards. They're criminals."

Amazingly, Manal had no reaction to this shocking information. It didn't surprise or upset her in the least. I couldn't believe it. She merely said, "Well, come to the prince and tell him yourself."

My anger transformed into strength; I stood up without assistance. "Quite right. I must talk to him. I must tell him everything." I got dressed and we went to meet my so-called husband.

The prince usually spends his evenings in a different palace from the one in which we were married. He owns many in Riyadh, and each is more magnificent than the other. Most of his palaces are copies of famous European ones, with Arabian and modern architectural "touches." The palace we traveled to stood on a small hill in front of a small oasis. It was in al-Dariya, the old district of Riyadh.

I was conducted into a room where the prince sat with three of his younger sons. Strangely, he greeted me with a handshake and introduced me to the children as a "new Mama." I didn't feel that this was my husband; it was like meeting with a stranger. After the children had left, he casually asked, "So how are you?"

"Not good at all. I'm sick."

"What's the problem?"

"I'm missing my parents, my brothers, and my sisters."

"I'll arrange for you to meet with them soon."

Encouraged by his reaction, I continued, "The head security agent for the villa raped me."

I expected an explosion of fury and anger. But absolutely nothing of the kind happened. The prince smiled, in fact leered at me, and acidly commented, "You undoubtedly provoked him to it with your beauty."

"I didn't provoke him! I was in the house! He came to the villa late in the evening to rape me!"

"Take it easy," he replied, unconcerned. "I'll have it checked out."

Then, suddenly, he became charming and attentive. "Let me show you this lovely palace," he said. It was a pretext, of course. We ended up in a bedroom. He shut the door and ordered me to undress and get into bed with him. I did as I was told and lay there passively. He said, "Play with me."

"No. I'm sick."

He hit me on the side of my head, put on a housecoat, and disappeared.

It was now clear to me that he would never regard me as a human being; I was just a sex object in his eyes. The man had no emotions, no humanity.

I left the room. Manal met me in the corridor, all excited. "My God, what have you done? The prince is angry!"

"Frankly, I couldn't give a shit."

"Be quiet! Don't talk like that!"

"So what's next, Manal?"

"Nothing. You're going to return to the villa immediately and keep a low profile."

Back at home, the security was stepped up. The house was watched around the clock not only by a guard but also by a secret service agent. The groceries that Ron brought in were searched.

Two days later, the Moroccan ambassador and his wife came to visit me. I was so happy to see him that I couldn't restrain my tears. I shared with them all my terrible experiences with the prince and in the villa. They listened attentively and comforted me; they understood my frustration and deep disappointment. I told them, "This is not a life. I am some kind of slave. I want to go home to my parents; I want a divorce." What was I talking about? I hadn't even seen any legal papers documenting the fact that I was married! The ambassador and his wife were visibly touched. He said, "Something has to change. But first of all, try to relax. Your first concern has to be your own health. The situation is a bit precarious just now. Let's wait until the prince calms down, then we'll see what can be done. But don't try anything yourself, and understand that I can't make you any solid promises. Remember—the prince is, at heart, a sensible man. I'm sure he will want to arrange a reasonable solution."

I was not allowed to leave the building; my husband had put me under house arrest. The telephone line was disconnected, and my only human contact was with Julia and Ron.

Three months later, the security was reduced and I was allowed to visit the Moroccan ambassador and his family. It had been a long time since I had had my monthly period, and I didn't know if this was due to stress or a pregnancy. I visited a doctor and learned that I had conceived. After this, my feelings were more ambivalent. When I thought about how the prince had used me in bed, and how I had been raped by another man, I wanted to get an abortion. Then I considered that, if I had the good fortune to give birth to a son, Prince Faisal might handle me with more respect. All I could do was hope for a son. But I couldn't stop wondering: who was the father?

The Moroccan ambassador conveyed a letter to me from my parents. My father wrote that the whole family missed me. They were very sorry about my situation. It was hard for them because they could discuss it with no one—the result would have been a big scandal and lots of gossip. People would say that my father had sold his daughter.

My parents had gone to the Saudi Embassy in Casablanca to try to get me returned home. The ambassador had told him that he knew nothing about my marriage. And that when Prince Faisal married, his brides were princesses, not office secretaries from Casablanca.

This did more than make me sad—it appalled me. It was a scandal for my parents, but it also put the al-Saud family to shame: how could they dupe and abuse an innocent girl like that? I decided that, under no circumstances, would I try to arrange an abortion. I wanted my son or daughter to be a living testimonial to the powerful Saudi princes' mistreatment of women. I wasn't the only victim. Julia and other Filipinas knew of many other young Arab women who had been preyed upon like me.

I wanted to flee the country, but the ambassador sternly warned me against trying it. Prince Faisal was capricious by nature. He could give me an exit visa at anytime, and perhaps sweeten it with a huge financial settlement. I should wait for exactly the right time to ask the prince to let me return home.

Finally, I went into labor. The pain from the contractions was terrible. Ron and Julia got me to the maternity hospital, where I gave birth to a daughter—the sweetest daughter in the world. I didn't want to inform my husband. He didn't like daughters, and he probably didn't even remember who I was. Since he had made me pregnant, he had married several more times. Or, as I put it, he had thrown wedding parties. Marriage was a concept he couldn't understand.

The only woman who came to visit me in the maternity hospital was the Moroccan ambassador's wife, Nadia. She brought me a big, beautiful bouquet of flowers. Over the past months, we had become close friends: she had given me courage, and I had benefited from her common sense. She wanted to help me get out of the country. Applications through legal channels had failed, and her husband feared political consequences if they pressed the issue too hard. After I returned home with the baby, the ambassador also came to visit.

One day, Nadia came to me and said, "We have an escape plan. You're going to be driven into Bahrain in the embassy's diplomatic car. You're going to use the passport of my housemaid, and sit beside the chauffeur. A friend of mine, who is also nursing a baby, will travel with us. She'll hold your daughter. I have arranged exit and reentry visas for those two passports. All three of you will veil your faces. Diplomats and diplomatic vehicles are not carefully searched, and neither are veiled women. What do you think of this?"

My heart beat faster than ever before. I was overcome by mixed feelings: fear and happiness. But more happiness than fear.

One week later, the escape plan was fully in place. Nadia came to get us inconspicuously, and the guards' suspicions were not aroused because she had often taken us to her home for a visit or out shopping. We drove to the city of Dammam, where the causeway bridge connects Saudi Arabia to the island state of Bahrain in the Persian Gulf. During the trip, we hardly spoke a word. It was a four-hour drive, and it seemed to take forever. As we neared the border, my fear intensified. Just before we reached the checkpoint, Nadia placed her passport on top of those of the other two women. The policeman riffled through a few pages of the top passport, peered into the car, and said, "Go ahead." No one in the world will ever understand the relief and sense of joy I felt as we pulled away.

In Bahrain, Nadia got me to the airport quickly. A seat was already reserved for me and my infant daughter. As I bade Nadia farewell in the departures hall, I was abject at leaving her behind. Truly, she had done so much for me. Her courageous action of smuggling me out of the kingdom was something that I would never forget for the rest of my life. I will love that brave woman forever. And she promised to visit me back home in Casablanca.

KARIN

Muna's story of her marriage to Prince Faisal demonstrates the horrors a woman faces when she is desired by a prince (much like we saw with the victims of Prince Nayef and Prince Mishel, as well). However, as Karin's experiences in Saudi Arabia demonstrate, it can be dangerous for any foreigner to become romantically and physically involved with a Saudi man, regardless of his political stature.

It was the beginning of 1992, and I was on my way home in Germany. The air smelled wintry and the sun slanted weakly through broken clouds onto the damp earth. The snow was melting, and water dripped from tree branches, some of which still held on to a few autumn leaves. Everything seemed to be saddened by the effect of the feeble sunshine. But I could see from the street that in our living room all the lights were switched on, and I already knew what was waiting for me. I shut the front door and went in to find Jochen, my husband, lying on the sofa. The room was a mess of abandoned, half-read newspapers and half-eaten snacks.

"Damn it, Jochen, I can't take this any more. I come home tired from work, and you're parked in front of the idiot box doing nothing. Couldn't you at least clean up, pick up your stuff, do the dishes?" I don't remember what else I said; I was furious. Every day was the same, and I'd had enough of it.

"Stop screaming your head off," Jochen snapped back. "I've had enough of you. Go to hell!" He clambered to his feet, stumbled into the bedroom, and slammed the door.

I picked up my handbag and went off to see Gabi, my best friend. She could always expect to see me when I had problems with Jochen, and lately those problems had been unending. Gabi offered me open arms, listening ears, and a warm heart; I unloaded all my unhappiness and fears onto her. As I stood before her door, tears of doubt were already streaming down my face. "What's happened?" asked Gabi. "You look so pale! Is it Jochen again?"

"Who else?" I blurted out. "I can't take it anymore, Gabi."

I came inside, and through my sobs I told her how Jochen was starting to drink, and how he lay around all day like some apathetic bum. Both Gabi and other friends of mine had managed several times to find Jochen a job. But it never worked out, either because he didn't like the position or because he lost it due to persistent lateness.

"Karin, you and Jochen need to take a vacation. Go away together for a couple of days—maybe that will help," suggested Gabi as she tried to calm me down.

"I don't know," I replied hopelessly. "I don't know if it will help. I'll suggest it, but he's so unmotivated. He just doesn't want to try anything..."

I had fallen in love with Jochen five years earlier, when he was still full of energy and happiness. He had been in his midthirties, and I was in my late twenties. We lived together for two wonderful years, and then we married. He was an electrician, and I was a teacher. There was a difference in our educational levels, as well as in the rhythm of our working days, which led to ever-increasing problems. It wasn't bad at first, but when Jochen became unemployed, we started to fight nearly every day.

A few days later, Gabi phoned me at work to tell me that she had seen an interesting job advertisement in a regional newspaper. She told me to drop by and take a look at it, so after school I went to her home. I read the ad but was doubtful that Jochen would jump for it. The job was in Saudi Arabia.

Gabi's husband, Hadi, was Iraqi. He was against the idea and told me that Saudi Arabia was a terrible country with a positively medieval regime. "Oh, come on," said Gabi. "You know, Karin, all Iraqis have hated the Saudis ever since the Gulf War. The Saudis let foreign armies base themselves in their country in order to liberate Kuwait."

I didn't know anything about Saudi Arabia; all I knew was its geographical location.

I put the ad into my purse and took it home.

Jochen, as usual, was flat out on the sofa. My blood pressure went up, but I put on a smiling face. I sat down beside him and prattled like a brainless kid. "Jochen, here is a newspaper ad. A German company is looking for electricians to work on a project in Saudi Arabia. What do you think? Would you like to give it a try? I'd come along with you." Jochen had been studying the *TV Guide* and was annoyed at being interrupted.

As his gaze transferred from the magazine to me, I pressed the ripped-out ad into his hand. He read it. He read it twice.

Then he asked, "So, where is Saudi Arabia? Isn't it in the Far East somewhere?"

"It's between the Persian Gulf and the Red Sea," I explained. "It's a big peninsula just east of Egypt."

"Oh . . . yeah . . . *that* place. It's all camels and sand, right?"

"And a whole lot of oil. Companies based in Saudi Arabia pay very well."

I cuddled up closer to him and read the ad again. "Look, it says here that you'll get a huge bonus for working overseas, a free apartment, and air tickets twice a year for both of us. That doesn't sound bad at all." I tried to animate him, to pique his interest.

"Yeah, but I don't speak Arabic," he countered.

"Oh, but you don't need it. This is a German firm, and you know enough English to get by. Anyway, this job is near Dubai. One of my colleagues at the school went on vacation to Dubai with her husband, and they really enjoyed it. We can also take a vacation there. And, you know, it will be fun to see a different part of the world. Why don't we give it a try? If we don't like it, we'll just come home."

After a lot of discussion back and forth, my powers of persuasion did their work, and Jochen agreed to call the firm. He was interviewed and then immediately offered a job doing electrical installations in Riyadh. Apparently the company was having difficulty finding candidates who were willing to work in such a culturally different foreign locale. Jochen signed a contract that gave him a generous salary, the use of a 2,150-square-foot, furnished house in a German residential compound, and an excellent medical plan. We were scheduled to leave in six weeks' time. I arranged for a one-year leave of absence from my school, bought books about Saudi Arabia, and got myself a credit card. We got inoculations against cholera and malaria while the company did the paperwork for our Saudi entry visas.

Jochen and I had always dreamed of living and working in a faraway, exotic land. However, I was more excited about moving to Saudi Arabia than Jochen. I not only wanted to experience a different culture and meet new people—I hoped that the change would refresh and restore our failing marriage. During those weeks of preparation, I made a lot of effort to emphasize that this would be a wonderful adventure for us. I downplayed or denied anything negative about the country. I collected publicity brochures full of glossy photographs of Saudi Arabia and shared them daily with Jochen. "Look, how beautiful! So much sunshine! How wide open these endless deserts are! Jochen, you'll be able to hit the gas pedal and drive like a madman. No rules, no stoplights, no traffic cops—just flat desert. Your dream comes true!" Jochen took some interest.

We decided to keep our apartment in Germany; Gabi agreed to look after the mail and the houseplants. Our bags were packed, and off we went, flying with Lufthansa via Frankfurt to Riyadh. It was the first time we had ever made such a long trip together, a six-hour flight.

Before we landed, the pilot made a special scripted announcement. Anyone caught smuggling alcohol or drugs into Saudi Arabia, or consuming them while there, would be heavily punished with either a long jail sentence or beheading. Jochen became afraid. "What kind of people are these?" he asked. But the man who was seated on the other side of us whispered to him, "Take it easy. They give you a lot of leash. I've lived here a long time, and believe me, I have a drink every day. One of the Saudi princes arranges for alcohol to be smuggled into the country."

"Then alcohol is available in Saudi Arabia?" asked Jochen, confused.

"You'd better believe it! The Saudis drink more than us Germans. But behind closed doors, of course."

A stewardess who was serving us our "last round" then entered the discussion.

"It used to be mandatory that we stop serving alcoholic beverages once we entered Saudi air space. And after landing, we always received letters from the morality police admonishing Westerners for the evil practice of drinking. But none of that happens nowadays. We're making progress."

We were met in the airport by company representatives: a German, a Saudi, and a Pakistani. I had already noticed at the passport control that I was the only woman without a black abaya. I knew that in Saudi Arabia I would have to wear one, even though I was a foreigner, or I would face problems from the morality police, who are strict Muslims. But, as a new arrival, I traveled without a problem to the German residential compound. It was the evening of March 18, 1992, and over 85 degrees Fahrenheit, but everything was air-conditioned—the airport, the overpass to the parking garage, the limousine. Only after arriving at the compound did we realize that we were living in a sauna.

Our new home was fully furnished, right down to the cutlery in the kitchen drawers. The compound consisted of forty houses, exclusively for German nationals, surrounded by a barbed-wire fence. The inhabitants lived a German lifestyle and strictly conformed to German codes of behavior. There was a supermarket that sold German food and German products. Each family valiantly attempted to maintain a garden, in spite of the desert conditions. In the social hall, current German newspapers and books were available and alcoholic beverages were offered on the sly. In effect, it was a perfect German ghetto in the middle of the desert.

Jochen went off to work the next day. He seemed to enjoy it. I busied myself with housework and tried to personalize our home by buying pretty pictures and artificial flower arrangements. In order to do this, Jochen and I traveled to downtown Riyadh's amazing shopping malls every evening. It was a consumer's paradise. Endless luxury boutiques displayed high-end goods from the West and Japan, from Meissner porcelain to the latest high-tech appliances from top companies. The prices were lower than in Germany—hardly a surprise, since Saudi Arabia had no sales tax and its people didn't have to support national social services. Even the cost of a loan was incredibly low. We bought a jeep and an all-terrain motorbike. After that, we often drove out into the desert, and every weekend

Jochen enjoyed high-speed rides on his new bike in wide-open, apparently borderless freedom.

One day our jeep got stuck in the sand when we were far out in the desert, with no sign of human life anywhere. We simply couldn't get the vehicle out, and Jochen started cursing his decision to move to Saudi Arabia. Then he discovered that the jeep's battery was empty. "What is this?" he complained. "It's brand new. The Saudis have cheated us." It became dark, and the sky filled with stars. We were afraid to spend the night in the desert, and lit a campfire, hoping that someone would notice it. The weather was lovely, and I enjoyed the silence, but Jochen just stared angrily into the fire. Toward midnight we saw a small light on the horizon that looked like an illusion. But it grew bigger. A car was traveling in our direction, and was about to pass us by. So Jochen took off his shirt and waved it frantically in front of the firelight. We were lucky. The driver took notice and came over to us.

Three Saudi men stepped out and greeted both Jochen and me. I was immediately attracted to the driver. His name was Satam, and he appeared to be around forty years old. He was tall and slim, with shiny black hair, dark eyes with thick eyelashes, a carefully trimmed beard, and a sensuous mouth. He opened the hood of our jeep and connected his car to ours with jumper cables. Jochen's vehicle sprang to life, and we were filled with relief.

Satam was very sociable and spoke excellent English. With typical Arab hospitality, he offered us a picnic: flatbread with a choice of hummus, cherry jam, yogurt, or sesame puree, and Pepsi Cola. We sat around the campfire and got to know each other.

"So, where are you from?"

"Germany."

"Oh, you're Germans! We love Germans. They make the best cars in the world—Mercedes and BMW's. You are hardworking, orderly, and responsible people." It was nice to hear Satam's praise.

"Really?" said Jochen, rather pointedly. "You're driving a Japanese car." Everyone laughed.

Then Satam proposed that we hunt a *dhubb*. "What's that?" asked Jochen.

"Well, let's drive around a bit to look for one. You'll see for yourself."

Satam attached a flashlight downward from the side-view mirror of his car and all of us drove off together. Shortly afterward, he stopped beside a hole in the sand. "A dhubb has to live in there. We'll get him out." He turned off the car, got a length of hose from the trunk, attached it to the exhaust pipe, and placed the other end in the hole. After running the engine for five minutes, he switched it off and waited for the dhubb to come out.

Slowly and looking very dazed, the giant lizard scrabbled out and looked around at us with large, tired eyes. Then he pulled himself up, puffed out his leathery cheeks, and I clearly saw the rows of sharp teeth as he hissed a warning in anger and fear. The dhubb was over three feet long and some twelve inches tall. I was suddenly overcome by fear. I ran to the car and quickly shut myself inside. From there I watched the ensuing scene unfold, overcome by horror.

Satam called to me laughingly, "Don't be afraid! He can't run *that* fast!"

Jochen approached the dhubb to get a better look at it. "Don't go any closer." Satam advised. "If he bites, he doesn't let go. We'll have to rip his jaws out of your leg."

Satam and his two friends gathered a pile of rocks. They started to throw them at the giant lizard. The first stones bounced off as if they had hit the surface of a tank. But the three men didn't stop. They threw the stones at it until it died. Satam grabbed the animal, tossed it into the trunk of his car, and we drove back to the campfire.

Using a knife, he then sliced what little meat the animal had from its bones, put it on a skewer, and roasted it over our fire. They offered me a piece. I declined and nearly vomited at the idea of eating an animal that had been tortured and killed in such a brutal manner. Jochen tried a piece but immediately spat it out. The meat had a uniquely disgusting smell, was stringy, and tasted terrible. But Satam and his friends ate the dhubb's meat and appeared to thoroughly enjoy it. Later, much later, I was to remember their brutal treatment of the animal.

Satam prepared tea over the campfire. While we drank it, we chatted about wildlife in the desert. Satam had happened to sit by me. He took a piece of paper out of his shirt pocket, wrote his name and phone number on it, and handed it to me. Jochen wrote down our phone number and passed it to him in return. Satam said that he would like to meet us again. "Certainly, why not?" replied Jochen.

The very next day, Satam phoned our house. He asked if Jochen and I had reached home safely after our desert mishap.

"Thank you," I answered politely. "We got back without a problem, and the jeep started this morning without any trouble." Deep inside, I wanted to get to know this man better; I was curious about him. I didn't know any Saudis at all, and Satam seemed to be a typical one, according to what I had heard.

"Do you like Saudi Arabia?" asked Satam casually.

"Up until now, it's been fine. But I didn't like the dhubb hunting." Satam laughed into the phone. I then added, "Frankly, I know little about this country and its people."

"No problem. I can show you Saudi Arabia and also tell you a lot about the Saudis," he offered.

"That would be nice," I responded, trying not to reveal my enthusiasm too much.

"Well, what are you doing today? I've got nothing planned. We could meet somewhere. Or I could pick you up." Satam sounded friendly.

"Not today, I'm sorry. How about tomorrow?"

"No problem. I'll pick you up. Where do you live?"

"In the German compound, in Rabua."

"I know where that is. I'll pick you up at 10 a.m."

"Okay. See you tomorrow."

I leaned back in the armchair and considered whether or not I should tell Jochen about the outing. But Jochen was easily roused to jealousy. He would probably make a scene; there would be a fight. I would tell him afterward. After all, did he expect me to sit around the house all day? I wanted to learn about this country and its people. Later, I'd be able to share all of this with my friends back home.

The next morning, Satam arrived at the compound gate. I was paged. "A Mr. Satam al-Jamil is here to see you?"

"Yes. Please admit him."

Satam drove in and picked me up at the house. He proposed that we go to the Sheraton Hotel's coffee shop. The morality police weren't allowed to enter its premises to check who was sitting with whom and whether all the women were veiled. We would be comfortable there.

We chose a secluded corner table. I ordered coffee. Satam then said, "I'll have a whisky, please." We both had a good laugh, since alcohol was forbidden—at least in public. He settled for tea.

"Unfortunately, many things are forbidden in Saudi Arabia. But the majority of Saudis are against all these restrictions. We want to live normal lives, like other people. The Mutawas—morality police—and other fundamentalists dictate how we have to live. They're running the scene. Because of them, foreigners get the impression that we're strictly religious and very conservative. But it isn't true at all."

"Would you sit here with your own wife unveiled?" I challenged.

The question irritated him, but he answered, "Certainly. But that doesn't depend on me. It's up to my wife and all our relatives. They tend to be conservative and put the pressure on me, too. Well, it's true, I'm a little conservative—because I was brought up that way. But I can be liberal in my outlook when I'm with Westerners. I know a lot of Westerners, mainly English. I work in a hospital, and I get to meet many people from the West." Impressed, I listened attentively.

Satam suggested that we make a city tour together. "I'd especially like to show you the old city—you Westerners like that. You can snap a couple of photos. I see that you've brought your camera along. Why don't you start by taking my photo? I'm like the old city—an old guy," he teased, and we both laughed.

We left the hotel. I began to consider whether I should do this. I hesitated before the open door of his car. "What is it? Are you afraid? Oh, I know what's bothering you. You think I'm going to kidnap you. Shall I give you my driver's license?"

"Oh, come on!" I interrupted and got into the car. I was willing to risk it. Satam's charm had calmed my fear.

As Satam negotiated through the traffic, he told me, "You know, women aren't allowed to drive in Saudi Arabia, which is absolutely ridiculous. I have to be a chauffeur for my own family. Well, it's true that I employ a driver, but nevertheless I have to chauffeur my wife and children a lot. And the Mutawas really dislike it when an adult woman is being driven around in a car with a man who isn't her husband. They say that a devil of temptation sits between every man and a strange woman. So, you see, there's a little devil sitting between us right now." We laughed.

Judging by the way the men handled their cars, I was amazed not to see a major accident every minute. "Let me tell you," I remarked, "even if I was allowed to drive in this country, I wouldn't do it. It's totally dangerous."

"Oh, you get used to it," said Satam, concentrating on the road. "I'd love to take you to visit the Museum of Traditional Folk Art, but it can't be done."

"Why?"

"Men and women are only allowed to visit the museum on alternate days. Some of us call it 'gender apartheid,' you know. Certain days are reserved for families. Today is a family day. But, unfortunately, you and I aren't a family. But if we lie, we can go in," he craftily proposed. I found the visiting regulations totally bizarre.

After a drive around Riyadh, we were ready for a meal. "I would like to invite you to eat in the family section of a traditional Saudi restaurant. You'll experience traditional dishes," my host proposed.

"What a lovely idea! Thank you!"

"But first I'll have to buy you an abaya—you know, like a bathrobe, but in black. Women really must wear it in Saudi Arabia if they don't want to attract anger and sexual looks from men here. I'm surprised that you don't have one. Oh, yes . . . I forgot that you've only recently arrived."

"I'm sorry. I actually do have one, but I forgot it at home. I'm simply not used to going out wearing a disgusting black tent."

"No problem," said Satam. Shortly afterward, he pulled over in front of a shop and asked me what size I wore.

"Thirty-six," I answered, about to step out.

"No, no—just stay in the car. You'll make the Mutawas angry. I'll go buy one for you. It'll only take a minute."

In less than five minutes, Satam returned with a lovely piece of shiny silk curtain material.

"Try it on," he said, opening the car door for me.

As I slipped into the abaya, I asked him how much I owed him. "Nothing. This is a gift from me to you."

"Oh, that's not necessary," I replied.

"Of course it is. Saudi tradition, Saudi style, made in China; the least I can do is pay for it."

I thanked him with a smile.

"How about something for something? When I visit Germany, you can buy me a pair of those short leather pants," he joked.

Just a few meters down the street, Satam parked again, in front of an oriental-looking house with a large sign on it in both Arabic and English: "Saudi Restaurant." Satam knew the restaurant and conducted me directly to the family section. The waiters greeted Satam and ignored me. We sat at a table behind a moveable screen, and Satam explained the menu.

"Have you eaten Arabic food before?"

"No. Go ahead and choose a meal for me."

As an appetizer, he ordered a salad of parsley, chickpeas, and eggplant paste, which was to be eaten with flat bread; for the main course, rice cooked with almonds and raisins, placed on top of grilled meat. Nearby I observed a Saudi woman eating her meal. Every time she ate a mouthful of food, she lifted her veil outwards with her left hand, shoved the fork in, and then dropped the veil while she chewed. Normally, the waiter would have stayed behind the screen to take our order, but because I was a Western woman with an uncovered face, he came to our table.

Later, Satam ordered a second main dish. "It's a meat dish called *mandi*," he explained. "The recipe was developed by the desert Bedouins. First of all, the raw meat is rubbed down with spices and placed in cardamom sauce for twenty-four hours. Then a hole, about a foot and a half wide, is made in the desert sand, into which hot coals are placed. The meat is wrapped in a cloth and buried in the hot sand to cook. It's ready to eat after two hours. Delicious." Satam licked the food from his fingers; he was eating with his hands. "Today, that dish is prepared in utensils specially manufactured in Japan."

"Isn't it sad, how modern appliances are taking over from the traditional?" I commented and tried to eat my meal with my fingers, like Satam.

The other families in the restaurant sat at their tables behind the Spanish walls. The waiters stayed out of sight. They were only allowed to speak to the male customers and took the orders from behind the screen. Dinner plates, cutlery, food and drink were deftly handed around the barrier. When a waiter wanted to indicate that he wished to speak to the people at a particular table, he grabbed the top of the Spanish wall, so the guests would see his hand. I kept an eye on these goings-on and was amazed by this method of communication and service. Satam ordered a lot to eat, and afterward a dessert, so I wondered if he expected me to try every Saudi dish in this one meal. After an aromatic cup of mocha coffee, I told him, "Unfortunately, I really must go home now. If I eat any more, I'm going to burst!"

"Well, we don't want that to happen! So let's meet another time when you're hungry again," bantered my escort. He paid, and we prepared to go out. A waiter passed me, and I said, "Good-bye." Satam snickered. "You undoubtedly made that waiter very happy. A woman said 'good-bye' to him! He never hears that from a Saudi woman!"

"Why is that?" I asked, taken aback.

"Well, some Saudis, as well as our religious leaders, believe that a woman's voice is a sexual organ. And, just like any other sexual organ, you don't expose it in public. You may as well have been showing him something else."

When we got to his car, I decided to go home by taxi.

"Why?" asked Satam with a smile. "Am I such a bad driver?"

"No, no; not at all; on the contrary. I just don't think that it would be right for my neighbors to see us together. What would they think of me?"

"Oh! Are German women just as conservative as the Saudi ones? I had no idea," he marveled.

"Well," I explained, "in Germany, just like here, it doesn't make a good impression if a strange man drives a married woman home."

"Hey! Tell them I'm your new chauffeur."

"Look, you have to understand that my neighbors don't know me well. I'm new here. . . . You know what? Forget it. It's none of their business. Feel free to drive me home, but please . . . just to the compound gate."

At home, I lay down on the couch and stared at the ceiling. A stream of thoughts about Jochen ran through my mind: "He has, actually, never treated me with love and affection, especially after he became unemployed, when his behavior was often simply insufferable. In the last few years, we seem to be just living in the same house. He has lied to me. He has cheated on me, which I found out purely by chance. Jochen and I have become friends; we are no longer lovers. I can't even think about love when I hear his name. We couldn't talk to each other about love even if we tried."

I stood up and went into the kitchen. I had to pull together a dinner for Jochen. In my mind, I could hear him complaining that a hot meal wasn't waiting on the table. When he had been unemployed, I had cooked for him every day after teaching school. He couldn't cook. He refused to learn to cook. Macho man. Just another jock.

Jochen came home in a bad mood. He complained about the Saudis; they were lazy, and when they actually did their work, the results were shoddy. A Saudi had ruined a machine by filling it up with petrol instead of diesel fuel. I tried to calm him down and cheer him up, but he suddenly became enraged. "It was your idea to move to this shithole of a country. Not mine!"

I suddenly needed to get back at him. I answered in an even voice, "Better than being unemployed, Jochen."

"I'd rather be unemployed than work for these bloody Saudis."

I tried to make sense of my experience with Saudis compared to Jochen's. "I think . . . we Westerners have to be patient with them. They aren't technologically as developed as us. But, in human terms, they know how to live properly. They've got it right. They're decent."

"How in the world would you know that?"

"Well, think of the men in the desert; the ones who rescued us. I bet Germans wouldn't be that kind. They probably would have passed us by."

"Saudis are also brutal and unkind. Didn't you see how they treated that lizard? You yourself said that it was disgusting. Now you're saying that they're decent people. You don't know what your own opinions are, Mrs. Teacher!"

I swallowed hard and thought, "Jochen's reverted to his old self. Narrow-minded. Judgmental. Impatient. Always looking for a fight. Flipping out over nothing."

I picked up a book I had brought from Germany and started to read.

Jochen felt shut out. "So where's the dinner, anyways?" he demanded angrily.

"It'll be ready soon."

"What do you mean, 'soon'? You had all day to get it ready."

"Well, look at it this way. When you were unemployed in Germany, I didn't exactly come home to a hot meal. Not only did I have to cook, but I also had to do the cleaning and the laundry. . . . Anyway . . . the meal is ready. Stop screaming."

Jochen got up and left our small house. I waited all night, but he didn't return. I became really worried and couldn't sleep. In Germany I had friends I could have phoned. I would have gone to Gabi's. But here? I didn't know anyone.

The next morning, I phoned Jochen's workplace. My call was answered by Mr. Schmidt, the director of the project. I asked to speak to Jochen.

"Sorry, he's outside at the construction site just now. Shall I get him in here to take your call?"

"No, no . . . that isn't necessary. Excuse me, but how long have you lived here in Saudi Arabia?"

"Seven years. Why?"

"Pardon me for my curiosity, but I want to ask you if you like it here?"

"Yeah, sure thing. Me, my wife, and the kids."

"That's lovely. Listen, my husband and I are new here and we hardly know anyone. Particularly Germans."

"Why don't you and Jochen come over to visit tonight? My wife would be happy to meet you two. We also live in the German compound, in House 21A. Tell you what, I'll tell Jochen when I see him."

"Why, thank you. Until tonight. Bye."

Jochen came home after work and apologized to me for "losing it" the day before. He had checked into a hotel and spent a sleepless night. Yesterday had been a tough day at work. Then he said, "Everybody who comes here from Germany has these reactions in the beginning." He was looking forward to visiting the German boss and his family.

I wasn't very impressed by his apology. Same old thing: he flipped out, and then asked for forgiveness. We sat down to a take-out Chinese meal that Jochen had picked up on the way home from work as a peace offering.

In the evening we made ourselves presentable and walked over to the Schmidts'. They welcomed us with warmth and kindness. Mrs. Schmidt had prepared a refreshing fruit cocktail using local dates, which was served by their Indian housemaid. It had been a scorching hot day—over 105 degrees Fahrenheit in the shade—but their home was pleasantly cool. Mr. Schmidt took it upon himself to initiate the evening's conversation. "You know, the first days and weeks are always the worst when you move abroad. You get used to all the differences very slowly, but, yes—in the end, you do adapt. When we came here seven years ago, everything seemed so desolate. But we've gotten used to it. For example, there are almost no cultural activities. If you want to live your life freely, you do it behind the closed doors of your house, in secret and closed clubs, at the homes of friends or else out in the desert."

"The good thing about living here," said Mrs. Schmidt, "is that you can earn more money than back home in Germany. You can also afford to take a lot of trips, including trips back home, on a regular basis. We travel four times a year just to Germany. There we visit our family and friends, and we go to the movies, to the theater . . ."

"In recent years we've hardly ever gone out to a movie or the theater," I mentioned. "So we hardly miss those activities."

The Schmidts shifted uncomfortably in their seats. "We also have a lot of friends here in Saudi Arabia," continued Mr. Schmidt. "We'll introduce you to them soon. The German Embassy has a 'Happy Hour' once a month. There you will meet many other Germans, as well as a few other foreign nationalities."

"Do they serve beer?" asked Jochen plaintively, half-jokingly, half in earnest.

"Yes, of course. . . . That's why we all attend! Alcohol is forbidden in Saudi Arabia, but if we are able to assist the embassy in any way, we get our thanks in the form of one or more bottles passed under the table."

At this point I commented acidly, "But surely one can give up alcohol for some time."

"I agree," said Schmidt. "The Saudis live without it, and they aren't at all unpleasant people. True, it's a Bedouin society, and they are still nomadic Bedouins at heart in spite of the modernization that started with the discovery of oil.

"Think of how much progress Germans have made in the last two hundred years alone. Saudi Arabia has had only forty years. A society requires time to ripen. And, to tell the truth, right now Germany needs a country like Saudi Arabia—incredibly wealthy but very undeveloped, a society that frequently messes up as it muddles through a process of learning and development. We can sell them a lot and we can earn a lot. It may sound cynical, but that's the truth. Every German car that they smash up on their roads requires a replacement. They are a benefit to our economy."

"They are terrible drivers," I mentioned. "They don't follow any rules, and they don't show any consideration for others."

"Actually, it's gotten better," commented Mrs. Schmidt. "When we first arrived here, the Saudis didn't even pay attention to the traffic signals. They would drive straight through red lights. Every time we traveled by car, we took our lives in our hands. But is this so surprising? These people made the transition from camels to Mercedes Benzes in less than thirty years."

"Driving on the streets of Riyadh is still downright dangerous," said Jochen. "You really need to have strong nerves, a talent for improvisation, and the agility of a tightrope walker. Listen to this: I was driving on a four-lane street when a local driver—I think he was a Saudi—came up from behind, passed me on the left at high speed, and then suddenly cut in front of me and took a right exit. I thought my eyes were playing tricks on me. How can they drive like that?"

"There are no rules of the road," replied Mr. Schmidt. "Well, no, that's not exactly true.... The rules are: be selfish, self-assertive, sneaky, and have a strong engine. Every second that you're behind the wheel here, you have to expect the unexpected. That's why there are so many car accidents."

"What about automobile insurance?" Jochen asked. "When we bought our car, the sales rep told us that it wasn't necessary. Is that true?"

"In theory, none of the cars in Saudi Arabia are insured. The religious experts are against it because the money collected is deposited into interest-bearing investments, which, according to Islam, is sinful. There are some authorized insurance companies; they are foreign, and under the control of one powerful Saudi prince or another. They very seldom pay out any benefits. Luckily, anyone who has the misfortune to be in a traffic accident, whether he is insured or not, will receive equal treatment. His car will be fixed without charge, and he'll get free medical attention," Schmidt explained.

The evening was so pleasant that we forgot that we were actually in a foreign country. The discussion with the Schmidts cheered us up and entertained us as we learned a lot about Saudi society. As we were leaving I commented, "You know, if another society is difficult and strange, it's a lot easier to live in it if you understand how it works."

The next day I met Mrs. Schmidt—Veronica—for a coffee. As we sat and chatted, a real and meaningful friendship grew between us. I learned that Veronica's sister was happily married to a Saudi and was the mother of three charming, black-haired boys.

One day when I was visiting Veronica she proposed a visit to her sister, Inge. She lived in a villa in an affluent district of Riyadh. Her husband was a doctor at the university clinic. After contacting Inge, Veronica had her chauffeur drive us over for a visit. During the ride, I shyly mentioned that I found it unusual that they could employ both a maid and a chauffeur. Veronica replied that capable servants in Saudi Arabia could be hired at very affordable rates.

Inge was pleased by our visit. Her husband and children had just arrived home from work and school, and they all greeted us in German. Her husband had studied medicine in Bonn, and the boys were growing up bilingual.

We sat in their spacious living room and discussed life in Saudi Arabia while we drank tea served by a Filipino housemaid. All of a sudden, the theme of the discussion became "marriage to an Arab." I summoned a little courage and asked, "Could you tell me, Mrs. Assaf," for that was Inge's surname, "I don't want to intrude on your privacy, but I have heard and read a lot about what it's like to be married to an Arab. Mostly I have heard that it's a bad idea for a foreign woman to marry an Arab, and a Saudi in particular.

"I also heard that Arabian women leave their father's jail only to enter their husband's jail. What do you think of all this? I mean, what's it like for a German woman married to a Saudi husband?"

"Well, if you marry an Arab, or a Saudi, your relationship has the same potential for happiness or unhappiness as with a German."

"Of course," I agreed.

"It depends on the circumstances of the decision to marry, and it depends on the type of man involved. Think about it: if he is modern and liberal in his thinking, independent of his family, and can afford to live alone (because most Saudis live with their parents), then, if the couple understand each other, why wouldn't the marriage succeed? Then, if you choose to live in this country, you accept that there will be certain restrictions. As a woman, you have to come to terms with the fact that you have left your own society behind, with all its hustle and bustle. You now live far away from your parents, your brothers and sisters, your friends, and everyone else. But think about it. . . . Here, over a period of time, you can also establish friendships and piece everything together until you feel that you actually feel that you have a new homeland. I myself am happy here in Saudi Arabia. I'm happy with my husband and with my children, while I'm hearing about friends and acquaintances in Germany whose marriages are falling apart."

"True," said Veronica, "but we have to remember that not all German women who are married to Saudis are happy. Think about Sabine. She is deathly unhappy with her husband, who continually threatens her and treats her like a slave. She's on the verge of suicide or a mental collapse."

"Quite right," I said. "Not everyone can be as fortunate as you, Mrs. Assaf."

We noticed that Inge was being distracted by the needs of her children, so we said our good-byes and returned home to the compound. I felt considerable sympathy for our chauffeur, who had had to wait for us in the Schmidts' car during our lengthy visit. But Veronica replied that he was used to it and had probably passed the time snoozing or working on puzzles.

Back home, I went to the kitchen and started preparing the evening meal because Jochen would return at any moment. Suddenly the phone rang; it was Satam. "I've been trying to reach you for hours. Where were you?" he asked.

"I was visiting an acquaintance. She's the sister of my neighbor, and she's married to a Saudi. I spoke with her husband, but only briefly."

"I bet he was shy."

"I don't know. I don't think so. Probably he was in a hurry."

"All Saudi men are shy."

"Well, you aren't!" I laughed.

I heard a noise at the front door and said, "I can't talk now. Call me tomorrow. Bye, bye."

Over dinner, I told Jochen about my visit to Veronica Schmidt's sister. "And how was your day?" I asked.

"Not too bad. Okay, actually. By the way, the German guys are going to meet at Henrik's place tonight to play skat."

"How boring!"

"Well, why don't you go over to Mrs. Schmidt's?"

"Because we were together nearly all day, that's why!"

"Well, what do you want me to do? Just go to work and sit at home every evening?"

"Forget it. No problem. I'll just stay here and watch TV or read."

But, in truth, I was annoyed. I had wanted to spend the evening alone with Jochen. "Wouldn't it be nice if Satam decided to call," I considered, as the evening hours crawled by.

At midnight, Jochen came home, drunk and stinking of beer. The taxi driver had to help him into our house. This reminded me of our years together in Germany, when he had often come home in the same condition.

The next morning, I had to wake him, and he crawled out of bed with difficulty. Half-asleep, he went through the motions of washing and shaving himself. The company's bus driver had to knock on our door and escort him out to the waiting vehicle.

Right after breakfast I got a call from Satam. It made me very happy.

"Did you sleep well?" he asked, in a loving, caring voice.

I couldn't hide my happiness that he had called. "Oh, yes! Yes, thank you!"

"What are you doing today? Can I invite you to a Saudi coffee shop? They serve the most delicious Saudi desserts there. Please, don't say no!"

"Fine! It's a wonderful idea!"

"That's just great. I'll pick you up."

"No, please don't. I'll take a taxi." I was afraid that Veronica Schmidt might happen to see us together.

"As you wish. Where shall we meet? How about in front of the Sheraton Hotel?"

"Good idea. See you soon."

One hour later, we met as planned. I was so pleased to see him; his face radiated happiness and good cheer. I wanted to get into the front passenger seat of his car and sit beside him, but he stopped me. "No, Karin, please sit in the back. Oh—I'm so sorry for using your first name. Well, now that I've done it, may I continue to call you Karin?"

"Why not? After all, we are dating each other," I replied lightheartedly.

"By the way, I only want you in the backseat to avoid any problems with the Mutawas. I want to protect you from them, no matter what."

"If that's what's best, I've certainly no objections. Anyway, there's lots of room to stretch out back here."

Satam started the car. A song was playing on the car radio, and he sang along.

"Do you like music?" he asked me.

"Yes, but Arabic music sounds a little strange to my Western ears!"

"You'll get used to it."

I enjoyed the ride. There were lots of people out and about in their cars ... admittedly, all of them were men. The day was very hot, but Satam's car was pleasantly cool due to its well-engineered air-conditioning system.

It didn't take long to reach the coffee shop. We got out of the car and entered. The décor was oriental, and all the waiters wore oriental costumes. I was completely charmed.

"Would you like to sit on the floor, Bedouin fashion, or on those lounge chairs?"

"I'll try the floor."

The restaurant was hung with intimate and authentic camel hair tents, and the floor was strewn with fine desert sand. In the middle of each tent was a large copper tray covered with glowing live coals. Nearby stood coffeepots, teapots, glasses etched with Bedouin motifs, and a basket of assorted types of fresh dates. Around the walls of the tent were long mattresses and many pillows covered in colorful handwoven wool. In front of each tent stood a potted palm tree. In the background, Arabic music played softly over loudspeakers. There were other guests in a few of the tents, but it wasn't possible to see them directly.

Fortunately, I was wearing my blue jeans under my abaya. We positioned ourselves on the low mattresses on opposite sides of the blazing coals. Satam ordered tea, coffee, and desserts. In this restaurant, which was visited by many Europeans, the waiters were allowed to enter the tents regardless of whether or not the women were veiled. They were even allowed to speak to female guests.

The place evoked in me an atmosphere of *One Thousand and One Nights*. Somehow Satam grasped this instinctively, for he suddenly said, "I feel that I am the sultan, and you are my Scheherazade," which made us both laugh. Then the waiter stepped into our tent with the food and drink.

As we sat there together, my thoughts wandered back to the reality of my life, and I couldn't suppress the anger and unhappiness caused by Jochen the previous night.

"You look sad. What's wrong?"

I struggled with the idea of revealing my marital problems to Satam; it could be misinterpreted. Yet I desperately needed someone to talk to. I longed for security, and maybe Satam would somehow provide that.

"Actually, you know, I'm having problems with my husband, Jochen. Last night he came home drunk. He drinks a lot, and I'm so afraid that his company will fire him if he keeps this up. Back in Germany he was fired— twice—for drunkenness. I thought that there was no alcohol in Saudi Arabia, so he would learn to live without it. But it looks like there are more drunks here than in Germany. Satam, one of my brothers is an alcoholic. It has destroyed his life. When he's drunk, he hits his wife and his kids. My family has tried everything to stop his addiction and nothing has worked."

"I have a glass of whisky once in a while, but I never let myself get drunk," said Satam.

"I don't know what I should do," I sighed.

"I would like to help you, but I don't know how I can. Our hospitals have special departments for alcoholics. Do you want me to inquire if they'll consider him for a therapy program?"

"Jochen claims that he doesn't have a problem with alcohol. I don't think he'll cooperate."

Our excursion was now overcast by a sense of gloom and oppression. Satam tried to lighten the mood by telling jokes, but I could scarcely pay attention to them; my thoughts were already at home, thinking about what I could pull together for the evening meal. We left the Arabic café.

As we stood outside, Satam said to me, "Listen, if you need me at any time, day or night, just call this number." He handed me a slip of paper. "That's my pager. You will always be able to get hold of me." I thanked him and stepped into a taxi.

"I'll call you tomorrow," he said and shut the car door.

Back at home, I entered the house and went into the bedroom to change. To my surprise, Jochen was lying in our bed.

"What is it? Aren't you well?"

He rolled over and replied weakly, "I took sick leave."

"Do you want some tea?"

"No. I just want to sleep."

I went into the living room, stood there, and didn't know what to do with myself. So I lay down on the couch, covered my eyes with my arm, and fell asleep. When I woke up it was already dark. I switched on the lights and went into the bedroom again. Jochen was still out cold. So I went back to the couch and tried to sleep some more, but it proved impossible; I was wide-awake. I pulled together a pile of newspapers and magazines and read until the small hours of the night. Then, suddenly, Jochen called out my name.

"I've got terrible pains. Can you make me some tea?"

I brewed it and brought it to him; he drank a little and then rolled over onto his other side.

"Does it still hurt?"

"Yeah."

"Should I call a doctor?"

"I dunno."

I went into the living room and dialed Satam's pager number. He called me back almost immediately.

"Yes, it's me. Can you send a doctor to our house? Jochen is really sick."

"Of course. Right away."

Half an hour later, Satam was at the door with a doctor.

"Please come in."

I took them into the bedroom. Jochen looked pale and was very weak. The doctor examined him and advised him to go to the hospital; his liver didn't seem to be functioning correctly. Satam and the doctor waited in the living room while I helped Jochen into his clothes. Ten minutes later we were all in Satam's car, speeding off to the hospital where he worked.

Jochen was examined, x-rayed, and put through tests. True enough, his liver function wasn't normal, and he had to remain in the hospital. During the procedures Satam had me wait in his private office. He showed a great deal of concern for Jochen and made sure that he got the prescribed medicines. He also looked after me, ordering in coffee and offering the use of a nurse's night bed if I was tired. Satam demonstrated energy, initiative, and concern for every detail. I was really impressed; I hadn't expected so much of him.

Then he offered to drive me home.

"You need your rest. Let me take you back to the German compound."

"No, you don't have to do that, but thank you. I'll take a taxi."

"As you wish, Karin. I'll call you tonight with an update on Jochen's condition. Don't be worried. Everything will be all right."

Satam escorted me to the taxi stand.

"Get home safely."

"Thank you. See you later."

When I got home, I immediately went to bed; I was really tired. Barely two hours later, the phone rang. It was Satam, asking how I was. Still tired and half-asleep, I answered, "Fine. I slept well."

"Jochen has improved. But I've spoken with his doctor, and he says that Jochen must stop drinking. Complete abstinence. Otherwise, his liver is going to give up on him."

"I'm not sure that information will convince him. Generally, he doesn't take advice from anyone," came my doubtful reply.

"Well, the doctor will tell him face to face. In any case, look after yourself. Tonight I'm invited to dinner at my neighbor's, so I'll phone you tomorrow to tell you when they decide to let Jochen go home. Just remember—phone me anytime. Do you need anything?"

"No, but thank you. You've already been a great help."

"Well of course; I'm always here for you."

"Thank you for that."

"I'll call you tomorrow."

"Bye. Until tomorrow."

The next morning I went back to the hospital by taxi. I inquired after Satam, but he wasn't there. Then I entered Jochen's private room. He was still asleep, but a nurse happened to be present, so I asked her when he'd be released.

"Tomorrow morning, I would think," she replied, making a professional guess.

Jochen moved in his bed, and as I shut the door behind the departing nurse, he woke up.

"Good morning. How are you today? Feeling better?"

"Yeah."

"You're going home tomorrow."

"That's great," he replied in a hoarse voice.

A different nurse brought him a calculatedly small breakfast, and she told me to make sure Jochen ate only light meals and drank only pure juices once he got home. I helped him to sit up. He ate a little and then asked, "How is it that the Saudi guy we met in the desert knows that I am sick? Is this a coincidence, or did you call him?"

"Oh . . . you mean Satam. . . . I called him, actually. You left his number on a piece of paper by the telephone, and I remembered him saying that he works in a hospital. So I phoned him. He's nice, isn't he? He's really helped you a lot. We have a lot to thank him for."

"Yeah, nice guy," mumbled Jochen.

Someone knocked, and I went to the door. "It's Satam!" I exclaimed joyously.

He shook both my hand and Jochen's, and told him, "Tomorrow you'll be back on your feet and on your way home. I hope that you're already feeling better? You look much better today. Your wife was really worried about you."

Then Satam turned to me. "I'll leave you two alone now. I have a few things to do. But please do call me directly if you need anything at all. I'll be in my office. See you later."

Jochen gazed at Satam in a dumbfounded way and as soon as he was out the door, he asked, "Why was he holding your hand for so long?"

"What? Really? I didn't notice."

"Strange. I've read it, and I've even seen it: Saudi men do not shake hands with women."

"I'm sure it's different if the woman is a Westerner."

"I don't think so," said Jochen. Then he settled himself on his side and shortly fell asleep again.

I went out to visit Satam in his office. As soon as he saw me, his face lit up and he ordered coffee for the two of us. A couple of minutes later a nurse came to tell Satam that he was urgently needed in the pharmacy. "Don't go away. I'll be right back."

The nurse looked at me quizzically and asked, "You're his new colleague?"

"No—my husband is an in-patient here." I smiled and asked her, "Have you worked here long?"

"Five years."

"Do you like it?'

"Well, it's not bad. I get paid a lot more than I would back home in England, and the professional environment is okay. Satam is the manager of the outpatients clinic, and he's very kind. Please excuse me; I have to go."

I waited in his office for over half an hour. It was boring, and I wanted to go home. I wrote him a brief note, left it on his desk, and took a taxi home.

I'd barely walked in the door when the phone rang.

"I'm very sorry that I stayed away so long."

"Think nothing of it. No problem."

"What are you doing this evening?"

"Nothing special."

"How would you like to get acquainted with a Saudi family? The family of my oldest sister? They would be delighted by your visit."

"Thank you—that sounds wonderful."

"Okay, then. I'll pick you up at six o'clock."

He came to get me and we drove to the home of his sister Sheika, who was in her midfifties and had eight adult children. Her oldest son was already forty; she had married at the age of fifteen. She lived with her children and grandchildren in one huge house. All the family members, except the men, were lined up to greet us. The children stared at me through wide eyes; they'd never seen a blond woman up close before. A few of them tried out English words and phrases on me. My reception was loud and heartfelt. Coffee and dates were served.

"So, what's this, Satam—a new love?" asked Sheika, both lethargic and bluntly acerbic in her tone.

"Oh, it's nothing. Her husband's in the hospital, and she needs a little distraction."

". . . And you need love."

"Why not? At my age, not much happens."

"Well, you know what you're doing. She's pretty and quite pleasant."

"I know."

I was busy with the children and didn't hear this conversation. Anyway, it was held in Arabic, which I hadn't learned. As a former teacher, being able to interact with children again brought me joy. They ranged in age from four up to twelve or thirteen. I was completely taken by the love and harmony that bound all the family members together.

Then dinner was served—in two locations. The men ate in one room, and the women and children in another. I found the situation very uncomfortable. And I was expected to eat with my fingers; there wasn't any cutlery. Sheika noticed my discomfort and brought me a knife and fork.

We said our good-byes at ten o'clock.

As he drove me home, Satam told me about his short conversation with Sheika and explained that she had been a widow for over twelve years now. Her husband had died of a heart attack. "Ever since then, I have been their financial support. In Saudi Arabia, widowed or divorced women don't get government assistance. They rely on help from their parents and brothers."

As we approached the German compound, I considered whether I should invite Satam in, or not.

"Well, here we are," he announced. "Let's talk on the phone tomorrow, okay? And don't bother to come to the hospital. I would like to help Jochen with the check-out procedures, and then personally drive him home."

"I think it would be better if I was there. But we could bring him home together. You know, he's a little sensitive."

"As you wish, Karin."

Before I got out of the car, I leaned over and gave Satam a goodnight kiss.

The next day we brought Jochen home. We helped him into and out of the car, and when he was in his own bed, I made tea and the three of us sat together. Satam and I chatted with each other because Jochen refused to join in. As soon as Satam had finished his tea, he got to his feet. "Jochen, get lots of rest. Everything is fine now."

I accompanied him to the door.

Two days later, Jochen was on his feet and back at work. I began to chat with Satam on the phone at least twice daily, and I often got together with him. I avoided spending time alone with Jochen. I often struggled with the desire to move back to Germany. I wanted to get away from Satam and this emotional bond that was drawing us closer and closer together. Deep in my heart I truly loved him; I longed for him; I wanted to speak with him and see him every day. But what would come from this relationship? How would it develop? At the same time, life with Jochen became increasingly intolerable. I wanted to return to Germany and divorce him. For some time I lived in a whirlwind of conflicting emotions.

From time to time, Jochen spent his weekends playing skat with his colleagues. He renounced alcohol and reined himself in for a while. On one of these weekends, when the clock showed one or two o'clock in the morning and Jochen hadn't returned, I became nervous and concerned. Suddenly the phone rang.

"This is the police. Is your husband Jochen Holtz?"

"Yes," I replied in total shock.

"He's been arrested for drunk driving."

"Is he all right?"

"Yes. So far."

"Where is he?"

"In detention in the al-Wafa police station. Tomorrow he'll be sent to jail."

"Which jail?"

"I don't know!" replied the policeman, and hung up.

Totally agitated, I phoned Satam and explained the situation. He immediately drove to the police station and phoned me from there. "Jochen is fine, but for the time being, he has to stay here." Then he drove over to our house, where he told me that he would phone influential connections in the morning to assure Jochen's release. Just after eight in the morning I phoned the German Embassy, but no one answered. "This is the weekend," Satam reminded me. He then left to plan his day visiting individuals with the kind of pull we needed. He phoned me in the evening. "I haven't been able to reach the right people yet. I'll keep trying."

The next morning I was able to speak to the German Embassy and explain the situation. The secretary replied in a cold voice, "I am sorry, but we cannot formally help you in such a case. However, it might be possible for us to reach a private agreement. Please understand that we can't promise anything. Give me your number; if there are any developments, I'll phone you immediately."

One week passed, and Jochen continued to be held in the police station. I wasn't allowed to visit him. Neither the embassy nor Satam could effect his release. Through a friend in the police force, Satam found out that Jochen's punishment would be one year of imprisonment, to be served in a jail somewhere in the south of Saudi Arabia. Secretly, deep inside, I was happy about this; maybe it would finally get him off the bottle.

Jochen's employers at the company believed he would be quickly released and immediately deported to Germany.

Veronica Schmidt came to visit me.

"I am so sorry about what has happened with Jochen. My husband and I are ready to assist you in any way. Please don't hesitate to call on us."

"Thank you. You're really kind. In my situation I appreciate any offer of help."

A difficult choice lay before me. Should I return to Germany with Jochen when he was deported, or should I stay in Saudi Arabia with Satam? He was already married. I had never discussed marriage with him. Maybe he didn't want to marry me. Actually, I didn't even really know if he loved me . . . but I believed that he did. I decided to talk to him openly.

I decided to begin with a test. I invited him to visit me at home. "Our friendship is coming to an end. I'll have to return to Germany with Jochen," I told him.

I had never before seen Satam look so unhappy. He looked deep into my eyes and said, "The idea of being separated from you—for any reason—fills me with deep sadness. Please tell me one thing. Are you happy in your marriage to Jochen?"

"You know that I'm not. You've seen that. Our relationship has gone from bad to worse."

"Karin, I love you."

"I love you too, Satam."

"Stay with me. Don't leave. Let's get married."

"You are already married," I pointed out.

"That's nothing. I'll get a divorce."

"I don't want to make your wife unhappy."

"My wife and I haven't been getting along for a long time now."

Satam stood up, came over to me, and embraced me. We kissed each other passionately.

That same evening I wrote my husband a long letter telling him that I was going to get a divorce and stay in Saudi Arabia. I gave it to Satam and asked him to pass it to Jochen. Satam phoned his friend in the police force and asked for permission to visit Jochen. He was already being held in the deportation area of the airport, waiting for the final paperwork and a flight to Germany with an available seat. Satam spent the night at my house.

The next morning I regretted my decision to sleep with Satam. Not because he was a bad lover—on the contrary, he was passionate and full of excitement—but because I had recalled a conversation with Veronica

Schmidt about marriage to a Saudi. She had told me that if a woman agrees to sleep with her husband before marriage, he considers her to be a loose woman who would go to bed with any man. I decided not to discuss this with Satam. After breakfast, he left for the airport to bring Jochen the letter.

Satam returned in the afternoon, looking depressed.

"What happened? You couldn't find him?"

"Yes, I found him."

"What's his problem? Did you give him the letter?"

"Yes. And when he read it, he fell apart. Even before I spoke to him I could see that he was in a really bad condition. I don't think you would have recognized him. His face was haggard and pale, and he could barely stand and walk. The minute I saw him, I was sure that he'd been tortured. He told me that the Mutawas came to his cell and wanted to convert him to Islam. They tried to force him to recite Muslim prayers. He refused, so they had him beaten. I saw blue welts on his face and back. He showed me everything. His feet are swollen, probably from direct blows. And he can barely see out of his left eye." Satam's face glowed with anger. "All that was done in the name of Islam. I am ashamed to be a Muslim and a Saudi."

I couldn't stop my tears.

"Jochen says that he refuses to give you a divorce."

"That means we can't get married."

"Of course we can. In Islam a man can marry many women, and he can be married to more than one woman at the same time."

"It's not like that in Germany."

"What's important, Karin, is that you stay here. I need to see you every day."

I had felt the same but hadn't had the courage to say it aloud. I needed to be near him. Without him, happiness was unimaginable.

It was late—close to midnight. Satam was not making any moves to go home. I yawned to show him that I was tired.

"Go to bed. You've had a stressful day. I'll sleep here on the couch," he said.

"Satam . . . I don't think we should sleep together until after we're married."

"Why? Didn't you enjoy last night?"

"Yes, oh, you know I did. But think about the neighbors. When they notice that a strange man is spending his nights here, how will I look?"

"I thought that Germans were used to such things."

"No, Germans don't approve when a strange man spends his nights with a married woman."

"But Karin, we'll get married soon."

"Yes. But until then, we have to live separately. That's what your culture expects, too."

"My God . . . you've already become a Saudi woman!"

"We have to respect our cultures," I replied with an indulgent smile.

"Good. Whatever you want." Satam got up to leave.

"Please, Satam, don't be angry. This is better for both of us."

"Do you want me to go, or not?"

"Yes. But kiss me first."

He gave me a brief kiss and went out.

"Call me!" I called from the doorstep.

The next day he didn't call. I was upset. I tried to reach him, but an impersonal recorded voice always reported that the party was not available. In the evening, I took a taxi to the hospital to look for him.

Satam was sitting in his office with a nurse, which piqued my jealousy. I walked right in. He stood up and greeted me in a restrained manner. The nurse left.

"Why didn't you call me? I've waited for your call all day. I tried to reach you many times."

"I was really busy."

"Were you busy, or are you angry with me?"

"Well, actually, both; but not anymore. Let's go somewhere and eat. I'm starving," he replied with engaging charm.

"My God, you're too sensitive. What is there to be upset about? Come over to my place. I'll cook you something nice, something German."

"Fine. Whatever suits you."

Satam unlocked a cupboard and took out a shopping bag. There were three bottles of wine in it.

Back at my house, I took two portions of rolled meat out of the freezer and heated them in the microwave. I prepared a salad and a delicious sauce. I set the table and put a red candle in the middle. We ate, drank, and enjoyed ourselves, focusing only on pleasant topics. "Marriage can be wonderful if the couple understand each other," I said with a smile and a little sigh.

"True, very true. But sometimes we burden our lives with worrying about what the neighbors think."

Both of us laughed. After dinner we went to bed.

I decided that, no matter what, I didn't want to lose Satam. It no longer mattered to me what others might say about my relationship with him; I had seldom, hardly ever, enjoyed my life as I did now with this man. And a few days later, I learned that Jochen had been deported to Germany. From then on, Satam often stayed overnight with me.

One day we arranged to meet in the old downtown marketplace so Satam could buy me a gold necklace; he wanted me to choose it myself. I took a taxi to our meeting point. As we entered this conservative district of Riyadh, the taxi was stopped by three Mutawas. The religious police don't like to see a woman traveling alone in a taxi. The driver and I were detained and taken to an investigation center run by the religious police. In addition to having committed a sin, I didn't have valid papers with me. They checked up on me in their computer, which was linked to the Ministry of the Interior, and discovered that I had overstayed in Saudi Arabia; both Jochen and I were listed as having invalid, expired visas. I requested permission to telephone Satam.

"Who is Satam?" asked the chief investigator in broken English and a threatening tone.

"A friend of mine," I replied, lightly and with pride.

"Oh, you have a 'friend'? You are a whore?"

"Excuse me, but I don't put up with insults."

"The whore is insulted! Did you hear that?" came the sarcastic response, directed to the other Mutawas.

"I want to speak to the German Embassy!"

"In our country, whores go to jail."

My face turned red with anger. "Damn you," I shouted, "I want to talk to the German Embassy!"

"Who is damned? Your own religion is damned. You Christians will burn in hell. But before you go there, here in the sacred land of Saudi Arabia you will live through a small piece of hell, just to get you ready for what you'll experience after you die. You can't damn us in our own land, because whoever talks like that gets beheaded by us. Understand?"

A strong Mutawa in a white robe that barely reached below his knees (because they believe that the prophet Muhammad wore something similar) walked up to me; he punched me with full force in my face. He hit me repeatedly until the blood ran. I began to scream and scream. My face throbbed with pain. I was filled with hatred of these men.

The chief investigator dragged me by my hair into the next room and raped me.

I was screaming, and the Mutawas in the neighboring room laughed hysterically.

Finally, when I was about to pass out from shock and stress, I was pushed into a prisoner transportation van with an inside temperature of over 105 degrees and driven to the women's prison. The van didn't have a window, it didn't have air-conditioning; there was only a small opening in the roof through which the hot outside air wafted in. I had no idea in which direction we were traveling. It seemed to me that I was inside for an eternity, suffocating and streaming with sweat. Then the van stopped and the doors swung open. I could barely stand up, let alone climb out. A policeman pushed me out of the vehicle like livestock.

The women's prison was a run-down building far away from Riyadh. High walls topped with barbed wire encircled it. The interior was dingy, moldy, and littered with trash. Since the sewage system was open, it stank of urine and excrement. Flies and every other conceivable type of insect crawled over the garbage heaps. You could hear the buzzing of the insects, and the moans and cries of the prisoners.

I was pushed into a cell that held many women. It was very dark. A small hole in one wall admitted a little light. The oppressive heat and the stink made me throw up. The women sat around the walls apathetically, like people in a madhouse, all of them dressed in black. One woman stood up and began to pelt me with hardened feces from the open sewer, as if to say, "There are already enough of us in this room . . . why did you have to come?" Another woman, who was quite old, approached me and began to kiss me unceasingly. Some of the women were groaning in physical pain; medical care was not provided. I was wide-awake. I shut my eyes and tried to convince myself that this was some kind of nightmare, and that shortly I would wake up to a normal life.

The Mutawa had told the truth; I was still here, in Saudi Arabia, but living in an unimaginable hell.

The Muslim call to prayer was heard. All the women in the cell lined up into rows, but I stayed in my place against the wall. A female prison guard entered the cell and hit me with a heavy stick. "Criminal, get up and pray with the other women." I did as I was told. After the prayer, I was punished with kitchen duty. A mountain of plates and spoons used by the five hundred inmates were waiting to be washed. Rats swarmed in the kitchen, animals the size of cats. I tried to scare them away, but my efforts didn't make the least impression on them. They were completely fearless.

At night I slept on the floor with the other women—not on mattresses, but on greasy and grubby mats. Because our cell had only natural light, as soon as it got dark we had to sleep. At sundown, a woman approached me who wanted to lie down beside me. She reached her hand between my legs. I pushed her away with a shriek and stood up. But where could I go? The room was full of human bodies and diseased minds. I felt like my very soul, my sense of personal dignity, was being raped. The experience of being there was more demeaning than anything I had ever imagined.

Nine days passed, and I heard nothing from Satam. Later I was to learn that he had looked for me everywhere. He had inquired about me in the German compound; he had asked his friends in the police force to try to locate me; he had alarmed the Germany Embassy. The embassy in turn had made a half-hearted attempt to get involved by telephoning the Ministry of the Exterior, but received no response. And according to the airport police, I had flown back to Germany with Jochen. In fact, the police officials at the airport had been given both Jochen's visa and mine. Without paying any attention, they had simply cancelled both visas. Satam was forced into the open: "That's simply impossible. I had an appointment to meet this woman downtown. And, shortly before our appointment, her husband was deported."

"Really?" came the crisp, slightly sarcastic reply from the voice at the German Embassy. "Well, maybe the Saudi Embassy in Germany will look into it."

Satam continued his search. He told everyone at the hospital and asked for advice. One of the nurses advised him to try to locate a women's prison south of Riyadh. She explained that a nurse who worked in another hospital had decided to take a taxi home alone at midnight and had been put in that jail. The mention of the taxi caught Satam's attention. He phoned a good friend with the police force and asked him to find out if I had been arrested.

One hour later he finally knew where I was.

He quickly put a plan into action. He gathered two male witnesses and went to see an elderly sheikh, who married the two of us in my absence and without my consent, with the legal date of the marriage set at one month previous. The terms became perfectly agreeable as a gift of money was slipped across to the old man. In any case, it is completely legal in Saudi Arabia to get married without the bride being present. Satam took the marriage certificate and headed off to the prison. When he finally located it, he went to see the director and demanded the release of his wife. As soon as he read the certificate, the director apologized for keeping me in detention for so long. He told Satam that, if he had known that I was married to a Saudi, he would have been immediately informed. But he also gave him some advice, since he was a new husband: to pay closer attention to my comings and goings, and never let me travel alone.

I was called into the office and suddenly treated with great respect, because my husband was a Muslim and a Saudi. "We just wanted to give you a little lesson. You should know that a Muslim woman must never be alone in a car with a strange man. The devil will tempt them. It is written in our religion!" Then he shook his finger at Satam. "And one thing more. Your wife has a boyfriend! A highly respected Mutawa in Riyadh informed me of this out of the goodness of his heart. Remember that women from the West, from places like Europe, can't be trusted. Islam has no place in their societies. Men and women associate freely and shamelessly in their countries. It's a scandal. The devil will follow this woman every day. Watch her, watch her carefully."

When I was first called from my cell, I experienced a panic attack, believing that something worse awaited me. I could barely walk from fear. When I saw Satam I jumped into his arms, held him tightly, and burst into tears. I was afraid it might be a dream, because I had dreamed of this meeting so often during my days in the cell. I stroked him repeatedly and kept rubbing my eyes. I was so weak and so happy, that by the end of our interview with the director I fell unconscious to the floor. Satam had me taken to a hospital by ambulance, where I was examined in the outpatients clinic. Apparently the doctor had stepped out of the examination room afterward to inform Satam of my condition. "I have two things to tell you. First of all, your wife is suffering from exhaustion and a gastric inflammation. She's going to need rest and a lot of vitamins. And now for some good news: your wife is pregnant."

I was transferred to a hospital room, but Satam was not allowed to visit me. The nurse greeted me kindly. Satam stayed in the hospital; he went to the cafeteria, where he drank coffee and chain-smoked cigarettes. From time to time he inquired about me. "She's in a deep sleep," replied the nurses. "A good sign."

He was allowed to visit me the following day. I looked a lot better and was overjoyed to see him. I could hardly believe that my nightmare was over. He sat beside me and stroked my hand. I began to cry and wanted to embrace him.

"It's all right, it's all right," he whispered into my ear. "I promise to never leave you." And he took me in his arms, although this was strictly forbidden in Saudi hospitals.

"Oh, I am so happy that you are here!"

A few minutes later, Satam asked me if the doctor had told me the good news.

"No. What news?" I asked, with tears in my eyes.

"You are pregnant!"

Unconsciously I pushed Satam away and replied, "What? What did the doctor say?"

"What's this? Aren't you happy?"

"Yes, but…" I stopped speaking and sank into my own private thoughts. I hadn't slept with Jochen in months. The baby's father was either Satam or the Mutawa who had raped me. Then, more out of duty than conviction, I said, "Yes, I'm very happy," and smiled.

Satam stayed with me. After three days, I could walk unassisted again. On the fourth day, just before my release from hospital, he brought me a beautiful dress and an abaya, since my own clothes had been soiled and ripped and stained.

In the car I sat quietly beside Satam, but my thoughts and emotions were in a turmoil that I did my best to hide. I was pensive and deeply depressed, but I definitely did not want to share anything with him. So much had happened: I had been raped, I had endured one of the worst prisons on the face of the earth, and I was pregnant. It was too much to accept. I was bitter and deeply wounded. I profoundly regretted coming to this country. Nowhere else in the world did such brutality and barbarism exist. A place where women were raped, with great pleasure, in the name of Islam. And when I recalled the prison, I became nauseous and began to tremble. Why didn't people in the West expose the human right abuses practiced in Saudi Arabia? There were no human rights here. None at all. People were simply walked on. Was it the oil that made Western governments so blind? Why wouldn't they fight the Saudis? Because they would turn the taps and shut off their oil exports? And what had happened to Jochen? He had been tortured. Was he all right? Had he recovered?

How would I forget or suppress these terrible memories? Would it be possible? That would only be determined in my future. The only thing that I needed to know at that moment was how Satam had found me.

He explained the whole story. He told me that we were now legally married.

"What? How was that possible? I wasn't even there!" I replied in outrage.

"Look, I had to do something! Without that marriage certificate, how would I have gotten you out of jail? And anyway, you know how much I love you. I wanted to marry you, Karin."

"Yes, but how is something like that even possible? I'm not even divorced from my first husband!"

"Well, according to Islam, a man can have more than one wife . . ."

"Well, that's not the case with us."

"Look, Karin, you are now a Muslim woman who is married to a Muslim man. Everything is legally in place."

I was completely amazed. "This is totally absurd."

"Tomorrow you're going to get new official papers and permanent resident status here in Saudi Arabia."

"I don't know about this. Everything is happening too quickly."

"Darling, stop thinking about it. Let's go somewhere and have a nice dinner."

Back in Riyadh, I was anxious to get back to my house in the German compound to see if everything was in order. "Well, we could drive by and take a look," suggested Satam. I took the house key out of my purse and tried to open the door with it, but at the same moment the door was opened from the inside by a strange woman. "May I help you?"

"Excuse me," I replied in shock. "Do I have the wrong place? I thought this was my house."

"Oh, you must be the lady who lived here before. Please come in. My husband was given your husband's former job, so we were assigned to your house. Your belongings are in storage with Mrs. Schmidt. Do you know where she lives?"

"Yes, of course," I replied and went with Satam over to Veronica Schmidt's.

"Karin! Where have you been? We looked for you everywhere!" she exclaimed, hugging me.

"It's a very long story. I'll have to tell you later."

"We thought that you flew back to Germany with Jochen when he was deported, that you didn't have time to say good-bye. We kept your belongings here and waited for you to contact us. Then Jochen phoned us and we learned that you were still in the country. We've been so worried!"

I introduced Satam. "This is Satam," I said—not "this is my boyfriend," or "this is my husband."

"Mrs. Schmidt, tomorrow I'll come by to pick up my things."

"Karin, you are welcome to stay here tonight. We have a guestroom."

"Thank you, but that won't be necessary . . ."

"When are you planning to fly? Shall we make a reservation for you? Lufthansa has a flight going out the day after tomorrow."

"I have to see. I'll take care of it myself." I said good-bye.

"All right, then; see you tomorrow, Karin."

Satam and I got back into the car. I was in a state of confusion and anxiety. I didn't know if I should fly back to Germany or stay in Saudi Arabia. "Where are we going?" I asked. "Do you have somewhere for me to stay?"

"Of course," replied Satam. "We are going home."

After a while Satam started to slow down. "We're almost there," he explained. He parked his car beside a house with high walls. We went in through the gate. It was a two-storied home, and the smell of roasting meat hung sharply in the air. A few small children opened the front door and called out, "Daddy! Daddy is home!" Satam kissed each one of them. They greeted me with shy handshakes and asked, "Who is she, Daddy? A new housemaid?"

"She's pretty!" said a little boy.

I didn't understand anything. Laughing, Satam translated all their comments for me. I replied with a weak smile.

Satam cleared a path through the cluster of children to the living room, where he told me, "Temporarily, we'll have to stay here, until I rent another apartment. I didn't expect the marriage to be so sudden." I didn't reply. I just sat down on the cushions placed on the floor.

Satam went upstairs to talk to his wife, who was with her three adult daughters. She already knew that her husband had brought a strange woman into the house.

"Who is she?" she exploded, skeptically, aggressively.

"The wife of a friend. She's having big problems. She lost her husband and was put into jail. I can't give you all the details now. But I married her to help her get out of the situation."

"What's this? You married her?"

"Pay attention! It was only to help her out! It's a marriage of convenience until she's able to legally leave the country. The prophet Muhammad himself did that. He married women temporarily, until their own husbands returned from war or long journeys. A Muslim man must always help women. But please . . . don't tell anyone that I have a second wife. It's better for you, it's better for all of us," he told her, and after he came back to me he translated what he had told his wife. "I had to tell her it is a marriage of convenience to calm her down," explained Satam.

"Karin, let's go upstairs to meet my family. Remember, we're going to live together somewhere else. And if she doesn't like it, I'm going to divorce her as soon as I find somewhere for us to live."

"How long will I be here?"

"Not long."

I accompanied Satam upstairs. He introduced us in a formal, reserved manner. His wife had gray hair that she had attempted to dye black some time before. It was tied back, and a few unkempt strands hung loose around her face. She was wearing a loose housedress covered with a pattern of huge, bright flowers on a loud, green background. Her feet were bare.

An Indian housemaid entered the room carrying a tray with both tea and coffee on it.

To relieve the tension Satam said, "It looks like the family has become bigger," and most of us smiled.

"Father, none of us speaks English. How are we going to understand this lady?" said Khaula, his oldest daughter.

"No problem. You teach her to speak Arabic, and she'll teach you English. Or, even better, German. But maybe that's not a good idea, since I don't speak German."

The daughters giggled. His wife sat stiffly in her place. Then she got up and went into a neighboring room. Satam followed her.

"Listen to me. If you don't accept this woman, I'm going to divorce you. Is that clear?" Satam paraphrased that to me later.

I started to come to grips with my new situation, and to show my good will I offered to give Satam's children their first language lesson. They fetched pieces of paper and pencils, and I taught them a few English words. The older daughters, Khaula, Najat, and Nadia, especially paid close attention. They were eager, enthusiastic, and had fun.

Satam returned and was pleased to see us getting along in a friendly manner. He told Khaula to set up and organize a spare bedroom for me.

The next morning, Satam left early for work. I had had a terrible, sleepless night, plagued by nightmares, and I woke several times bathed in sweat. The hell I had experienced in the women's jail had penetrated to the core of my being. I wasn't able to really fall asleep until dawn, and I was wide-awake a few hours later. I got dressed and left the bedroom. The housemaid, Mimi, was in the hallway, and I discovered that she spoke very good English. She directed me to the kitchen.

Satam's wife was there. She gave me a withering and hateful look and told me to get out of her kitchen. Mimi translated this with embarrassment. I returned to the bedroom, phoned Veronica Schmidt, and asked if I could come to see her.

I ordered a taxi and left Satam's house.

"How are you?"

"Truthfully? . . . Not good."

"What's bothering you?"

"A trauma. I've experienced a terrible trauma, Veronica, and I can't deal with it. Whenever I think about it, I start to tremble." And then I told her the truth about the previous weeks.

"This is disgusting! Simply disgusting! Unimaginable!" she exclaimed. ". . . And what do you want to do now?"

"I don't know. I'd like to return to Germany, but I'm afraid Jochen will terrorize me. He did that once before when I decided to divorce him. My life was a living hell. On the other hand, I love Satam. He's my new love. But I don't want to be his second wife. And, frankly, I'm afraid of his first wife."

"Is he willing to divorce her and keep her away from you?"

"He promised me that. But I don't know if he's actually going to do it."

"Well, wait a bit. Give him a chance."

"Veronica, he married me without my knowledge while I was still in jail. Furthermore, I'm still legally married to Jochen. What kind of unbelievable mess is this?"

"I don't believe that this is allowed," she said.

"In Saudi Arabia? . . . Yes, it is!"

I asked her if I could phone Satam to come and pick me up. When I spoke to him, his voice was acid with anger when he heard that, once again, I had traveled alone by taxi. He asked me when I would learn that that was dangerous, and told me to never do it again.

Shortly, Satam arrived in his car. He loaded my belongings into it and we headed back to his house. During the drive I told him about my encounter with his wife in the kitchen. "Look, she's an idiot—an absolute idiot. But have a little patience. I'll divorce her soon." Then he added, "I have a request to make of you. Please—never leave the house alone. Anywhere you want to go, I'll drive you there."

I got through the boredom of the long days inside the house by watching the English-language television channel and reading books on Saudi Arabia and Arabic culture and literature. I learned Arabic by pointing at objects and having Satam's daughters tell me the words. They also tried to teach me to read and write. On weekends, I often went to visit Mrs. Schmidt; Satam drove me there. I began to be completely, utterly bored. I started to sleep a lot and to spend more and more time in my room. I felt like a prisoner in my own skin. Satam would often go out with the whole family, and I stayed behind, all alone. I asked Mimi to bring the meals to my room. From time to time, Satam took me out to a restaurant in the evenings. I drank a lot of coffee and smoked a lot of cigarettes. Satam bought me a water pipe, since his first wife also smoked one. For the most part, I only communicated with two people: Mimi, the housemaid, and Jawaher, a younger sister of Satam who was married and lived in the neighborhood. Jawaher taught me a lot about the life of a woman in Saudi society. She had been married for over ten years and worked as a teacher. She was intelligent, and, to my surprise, believed in women's rights. One day, after we had spent an hour or two together, she actually gave the following speech:

"Saudi women don't live normal lives. Both tradition and religion keep us ignorant and uneducated. We only realized this after satellite television was introduced. Before that, we thought that all women in the world lived like we did, huddled together on the dark side of the house, with a wall separating us from the men's quarters. Now we know that men and women can caress each other, can kiss each other with passion and love. Now we know that there are actually men in the world who can treat a woman tenderly and kindly. Our men appear to be serious and strong, but in reality they are shallow, fragile, and naïve. They hide these characteristics behind serious faces that look like they are carrying all the world's problems.

"And consider the fact that we practice total segregation of the sexes from the onset of puberty. This means that women have no idea what a man is thinking. And, in my opinion, our men don't have any idea what a woman is thinking, either. They think we are only useful in bed or for cooking, cleaning, and doing laundry. I have never, in my lifetime, spoken freely with a foreign man, but when I watch men and women talking on television, I wish I could do the same. At the very least, I'd like to get to know my own husband. I don't know what his thoughts are. I don't know my brothers, either. My husband comes home, wants his dinner ready and waiting, asks how the children are, and that's it. I don't know what he does at work. I don't know what kind of problems he faces. And, in turn, I never talk to him about my work in the classroom. We just don't communicate. After dinner, he takes a two-hour nap; then he goes out to visit his relatives and friends, who are all men.

"But this is not just my story. Most of the wives in our country, rich or poor, have the same lack of connection to their husbands. I would love to love and be loved in return! I want to be seductive and playful! But I don't even know how to do that. Sometimes I dream that I am looking into the eyes of a handsome strange man, which will never happen in reality. We look outside and see the house walls. When we go beyond them, everything is obscured by the black cloth of our veils. We can't even breathe fresh air because of that cloth. I want to be like you. I don't want to wear a veil. On the television, I've seen people walking dogs on leashes. Sometimes I think that Saudi women are kept on leashes, too. That's why, in this country, more women than men get sick. And you know, my mother's generation had a better life. Because they believed that every woman in the world lived exactly like they did. That women all over the world existed only to serve men. You are lucky—so lucky—that you're not a Saudi woman. To tell the truth, I'm surprised that you love him so much. I think he's just another chauvinist."

"In that respect, you're wrong. Satam is very kind and loving," I retorted.

"Maybe that's because he works a lot with Western men and women. That's changed him. And, as a man, he can look for love wherever he wants. Imagine what would happen to me if I had an affair. I would be stoned to death."

As time passed, Satam lost interest in me. He came to sleep with me less often; he seldom drove me to Mrs. Schmidt's, or anywhere else, for that matter. Sometimes he came home very late, or not at all. Apparently he was very busy at work. He didn't divorce his first wife. We fought loudly and often.

One time, when Satam didn't come home by late evening, I phoned the hospital where he worked. He wasn't there. I asked his daughter to locate him, but she had no idea where he might be. Finally, late in the night, he showed up—drunk. When I asked him where he had been he laughed hysterically, slapped me on the side of my head, stuttered a few words in Arabic, and collapsed into a deep sleep on our bed. It brought back memories of my relationship with Jochen. I could barely sleep. I agonized over my situation all night, totally depressed and disappointed, overwhelmed with regret at my decision not to fly back to Germany.

The next morning, I asked Satam once again where he had been.

"What is this? Are you trying to control me?"

"No. I was worried about you."

"You didn't need to worry about anything. See—here I am. I had a lot of work to do, and afterwards we had a little party in the hospital."

"Satam, I have to tell you something. I feel like I'm living in a jail."

He became furious and snapped back, "I should have left you in the jail! I saved your life, don't you remember? You've got everything you need. What more do you want? You don't know what you want—that's the problem. I've had enough of you, you thankless bitch!" He slammed the door and left.

I collapsed into a chair, sighing in deep resignation. I felt so alone, helpless, and empty. Suddenly I was overwhelmed by a new idea: that all the love and charm that Satam had shown me had been merely theatrical, simply a mask hiding his vulgar meanness. But now I had seen his true face.

Satam's first wife was pleased by these goings-on; Mimi told me. She had put a cassette of Arabic music and singing into her tape recorder, punched the start button, turned up the volume, and started to dance. And she thought out a plan. She sent her children and the maid on a visit to one of her sisters in another city. She knew, from experience, that when Satam was angry, he stayed away from the house for a few days. She also knew that I was pregnant, and she wanted me to lose the child.

Around midnight, she crept into my bedroom and slammed a massive stick down onto my stomach. I jumped out of bed in shock and screamed for help. "No one is going to hear you, *gahba*!"—whore—she yelled, and swung at me again and again. I grabbed a chair and managed to throw it at her in such a way that it hit her directly. She fell to the floor and had difficulty getting up. I used the opportunity to throw on my abaya, grab my purse, and run in the direction of the house door. I ran to a main street and waited for a passing taxi. Two minutes later, I flagged one down and had the driver take me to Mrs. Schmidt's.

Mr. and Mrs. Schmidt were horrified. I had to return to Germany; they were adamant. I spent the night at their home, and the following day Mr. Schmidt booked me onto a flight. "Thank God," he said, "I've got you a seat going out the day after tomorrow." I cried incessantly, and Mrs. Schmidt told me to calm down. On the day of the flight they accompanied me right to the passport control, and they planned to stay in the airport until the plane took off. But I received a paralyzing shock when I presented my passport, one that I hadn't even imagined. As the wife of a Saudi, I was forbidden to travel alone. I needed my husband's consent.

We were all left speechless.

Mr. Schmidt phoned the German Embassy. The consul said that he would try to intervene and told us to stay at the airport. It was getting late. The flight was delayed to see if anything could be done on my behalf. Nothing. The plane left.

On the trip back into Riyadh I felt that I couldn't breathe properly, I couldn't swallow, and I couldn't think straight. We went to the German Embassy and met with the consul.

"I am sorry that you couldn't leave the country," he told me. "We'll try to get this taken care of, either by approaching your husband directly and securing his consent, or by dealing through our contacts in the Ministry of the Exterior. Could you give me your husband's telephone number, Mrs. Holtz?"

"Certainly. This is it."

The consul phoned Satam and attempted to convince him, in a friendly manner, to let me travel to Germany. Satam wanted to know where I was, and why I hadn't informed him that I wanted to travel abroad. He said that he was quite willing to give his consent, but that first I should come home to have a little talk with him and say good-bye.

I was afraid of being locked in the house and facing another attack from Satam's wife. I didn't want to return. The Schmidts said that they would accompany me, but I only accepted their offer reluctantly.

They reached Satam by phone, and when we arrived at the house, he was waiting for us. His greeting at the door was friendly, and he escorted us to the living room. Coffee, tea, and cake were served. Satam then began to speak. He told us that it is normal for family members to quarrel and fight from time to time. He loved me very much; that's why he had married me, in spite of the family difficulties it had caused in consequence. He wanted to divorce his first wife and live with me in a different apartment, but at the moment he didn't have enough money to do this. Somehow or other, however, he would get the money and we would move out. He promised to treat me well. Unfortunately, his family would very much disapprove if I ever traveled alone. Therefore, if I wanted to visit Germany from time to time, he would be happy to accompany me. That way he could get to know my homeland and the members of my family.

At this point I dug in my heels and insisted that he provide me with my own apartment. I couldn't live in that house again; I was afraid—so afraid that I was having panic attacks.

"All right," said Satam. "Let's make a compromise. I'll get you your own apartment now, and the trip to Germany will come later."

I instinctively hesitated and held off. But then I said, "That's all right, then. I accept."

"Good. Tomorrow I'll go to the bank and arrange a loan to cover the cost of renting and furnishing your new apartment."

"Until it's ready, Satam, I'm going to live with Mr. and Mrs. Schmidt."

"Okay," he replied with a dry smile, a habit of his which I had been seeing more and more of since our marriage.

I went home with the Schmidts and stayed there for five days.

The apartment was rented and furnished. I was happy to hear that I would be moving in. It was small and not really in good condition, but I decided that I could decorate it and make it a pleasant place to live. This kept me busy and preoccupied for a time.

Satam's wife continued to harass and terrorize me. She often telephoned and launched into a tirade of verbal abuse. She spread rumors that I had a boyfriend who secretly came to visit me. Once, when Satam was at my place, she arranged for a friend of her younger brother's to telephone. He asked to speak with me and told Satam that he was my boyfriend. She had made an agreement with him; if he could get Satam to kick me out, he would get my apartment. She arranged to be driven past the entrance door to my apartment with her daughters in the car. This young man, with his face hidden by an Arabic headscarf, pretended to be leaving my place and running nervously away just as the car passed by. The daughters reported what they had seen to their father.

Satam didn't fall for these tricks. But he began, increasingly, to neglect his duties as the man of the house. I received less and less money for household expenses; he neglected to pay the rent for months; I had to withdraw money from my bank account in Germany to cover costs. I wasn't allowed to go out alone. I wasn't informed about what was going on, and often he didn't come to see me or even call for days on end.

My only support was the Schmidts, who visited me occasionally. My friend in Germany, Gabi, sometimes wrote me a letter. She told me that Jochen walked around in filthy clothes—he had become emotionally distraught. My replies were long and detailed, as I explained everything I had endured since Jochen's deportation. Gabi now took to heart her husband's warning and advice not to be lured to Saudi Arabia. But she also gave me courage, and she encouraged me to find some way to get out of the country as soon as possible.

My pregnancy was advancing, and doing the housework became more awkward and difficult. I asked Satam to send his first wife's housemaid, Mimi, over to help me out. Satam arranged for her to come two days a week to clean and do my laundry. At first I was very happy—I regarded her as an old and trusted friend, and it was a joy to see her again. Satam's wife was furious with this arrangement, not only because I was getting the use of her maid, but also because Mimi and I liked each other. She plotted to destroy at least one of us.

She observed the house on the days when Mimi worked for me and noted that I would sometimes send the maid out to the tiny grocery shop next door. Then she contacted a Mutawa, a member of the religious police who regularly patrolled our district, and denounced the girl. She claimed that Mimi slipped into the store for a secret romantic tryst with the two Indian shopkeepers, usually during the prayer times, when the store had to be closed and shuttered. This reference to behavior insulting to the Muslim religion—in addition to the accusation of fornication—was designed to arouse the Mutawa's wrath.

The Mutawa wanted to know where the shop was, and he wanted to have evidence that Mimi went to shop there.

One day shortly before noon when I sent Mimi out to buy fresh bread and vegetables, Fatima, Satam's wife, was waiting for her in a taxi. She paid the driver, dismissed him, called the Mutawa, and entered the shop. She greeted the surprised housemaid and let her make her purchases. Then she engaged her in a long, friendly, detailed conversation. Mimi was puzzled by her behavior and waited patiently for Fatima to finish speaking.

Suddenly three Mutawas entered the shop. They were strong men with long, unkempt beards that reached practically to their navels. Fatima announced in a loud voice, "This is she!" and pointed at Mimi. One of the Mutawas grabbed her by the back of the neck, just like an animal, and bundled her out toward their waiting car. Mimi began to scream incessantly, and she was heavily slapped twice across her face. The other two Mutawas handcuffed the two bewildered Indian workers.

The Mutawas then thanked Fatima for her vigilance in protecting the purity of their religion. "May Allah praise you for your actions. The girl has sinned against God, and will be stoned to death," said one of them.

I was upset and confused when Mimi did not return. Four hours passed. Finally, I called Mrs. Schmidt.

"I simply sent her out for a few things."

"Maybe she went to visit friends," suggested Veronica.

"She doesn't have friends in this neighborhood. And anyway, she wouldn't do that without telling me. What should I do?"

"Call Satam's wife. Maybe she went back there."

"Not a chance. I'm afraid of that woman."

"Then speak to Satam. And call me back when you find out what's happening."

I was afraid that Mimi had been snapped up by the Mutawas, just as I had been.

Satam came home, and I immediately asked him about Mimi.

"What are you talking about?"

"She's disappeared!"

"Disappeared?"

"She's been gone since morning, Satam!"

Satam phoned Fatima, who snapped back that she hadn't seen Mimi since he drove her over to my place. "You swore to me that you would destroy that girl. So let's hear the truth. What did you do with her?"

"To hell with you, and to hell with your maid!" she replied and hung up.

Satam was furious. He drove over to her house and demanded an answer. Without meeting his eyes she replied that both Mimi and I were having illicit relations with men. That we were carrying on like a couple of whores. That the Mutawas had caught Mimi in the act in the back storeroom of my neighborhood food shop.

"That's a lie, you stupid woman. You denounced her to the Mutawas yourself, didn't you?" He hit her in the face and left the house.

Back at my apartment, he decided to contact his friend who worked for the police. The policeman phoned back soon with information that was also reported by the Saudi radio: Prince Salman, the governor of Riyadh, had already passed sentence against Mimi. She was to be stoned to death.

"For what reason?" Satam demanded.

"Probably for fornication."

"Where? When? With whom?"

"I've got no idea," he replied in a bored tone. "I've got to go now."

When Satam told me the details, I collapsed onto the living room couch, distraught and totally paralyzed by shock. I could feel anger rising in me like a river. When I looked up at Satam, I realized that he was just as stunned and unbelieving. After a period of silence, I begged him to do something to save Mimi. He began to pace the living room with the frustration of a man locked in a jail cell. "After Prince Salman signs the death warrant, no one—absolutely no one—can do anything to get it changed."

"My God, is a sentence of death passed so quickly in this country? Can't there be an appeal?"

"Damn it, Karin, we're not in the West. We don't have proper courts, and we don't have a justice system. The prince makes rulings on everything."

"What kind of country is this? How can it be run like this? There was more justice in the Middle Ages."

The two Indian shopkeepers were each sentenced to one hundred lashes. The sentence was carried out on Friday, the Muslim day of rest, after the noon prayers, in a large public square outside a magnificent mosque in central Riyadh. Naked from the waist up in the scorching heat of the early afternoon, they were roped to concrete posts with lengths of chain that encircled them from neck to ankles to ensure that they couldn't even attempt to avoid the whip. An Islamic cleric read the prince's sentence aloud to the gathered crowd in a cool, official tone. His speech was scattered with phrases from the Qur'an. To conclude, he proclaimed: "In the name of Allah, and according to the laws of Islam, the two Indians Farhat Sahti and Jeved Iqbal will now receive one hundred lashes for fornication with a woman. Begin now."

A tall, muscular man began hitting the men with all his strength. The lash of the whip was made from wool and metal. A couple of times, the whip hit their faces. The men's faces and backs ran with blood, so that their pants were soaked and dripping bright red. As the punishment was carried out, some men in the crowd shouted from time to time, "Allah akbar! God is great!" and others exclaimed, "Long live the justice of Islam!"

The following Friday, Mimi was stoned to death. Before that she was taken to a hospital for a medical examination—not to determine whether she had indeed slept with the men, but to determine that she was not pregnant. If she had been, they would have killed her only after the birth of the child. The Egyptian doctor ascertained that Mimi was not pregnant.

On the day of her execution, Mimi was brought to the same place at the same time, dressed in black from head to toe, and with her hands bound behind her. She couldn't walk, so she was dragged to the middle of the square by a chain attached to her neck, as though she was the carcass of an animal. Her head was positioned on a pedestal, face up, and tied into place with wire. Once again, the sentence was read out to the assembled crowd. "It has been determined that Mimi Wardllah is guilty of fornication. She is sentenced to death by stoning." Verses from the Qur'an were read, and the cleric then declared, "Begin the stoning!"

A large pile of stones had been bought to the square by a dump truck. The men, who had just come from their noon prayers in the mosque, rushed to the pile and chose the best they could find. They threw them at Mimi's immobilized head, while shouting "God is great!" in jubilation. Everyone strove for a direct hit.

Mimi soon lost consciousness. Her head and body soon lay motionless under a pile of sharp rocks. The men continued to shout and pelt her until they were informed that the condemned woman was dead. One hour later, a doctor was summoned to take her pulse and make a medical declaration. "The stoning has been successful!" announced the cleric, with pleasure in his loud voice. "Thanks be to God!" commented a representative of the Ministry for Religious Affairs. "Last time we had to wait over two hours for the whore to die."

One day I experienced sharp pains. I called Satam at work, and he hurried home to take me to the maternity hospital. I was in labor for many hours, but in the end, I delivered a baby boy with no complications. Satam and I were filled with joy. I felt very lucky to have had a son. I couldn't imagine what life for a daughter would be like in Saudi Arabia, as I remembered my arrest and imprisonment, and the stoning of Mimi. Now, at last, I felt that I could understand why Saudi couples in this sexist society were truly sad when they had a daughter. Satam, because he was a man and therefore responsible for all family decisions, decided to name our son Harun.

One week after the birth, Satam brought us home. Sheika, Satam's sister, came over to visit with her two daughters and Satam's daughters by his first wife. In accordance with Saudi tradition, they brought gifts for the baby and spices for the mother. Sheika prepared mint tea with walnuts for all of us and presented me with a small kettle full of cooked garlic cloves, telling me to eat them to get my strength back. I ate one or two and refused the rest. Sheika told me that Satam had already arranged for the circumcision of Harun and one of his newborn nephews on the very next day. "A circumcision?" I asked, puzzled.

"Yes, according to our traditions and religion all baby boys must have their foreskins removed."

"No—I'm not going to allow this."

"That's impossible. Your son must be circumcised."

The next day, Satam drove the baby and me to the circumcision ceremony at Sheika's house. A crowd of Satam's relatives attended, and we were segregated by sex into two separate rooms. The house had the atmosphere of a bazaar: everyone was laughing and speaking loudly, and the aroma of cinnamon, cardamom, and coffee hung in the air. Harun was circumcised by a doctor in the presence of the men. He screamed and cried, but I wasn't allowed to go to my own son, because he was with the men. After the cutting of the foreskin the men cheered, congratulated Satam, and threw gold pieces in the direction of the baby. The women in the adjoining room ululated. Finally, Satam brought Harun to me. I began to breastfeed him and attempt to calm him down. I found the circumcision abominable and completely unnecessary.

Some time later I was obliged to attend the genital mutilation ceremony of one of Sheika's daughters, which only occurs when a girl is ten or twelve years old, at the onset of puberty. I found it inhuman and in complete violation of human rights. An older woman who had learned this "profession" from her own mother presided at the ceremony. While the women trilled and sang, the girl was brought out into the middle of the room, stark naked, where she was forcibly laid down on the floor. Four heavy women held the girl immobile by sitting on her outstretched arms and legs. The terrified girl violently tossed her head from side to side, begging the women not to do this to her. As the woman in charge began the operation, the girl began to scream and weep from the extreme pain. Immediately, the women in the room sang and trilled as loudly as they could to drown out her voice. The head woman, who was also a practicing midwife, sliced off the girl's clitoris. She then stretched out the two lips near the girl's vagina and quickly pierced both of them, well in from their edges, with a needle. She tightly stitched the two lips together and then, taking the same sharp razor used before, she amputated the soft flesh above the stitches. The wounds were then dabbed with a solution of bright red iodine. Afterward, the women continued to sing and dance. Sheika received hearty congratulations and accepted presents on behalf of her daughter. I asked a woman sitting beside me what the purpose of this was. She replied that it helped the young husband to enjoy the sex act more. Amputation of the clitoris and labia made a woman sexually frigid, so it really didn't concern her how demanding (or undemanding) her husband would be in bed, or how well he performed, for that matter. Then she gave me a smile.

At home, the baby preoccupied me. One morning I called the German Embassy and requested to have him registered as a German citizen.

"Is the father German?"

"No, he's Saudi."

"Then please bring us his birth certificate and a statement from the Saudi Ministry of the Interior proving that your child has not been registered as a Saudi citizen. If he has been registered, then we'll need a statement that the parents have legally removed his Saudi citizenship. Germany does not allow dual nationality."

When Satam came home, I told him about this.

"Well, it's out of the question, of course. He's been registered for a long time, and that isn't going to be revoked. Saudi Arabia also doesn't allow dual nationality. Harun is Saudi, and he's going to remain a Saudi." And he glared at me in such a way that I knew further discussion on this point was out of the question.

I was deeply disappointed but eventually I began to view the situation differently. I decided that, as long as Harun learned to read, write, and speak German, he would be a true German—whether or not he had official papers. Most important would be to keep him healthy and teach him all about German culture. The rest I left to the winds of chance. The baby gave my life a sense of purpose and brought me joy. Looking into his adorable little face, I forgot all my problems with Satam.

Like a typical Saudi, Satam took little interest in Harun or me. If the baby woke up crying in the middle of the night, Satam rolled over in bed and went back to sleep. He became surly, claiming that my apartment was too small, and he much preferred the spacious home of his first wife. There, if the baby had cried at night, he would be able to just go and sleep in another bedroom. For this reason, he slept at my place more and more infrequently. Formerly he had kept my fridge stocked with food; now it was empty. He stopped paying my rent again. He refused to discuss financial support for our son and me. He claimed that he was broke. But, in fact, he had lots of money—for parties, restaurant meals, and even alcohol.

There were times when I didn't see him for weeks and seldom got a phone call from him. In the mean time, I got acquainted with a number of Germans and other Europeans. They all lived in a beautiful, new, Western complex, equipped with an amazing range of amenities: swimming pool, children's playground, health club, hair salon, restaurant and supermarket. Saudis were strictly forbidden to enter, as the owners did not want the Mutawas to get access to the building.

One day a foreign nurse at Satam's hospital mentioned that she had visited people who lived in the complex during the weekend. She described a German lady who had a young child whose father was probably Arab. The mother and son had been in the pool, and she remarked on how well the toddler swam. Apparently the two of them went swimming there every day. Satam suddenly became attentive and said, "That was my family. So, where did you say you saw them?"

"In the Sahara Towers over in al-Olaya District. It's a really lovely complex," enthused the nurse.

Satam dropped his work and went to the Sahara Towers. He drove up to the parking lot barrier and honked the car horn impatiently. The porter would not admit him; it was a private complex, and he could enter only by invitation. Satam told him that he was there to visit friends.

"Who are they?" asked the gatekeeper. Satam didn't answer. He backed up, parked beside the building, and walked over to the pedestrian entrance. When the security guard challenged him, Satam attacked him. After a short scuffle, Satam punched him so soundly that he fell to the floor.

He ran into the complex and looked for the swimming pool.

There were a lot of people at the poolside—children, women, and a couple of men, all in scanty, Western swimwear. Satam certainly looked odd in his long, white Saudi gown. I spotted him and came over.

"Hi!" I said with a smile. "Have you come for a swim?"

Satam came at me with fiery eyes and slapped me with full force across my face. "Where's the boy?!" he yelled. "Where's Harun?" Many people observed this and stood paralyzed and speechless. Monica, one of my friends, spirited Harun quickly up to her apartment. Two women rushed to my side to help me as I began to collapse. Satam spun around and ran out of the complex. I was hurt, frightened, and deeply humiliated.

I was afraid to go home.

Two of my friends, Monica and her husband, Gert, advised me to stay in the complex since God only knew what would happen to me if I went to the apartment. I agreed to stay. Now, more than anything in the world, I wanted to get back to Germany.

But I needed my passport.

Monica suggested that Gert could go to my apartment to pick it up. But I didn't know for sure where I had put it away. They offered to accompany me, but I declined.

"Listen, let me leave Harun here with you for a few hours tomorrow morning; I'll go there by myself while Satam is busy at work."

"Out of the question! I saw how he assaulted you in public! What will happen to you if you find yourself alone with him? We'll leave Harun here with the housemaid, and we'll go together."

"All right, if you insist . . ."

The next morning, Gert drove Monica and me to my apartment. He waited in the car while Monica and I went up. I quickly looked for my official documents—and found nothing.

"Karin, come on, give it up. Let's get out of here. The embassy will issue you a temporary passport," said Monica, who was becoming afraid.

"The pig! The pig! He's taken my passport, all my jewelry, and my money!" Tears ran down my face. I grabbed a few belongings for Harun and myself, and we rushed out to the car. Gert started to drive back to the security of the complex but then decided to head to the German Embassy instead. "Let's request a new passport right now."

"Good idea," Monica agreed.

In the embassy, I asked for a passport for my son as well.

"That's going to be difficult. Your child is not registered as a German citizen. He needs a Saudi passport, and, as a minor, the written permission of his father. And you, as the wife of a Saudi, will need permission to travel."

"No, I don't, because I'm going to divorce him."

"If he agrees to that, and you become an independent German citizen, you'll be free to travel."

"How do I apply for a divorce in this country?"

"This isn't Germany, I'm afraid. Here in Saudi Arabia the decision to divorce is made almost exclusively by the husband alone. A woman who requests a divorce will have to wait many years to even see her case presented in the courts. And most of the time, it's rejected."

"Okay. What if my son and I leave the country under a different name?"

"We can't falsify a passport!"

"You could do it on humanitarian grounds," interrupted Monica.

"That's simply impossible. We would get into trouble with the Saudi Ministry of the Exterior. And secondly, it won't be possible because the data in the airport computer system won't match up. You'll be asked when you entered the country, and they'll check it in the system. The Saudi Ministry of the Interior is really well organized. The system was built by German technicians."

"Bad luck," commented Gert.

The consul turned to me. "You've only got one choice. Get your husband's consent."

"If I meet with him, things will go badly," I predicted.

I considered my options. I didn't want—under any circumstances—to meet with Satam. My heart had turned to stone; I hated him. He no longer took any interest in me. He hadn't remained a good lover, and he hadn't become a good husband. But how could I convince him to divorce me, how could I twist his arm? I had to do it without provoking his anger. The entire situation was under his control. Maybe, I thought, I should send Mr. and Mrs. Schmidt to meet with him. At his previous meeting with them he had been charming and quite flexible. If he behaved in the same manner with them again, he might accept the idea of divorcing me.

Gert drove Monica and me back to their apartment in the Sahara Towers complex. There we discussed the next step. I suggested involving the Schmidts. Monica called them, and they decided to come over. One hour later, they arrived.

Mr. Schmidt was prepared to talk to Satam, and, without further ado, simply called him and arranged a meeting later that evening. His wife decided to go along, just to "soften up" the atmosphere. I was told not to come; if we saw each other, we would see red.

They met in the Sheraton Hotel's coffee shop. Satam arrived first. When the Schmidts arrived, they greeted each other, shook hands, and ordered coffee. Satam looked both disgruntled and sad. He began to discuss the situation without waiting for the Schmidts to make the first move.

He was very angry that I was visiting the Sahara Towers without his knowledge and consent, swimming in a pool with strange men who were almost naked. This was not normal behavior and was forbidden by Islam. Mrs. Schmidt kept quiet, but she really wanted to tell him that he almost never came to my apartment and wasn't providing us with support money. She was pulled back from her thoughts when Satam announced that I should return home, since he wanted me back and wanted us to have a happy, married life together.

"Why don't you take a vacation in Germany with your wife and son? You'll recover from all this stress and your marriage will get back on track. Karin will give you a tour of the country; it really is very nice. I remember the last time we met—you promised Karin a vacation in Germany. This would be a great time to honor that promise," said Mr. Schmidt in a flattering and easy tone.

"Of course, but not now. Harun is still too small; we won't enjoy the trip. Maybe in a year."

"Well, let Karin make the trip on her own. She's homesick, you know."

"I understand. But not now."

"She's having a hard time. She's on the verge of a nervous breakdown."

"That's her problem."

"Listen, Satam, why don't you consider divorcing her. Karin would agree to it."

"I can't do that. She has to raise our son first. When he's grown up, I could consider it."

The conversation started to become tense and more aggressive. They had reached a dead end. Satam then announced emphatically that he was sorry but that he was in a hurry to get home.

I lived in Monica's apartment for a week. I thought to myself that, somehow or other, this has to reach a resolution. I couldn't continue to live without getting a job. My German savings account was almost empty. I inquired if I could get work in the German Embassy or German International School, but nothing was available.

Mrs. Schmidt called Monica to tell her that Satam was looking for me. He had just come to the Schmidts with two policemen and was now heading for the Sahara Towers. He wanted me back. Gert wasn't home from work yet. Monica spoke to a Swedish friend of hers in the same complex, who agreed to hide Harun and me in her apartment. We quickly gathered our belongings and made the move.

The porter spoke to Monica over the intercom, telling her that policemen wanted to come up to speak to her. She replied, "No—my husband isn't home yet." Two hours later, a policeman called and asked for "Mr. Gert." He picked up the phone.

"Can I help you?"

"We are looking for Mrs. Karin Holtz and her son. Is she there?"

"No. Absolutely not."

"Where can we find her?"

"I don't know. I can't help you."

The policeman hung up.

Harun and I moved back in with Monica and Gert. Three weeks later, the German Embassy contacted me. They had received a letter for me from the Saudi Ministry of the Interior. It read as follows: "At the request of Mr. Satam al-Jamil, his marriage to Karin Holtz is terminated. Mrs. Holtz must leave Saudi Arabia within 48 hours or serve up to one year in jail as punishment." It was signed by Prince Nayef Bin Abdulaziz, the Saudi minister of the interior.

I was filled with ambivalence. On the one hand, I had succeeded in getting the divorce; on the other hand, I would have to abandon my son. I was overcome with horror at the realization that I might never see him again. Only a mother can imagine the terrible emotions that ripped me apart, and my hatred of this brutal system that could coldheartedly deprive me of my own child. That night, as I put Harun to bed, I couldn't stop kissing him. I held him in my arms. I tried to suppress the reality of our separation, fearing that my heart would break. I broke into tears, and Harun, feeling my distress, also began to cry.

Because I had become a "foreign national" in Saudi Arabia once again, the German Embassy had dutifully informed the police where I was living. The phone rang. It was a policeman, warning me to fly out today, or face imprisonment. I didn't believe him; I was sure this was a setup pulled together by Satam.

"We had better get Harun to a safer place," advised Monica. I moved him in with Gudrun, Monica's Swedish friend.

That evening, Monica, Gert, and I sat in their living room, discussing my situation but finding no way out. Suddenly the doorbell rang. Gert looked out through the spy hole and whispered to us, "It's a policeman!"

He began to pound with full strength on the door. The noise was unbearable. Finally Gert gave in and opened it; there were two policemen there, and they didn't say a word. They just handed him a warrant for my arrest. Monica went into the front hall, saw the situation, and rushed back to me in the living room. I ran and locked myself into the bathroom.

The policemen pushed their way past Gert, paying no attention to him. One of them said, "No English." They searched the rooms and noticed that the bathroom door was locked. They hammered on it; I shook with fear, but kept quiet. Then, after a quick, quiet discussion in Arabic, they started to break the door down by force.

Monica was afraid that I would be injured when the door collapsed inward on me. She went to the door and shouted, "Karin, open the door. They're bashing it in. You'll get hurt!"

With tears streaming down my face, I unlocked the door and came out. Monica grabbed me and hugged me tightly.

One of the policemen made a quick phone call. A few minutes later, three more policemen and a Saudi man in civilian dress, probably a detective, stepped off the elevator. All three of us were handcuffed. I resisted and was hit across the face. The detective spoke English. He asked Gert where the child was. Gert said that he didn't know and angrily asked what was going on.

"Really? You don't know?" commented the detective. "Shortly you'll be the one telling us everything."

"I want to use the telephone!"

"Not allowed."

"I want to speak with my embassy, damn it!" yelled Gert, absolutely furious.

The three of us were led out like criminals. Many of the neighbors— mostly Europeans—had come out due to all the noise and were gathered around our apartment door. The murmur of conversation rose into anger and shock when they saw us in handcuffs. Some of them shouted aloud, "Barbarians! Get out of here! Get out of our building!" A Dane telephoned his embassy and asked the secretary to quickly convey the news of what was happening to the German Embassy. Outside, we were pushed into the back of a police van and driven to a police station.

We were put into separate cells and called for questioning separately.

"Where is the child?" they asked, over and over.

Gert was slapped and punched. The blood ran, but he refused to answer them.

That evening, the German consul came to the police station and met with the officer who had arrested us. He was told, point blank, that no German citizens were being detained there.

The next morning we were taken to the airport and forced onto a plane bound for Cyprus. Without any legal papers, without our passports, without our money—it was the perfect way to dispose of us. Gert, Monica, and I sat on the plane in stunned silence—we couldn't find any words to describe what had happened to us. It didn't match my previous experiences, and it didn't match anything else we might have imagined.

Satam still didn't know where Harun was, so he decided to take the law into his own hands. He drove to the entrance gate of the German compound where the Schmidts lived and waited there. As soon as the school bus arrived, he boarded it and asked which student was their son, Thomas Schmidt. He grabbed the seven-year-old out of his seat and got him off the bus so quickly that the driver couldn't think how to react. Satam bundled Thomas into his waiting car and sped away. The Schmidts were in a state of panic and contacted the embassy immediately.

The next day, headlines screamed across Saudi newspapers: a mentally ill German woman had attempted to abduct a Saudi child to take him abroad. Her plot had been found out and she had been deported, but she had hidden the child. The police needed help to find the little boy. Anyone who detected anything suspicious, any possible trace of him, should contact the closest police station.

Not one word was written about the abduction of Thomas Schmidt.

Satam called the Schmidts. He told them that their son was in "safe hands." If they located Harun and passed him over, Thomas would remain unharmed. If they contacted the police and told them that he was the man who had taken the child off the school bus, something extremely unpleasant and regrettable would happen to Thomas.

The Schmidts went to the Sahara Towers and soon discovered that Harun was staying with Gudrun. They drove him back to their place and waited.

Satam called again. He told them to take Harun to his first wife's house and wait there for his call—in return, he would tell them where they could find Thomas.

They went to Fatima and gave her my son.

The phone rang.

Satam reported that their son was already inside their house in the German compound. Veronica Schmidt quickly dialed her own home. Thomas picked up the phone.

❖

In Cyprus, Karin and Monica, terrified and in tears, and Gert told the migration officers of their ordeal back in Riyadh. The German Embassy was alarmed. Officials from the embassy rushed to the airport and helped the three victims fly immediately to Frankfurt in Germany. Back in Germany, Karin sank in deep and incurable depressions. And a few years later she died. Before her death, I talked to her several times. She told me that she wished to die. Life after her nightmare and leaving her son, Harun, back in Saudi Arabia did not make any sense.

SALEH

Marriage à la Saudi

S ocieties still exist where women are virtually raised at home like plants in commercial greenhouses: isolated, protected, and haggled over when the time comes for them to be put on the market. They can't openly be seen by almost all males, as that would corrupt and contaminate them. If women are obliged to be in the presence of a strange man, or if they step outside of the house, they must be shrouded from head to toe. Many women get so used to this that going out of the house unveiled feels like going naked in public. Their understanding of the realities of the world beyond their doorstep is obscured by a piece of muffling black fabric. Therefore, going outside feels like staying home. Many men prefer "greenhouse" women—and the younger, the better. Others rebel against this cultural practice and consider it tiresome and demeaning. Saleh belongs to the latter group—after his stay in the United States, he changed and rejects "greenhouse" women.

Saleh is a forty-year-old Saudi, and, in fact, a Bedouin, but his bright and lively face shows that he received the stimulus of education. He wanted to share with me the memories of his wedding, which had taken place fifteen years previous. He wanted to tell me about his relationship with his wife. This is his story.

After completing my university degree, I wanted to get married. However, I didn't know any women. The only ones I knew—and had actually seen—were my mother, my five sisters, and my three elderly aunts. I also had two aunts who were younger than me, but I was not allowed to see them or even hear their voices. We had been together in the same room on occasion, but they had always been fully veiled, including their faces. My older brothers had been married for more than six years, and their wives lived in our family home, but I had never seen them and had no idea what they looked like. In our family, girls over the age of five are treated like grown women. They are allowed to play only with other girls. We are afraid that they may be sexually abused by male members of the family or by any man in general. Therefore I had almost never experienced direct contact with a woman.

Our houses are architecturally divided into two separate sections, even if the family has limited means. On one side live the women, girls, and boys up to the age of about five; on the other live the men and older boys. Each section has its own living room, bedrooms, and bathroom. The kitchen is on the women's side because the preparation of food is strictly women's work. In well-to-do families, meals are brought over to the men's section by housemaids. In ordinary families, the women bring the food across in the absence of the men, prepare the table, call the men to eat, and then quickly disappear. If the men need something, the women reach into the room and hand it over without revealing their bodies or faces. In fact, women never cross over to the men's side of the house unless they are fully veiled.

To tell the truth, I can't remember ever being in our kitchen. Maybe, when I was a young boy, I had raced through during my hours of play. Food preparation is women's work, and it is held in low regard; even if a meal is very tasty, the men of the family never considered praising it. Saudi men are brought up to obstinately take the labor of women for granted, even pregnancy and the delivery of their children, according to the unbending dictates of age-old traditions.

In Bedouin families, the men leave home to take their flocks to pasture, to market, and to barter for other goods. Women are persistently regarded as the weak and incompetent half of the family. They must stay in the house, cook, bear children, and look after the infants and small children.

Our family never sat together as a group, even when we celebrated holidays. I believe that my father usually saw my mother only at night, and each time he was with her for only a short period of time. The men and women sat in their separate living rooms until they were tired; then they went to bed. There was little interest, and even less energy, for spouses to indulge in relaxed, private conversation. Most nights my father—a silent and serious type—slept together with my brothers and me on the living room floor. How and why would I ever get a chance to see a woman?

As I mentioned before, I wanted to marry; a man is not a fully worthy and accepted adult male in our society unless he has a wife. I was already twenty-five. To be that old and without a wife and children was verging on the edge of anomaly: people were beginning to wonder what my problem was. Perhaps I was a homosexual, which would shame my entire family because that was a perversity common only in decadent Western societies. They also speculated that I was impotent, that I couldn't get an erection. Not once did they consider that maybe I hadn't yet found a woman whom I wanted to marry.

After all, it's easy for a man in Saudi Arabia to get a woman. Interest is publicly indicated, and offers and negotiations begin. Overall, we have more women than men, especially unmarried women. And every woman wants to be married because a single woman is considered cheap, shoddy, and inferior—and she is spied on all the time. Skeptical gossip follows her every move. Where is she going? With whom did she speak? Every time she leaves her house, the event is registered with excited and intensely cynical analysis. Also, a single woman is a burden to her family. In spite of the modernization of our country, men only grudgingly allow their daughters and sisters to work outside of the family home. In their opinion, it borders on prostitution: mixing with men in the workplace, talking to them, smiling at them—it can only lead to immoral behavior. That would insult the honor of the family and fly in the face of tradition. Therefore, a man has only to mention that he is looking for a wife and very shortly he'll find himself offered a vast range of available females.

Most of my friends and acquaintances were married. They persistently badgered me about my single status. I liked to reply, why do I need a wife? My servant, Philip, looks after me better than any woman. He cooks, cleans, and goes shopping for me. Then they would laugh and say, how does he look after you in bed, when you get the urge? Or do you use a prostitute with a venereal disease? Our religious leaders were always preaching about prostitutes and homosexuals, claiming that they were devils in human form.

Everyone in my family wanted to see me married. Whenever my mother and sisters were invited to a wedding, they would return with glowing descriptions of the lovely available girls at the party. They would describe each of them in turn and praise her personality: "Nawal suits him. . . . No, Hala would be better." Each was apparently more beautiful than the last, and I'd better jump before another man got her. My grandmother was over eighty years old and doted on me because I was the only grandson who had gone to university. She repeatedly told me that before she died, she wanted to see me married and the father of many children. In turn, my mother pleaded with me, with tears streaming from her eyes, to fulfill the elderly woman's last wish. My father was starting to make acid comments to the effect that people who study too much develop complicated and skewered personalities and are unable to function in the real world. My brothers regaled me with enthusiastic speeches about how lovely marriage was and how it was even better to be a father because children were life's greatest delight.

Because I couldn't continue to take the family pressure and the mounting social stigmatization, I decided to go ahead and get married. In the meantime, I received an offer to study toward a master's degree in America. That strengthened my resolve because experienced Saudis who had lived abroad always advised that it was easier to handle the culture shock with a wife at your side. It would also protect my moral purity. She would wash for me, cook for me, and look after my sexual needs. Otherwise, I might get involved with a Western woman, and God would only know how many men she had already slept with. A Saudi woman would be pure.

I had heard that an uncle of mine—part of the extended family and someone I barely knew—had a large number of daughters who were pretty and unpretentious. I decided to make a trip to visit him, to get some indication of whether he would arrange a marriage for me. He lived in al-Qaseem, about 220 miles north of Riyadh, in the very conservative region of the country where the facial veil originated.

It had been a long time since our last meeting. We had met at a cousin's wedding in Riyadh two years previous. He was a typical Saudi: conservative, deeply religious, and cheerful by nature. He was very proud of our family tribe and therefore took a great interest in all its members. He knew almost everyone from the older generation. I received a hearty welcome and was conducted into the living room. For hours on end, we chatted about life in general, my studies, and my job. I hoped that he would bring up the theme of marriage himself, but he didn't. Gradually, I developed the opinion that he had guessed the reason for my visit but wanted me to take the initiative. Fathers of girls tend to avoid the subject of marriage, so it doesn't look like they are desperate to marry them off. Finally, I found myself blurting out: "Uncle Nawaf, I want to get married."

His face lit up with joy, and he replied, "May God bless you."

"I would like to marry one of your worthy daughters."

"Which one?" he queried, with a serious face.

"I don't know. Anyone that I deserve."

"I have seven daughters. You are welcome to choose any one," he replied generously.

"No—you choose one for me," I responded, feeling shy and embarrassed.

"All of them are good girls who are already grown up. No problem. I will do this for you."

Suddenly we heard the noon call to prayer from the local mosque. Uncle Nawaf got to his feet and said, "Let us go pray for guidance in this matter." We walked to the nearby mosque, where Uncle Nawaf greeted the imam and invited him to his home for the midday meal. Afterward, all three of us returned to Uncle Nawaf's. After we had spent a few minutes in the living room, he told the imam, "My nephew Saleh would like to marry one of my daughters."

"With God's blessing," replied the religious teacher.

The imam withdrew a Qur'an from his pocket and read a few verses aloud. Then he said to my uncle and me, "My warmest congratulations." And with that, I found myself a married man. I had no idea who my bride would be. I didn't know her name or even what she looked like.

The meal was served, and we ate with gusto. Afterward, Uncle Nawaf said to me: "Bring your parents to dinner next week. I will be waiting for them."

I drove back to Riyadh. First, I went to my small apartment to claim a little space to think and reflect. My servant, Philip, always kept it clean and orderly, and the fridge was always full. I felt good there. My parents didn't know that I rented it because our society believes that a bachelor who lives outside the family circle in an apartment only maintains it so he can bring prostitutes there. I owned a food shop run by two Indian employees near the apartment. With the profits of my business, I paid the rent and kept the matter a secret from the family. After a few hours, I went home to inform the men of my family that I had married. In the evening, I chatted with them about the details of my visit with Uncle Nawaf. All of them were very happy that they had been invited to his distant home.

One week later, all of us traveled to al-Qaseem—both my parents and all my sisters and brothers. We stayed for the weekend. On the men's side of the house, we discussed every topic under the sun except my marriage. At the end of the visit, as we were saying our farewells, Uncle Nawaf casually said, "Take your bride, your new wife, with you."

"I don't have an apartment for her, Uncle Nawaf. I plan to build a new extension on the family house for her."

"Don't be so modern! In earlier times, we all married and lived in tents," he scoffed.

"What about the wedding festivities?"

"Don't worry about that. We'll celebrate them later."

I had mixed feelings about this situation. On one hand, I was excited because I wanted to speak to an unknown woman. Hopefully she was pretty and matched my tastes. On the other hand, the marriage wasn't yet fully official. It had to be legally registered in the Justice Ministry, with two witnesses in attendance. If any problems surfaced during the marriage process, I could annul it and return the girl to her parents.

In the end, Nuha—that was my bride's name—came with us back to Riyadh. She was fully veiled from head to foot and sat quietly beside my sisters in the back of our vehicle. Occasionally she spoke very softly to one or another of my sisters, but I couldn't hear her. She didn't speak to me, and I had no idea what to say to her.

In Riyadh, we clambered out of our vehicles and pulled ourselves together after the long journey. With the help of my mother, a bedroom in the house was freed up so that Nuha and I could share it.

After sunset, my mother brought Nuha's personal belongings into our room. I was excited. I had no idea what I ought to do. I left the bedroom and went into the living room, where I sat down with my father, grandfather, brothers, and uncles. For them, it was an evening like any other. We, the men of the house, sat in our living room, and the women sat in theirs. Eventually we settled down and got comfortable watching TV shows.

Actually, since our purchase of a television, we had developed the tendency to avoid conversations. Most of us just drifted off to sleep in front of the TV. Many of us stayed, dead to the world in our seats, right through to morning. Tonight was like any other, and my relatives drifted off into slumber. I alone stayed awake, full of repressed excitement. I wanted to enter our shared room, our bridal chamber. But I also didn't want my relatives to notice me leaving.

I stood up and sneaked out of the room. Softly and carefully, like a thief, I opened the door of my room. Nuha was cowering on a corner of the mattress. The only item in the room was a large mattress—there were no chairs and no bed. We Saudis prefer to sit and sleep on the floor. Many families furnish their homes with beds and armchairs, and then spend most of their time on the floor. Nuha sat there, fully veiled. I thought to myself, "This is the hour of truth," and my heart began to race. I knew nothing about her except her name.

As I had entered the room, Nuha had averted her head.

"Good evening!" I said in a friendly tone.

There was no answer.

In Saudi Arabia, women are taught how they should behave with their new husband on the first night of their marriage. The bride must demonstrate great shame, and under no circumstances show any interest in her spouse. Absolutely none. She has to act as though she has no understanding of the sexual act, and she has to be guided and taught how to make love. This is accepted as proof that the girl is a virgin, pure and inexperienced. Her behavior is supposed to make the wedding night's sexual experiences very thrilling for the husband.

"Do you like this room?" I asked Nuha.

There was no answer.

I walked over to her. She pulled her arms and legs in closer to her body.

The closer I came, the more I was overcome by excitement and curiosity. She was like a veiled statue about to be revealed to the waiting eyes of the public. I had no idea what she looked like and I couldn't even imagine her appearance. I felt that if I could see her face, I would understand her personality. I wanted to see her face. I was as impatient as a small child who has been promised a present and sees it all wrapped up, but has no idea what is inside. Of course, I hoped that she was a beauty. Every man has his own idea of feminine beauty, and I was anxious to see if her face matched my dreams. Finally, I was so close that I could reach out and touch her, but I hesitated. I didn't want her to be terrified by the sudden grasp of a strange man. As excitement mounted in me, I slowly extended my right hand and raised the veil off her face. She turned away, but with that same hand I took hold of her chin and turned her face toward me. She kept her eyes cast down toward her cheeks. She didn't raise them for a second. But now, I was able to see my wife's face for the first time.

"My God!" I exclaimed, absolutely appalled. I was looking into the face of a child. She couldn't have been older than twelve or thirteen. I instantly realized that she was terrified. She glanced at me with horror, as though at a ghost. She was so paralyzed by fear that she couldn't even cry or scream. She was clutching desperately at her doll, which she had smuggled out of her parents' home with her other belongings. Marriage to a child? Sexual intercourse with a child? Those two sentences pounded in my brain.

I was appalled. I left the room. My mother was up, and she saw me.

"Where are you going?" she asked.

"I'll be back soon. I've got a couple of things to do."

"Now? It's after midnight."

I got into my car and drove aimlessly around the city for the entire night. I just wanted to get away. I went to my own apartment and tried to settle down, but sleep continued to evade me, so I got back into my car and continued to drive. Nuha's face was imprinted in my memory. Her fearful glance followed me through those long hours, as though she were speaking to me: "How could you marry a child? I'm only a child! Don't hurt me! Let me play, let me enjoy my childhood! Why do you want to snatch my childhood away?" The more I envisioned her face, the more I felt pity for her, and the more my anger toward Uncle Nawaf increased.

But, in another respect, I could hardly blame him because this hadn't been entirely his decision. Our traditions allow children to be married off. I decided to return Nuha to her parents. My father would be disappointed, as he was also a traditionalist. People would gossip about me, saying, that's what happens to boys who get too much education. His two older brothers took child brides, and neither of them philosophized about it.

I spent the night outside, but at daybreak I returned home. I wanted to talk to my father about this.

My father, my two older brothers, and my mother were standing at the door waiting for me. They had guessed that I was facing a big problem.

"What's wrong? Where have you been? Is everything all right?" asked my father.

To give an honest answer would have been pointless and would only make the situation worse. My father would return to his usual diatribe against education. So I came up with a good lie, using the weight of tradition instead of a logical and commonsense objection. I said, "Nuha refused to have sex with me, and I will never share my bed with any woman who even once refuses me. I don't need her. I have my pride."

"Son, she is still a child. She has been crying incessantly since you drove off at midnight but wouldn't explain what went wrong between the two of you." My oldest brother, who was quite macho, came to my defense. "Saleh is right; this is unacceptable. If she has refused him, and the marriage is not yet fully legalized, we must return Nuha to her parents."

After I got all the family members on my side, I ventured this comment: "And anyway, Nuha is just a child. I want to marry a woman, not a child."

"Come on, that's not a big deal. She was Uncle Nawaf's choice, and he knows what's best for you. The younger the bride is, the better. However, no problem; we'll return Nuha, if that's what you want," replied my father.

"Yes, that's what I want. Right away," I said stiffly, but in my heart I was very relieved.

I considered speaking to Nuha about the situation but decided against it since she was just a child and probably didn't even understand what marriage was. My mother and sisters cried a lot. They believed that I would never get married. With tears in her eyes, my mother begged, "Please don't send Nuha back. She must stay with us. She likes living here." Later we were to learn that Uncle Nawaf's second-to-most-recent wife, Abla, had wanted to rid herself of her daughter. She had pestered Uncle Nawaf to marry the girl off. Every mother in Saudi Arabia is anxious to get her daughters married as soon as possible. Uncle Nawaf had four wives, and they competed with each other. The three oldest wives lived in the same house, but his youthful fourth wife lived in a different house in the same neighborhood.

Accompanied by my parents, I drove to al-Qaseem to return Nuha to her family home. During the trip, no one said a word, and the journey seemed endless. I wanted to put this behind me and never, ever again mention that I was interested in getting married. We finally arrived, and Uncle Nawaf received us in a friendly way but somehow guessed that our visit had something to do with the marriage. He accompanied my father, my brothers, and me into the men's living room and repeated, rather too loudly, "Welcome. You are most welcome."

My father began to speak. He opened the discussion with a long and complicated introduction. In our culture, this is normal when a problem will have to be solved. "Nawaf, my brother, I don't know how to tell you this. You know, we are a family. Your family and my family are part of a bigger family. We have hardly ever had differences of opinion, and never will. I want you to have exactly what I want for myself: nothing but happiness and success. Our mutual daughter Nuha is still too young for Saleh. She is too afraid of him. We have no intention of declining her—heavens no, in the name of God—but we will take her later, as the bride of one of my younger sons. Can you offer Saleh one of your older daughters instead?"

"My dear brother, not a problem! Of course! My daughters are your daughters! You can do with Nuha as you please. Take Hind instead. I think that she is eighteen years old," suggested Uncle Nawaf.

I had hoped that the negotiations would fall through. But there I was, stuck. There was no way I could refuse; if I did, Uncle Nawaf would consider me a person who couldn't be taken seriously.

Then my uncle gave me a pep talk. "You know, Saleh, there is nothing nicer than marrying a young woman. She's fresh and luscious like ripe fruit. I'm now fifty years of age, and last year I took a seventeen-year-old as my fourth wife. Of course, I keep her separate from my other three wives. But it's great. Just touching her makes me grow younger every day."

My first task was to get myself divorced. The imam from the local mosque—the same one who had married me—was called back in. In his presence, and in the absence of my wife, Nuha, I repeated the words "Nuha, you are divorced," three times. Now my first marriage was annulled. Then I was promptly married to Hind, in her absence and without her knowledge. The imam followed the same procedure as before. He pulled his copy of the Qur'an from a pocket and read a couple of verses aloud. In conclusion, he said, "Congratulations" and asked Allah to bless the marriage.

That night we drove back to Riyadh with Hind. My marriage night went off without problems. I didn't have high expectations and wasn't overly excited about the entire situation. It was easier to remove her veil, as she was quite passive and unresisting. She was older, of course, but to tell the truth, her body type didn't appeal to me. It took me a long time to warm up to her a bit and accept her as my wife. She almost never looked me in the eyes. No matter what I tried, I felt that I was married to a stranger. She wasn't talkative and had very little general knowledge; she could barely read and write. She only spoke if I asked her a direct question. Well, to be sure, she was still very young—eighteen or maybe nineteen. She was sexually frigid, and I slept with her only two or three times. This was not a happy marriage for me, but I couldn't share my feelings with anyone, because such discussions are frowned upon in Saudi Arabia. Many Saudis say that a young virgin is like a batch of dough—you can form and fashion her any way you want. And if a man can't do that, he's not a man's man—he's a weakling.

At that time I was working as a teacher, and of course I had my business, the small food store, on the side. I spent most of my time outside of the house or else with the men of the family. I saw Hind only at bedtime. And I usually acted as though I was very tired and needed to get to sleep immediately.

Then I found out that Hind was pregnant. I wasn't totally overjoyed at the news. The woman was like a stranger in my bed. But I thought to myself, maybe after the birth of our child she will change and become warmer, more demonstrative.

In the meantime, my scholarship for the United States came through. I would continue my studies over there and have to write a thesis. I was extremely happy about this. It meant that I wouldn't have to see my wife for a few months—maybe a few years—and then we would see if our married life had improved.

One day, Hind asked me a question.

"I have heard that you are going to America to study. Is that true?"

"Yes. But I'll be coming home every couple of months."

"Don't you want me to go with you?"

"Later, maybe . . . when I've settled in."

"Your mother thinks I should accompany you from the beginning," Hind reported.

"That's out of the question. I have to focus on my studies. The beginning will be especially difficult and stressful," I explained with determination.

I immediately went to see my mother, who was sitting with my father in their bedroom. "Mother, I am not going to take Hind to America. First of all, she's pregnant, and second, I'll have to concentrate on my studies, especially at the beginning. Hind is going to stay here."

"And who is going to cook and clean for you?" she replied with concern.

"Don't worry about it. I'll look after it myself. I can clean my own room, and I won't need to cook. I'll eat in the university cafeteria. It's not expensive."

I flew to America—to New York. There I picked up my student documents from the Saudi Embassy and then continued with a flight to Oregon, where I'd been offered a place at the university. In Saudi Arabia, I had been warned that I would experience unavoidable culture shock. That was the only thing I was afraid of. Aside from that, I was overjoyed to have the opportunity to study in America. When the plane landed in Portland, a Saudi exchange student met me at the airport and took me directly to the student residence. I arrived late in the evening and was completely tired out.

The next morning I glanced out the window and received the shock of my life. In contrast to Saudi Arabia, there was rich greenery everywhere. It was like being in paradise. The second shock was that both men and women were living in my student residence. My religion had taught me that unveiled women drive a man wild with sexual desire and lead him to sin. I was confused and unsettled by the sight of unveiled women, but I didn't go wild and had no sexual reactions at all. Everywhere around me, men and unveiled women were heading off to work as though everything was normal. In Saudi Arabia, a woman has only to show her ankle in a public place and men drop whatever they're doing to chase her through the streets.

I met with my Saudi colleague, who had picked me up at the airport, in the university cafeteria.

"You are amazed to see men and women socializing together, aren't you?" he said. "Well, it's normal here. You'll get used to it."

"Tell me the truth, Obaid. I've heard that it's really easy to get a woman here."

"Well, yes, but only if the man and woman mutually like each other. Otherwise, forget it. Women are free in this country and do whatever they want. You can't control them, like back home in Saudi Arabia. Most women here are both self-confident and self-reliant."

"I can't believe how much bare skin they're showing. Don't they get raped?"

"What? Oh, the number of rapes here is much lower than back home."

"Actually, I think it's nice here."

"I'm going to play tennis this evening. Want to come along?"

"I don't know how to play tennis."

"No problem. You'll learn fast. The most important thing is you speak English well."

"That's true. Otherwise, I wouldn't have been accepted into this university."

That evening, I went to play tennis with Obaid in a huge indoor hall. The courts were quite full, and both men and women were playing. Obaid got me a racket and some tennis balls. An American female student waved at him from a distance. "Judy!" he yelled, returning a wave and a smile. She came over to us, and he introduced us. I wasn't used to such a thing, so I averted my eyes. Obaid noticed and prompted, "Don't behave like you're back home. Here you look a woman straight in the eye—otherwise, you're being rude." Then Obaid asked Judy if she could teach me a little tennis. She agreed and took me to a free court. After a couple of attempts, my tennis balls were gone, and two of them had landed on top of an air-conditioning unit. We gathered up the stray balls again, and I said to Judy with innocent concern, "Two of my balls are up there."

Judy doubled over in laughter. When she finally calmed down, she tried to explain the double entendre I had stumbled into.

"In English, these things we are playing with are called balls. But it's also what we call the two things hanging between a man's legs."

I was amazed that an American woman could speak so naturally and openly about that without any shame.

Over time, a friendship developed between Judy and me. As for Obaid, he actually had an American girlfriend. We would often meet and set off on various activities as a foursome. When I was alone, I would sometimes find myself thinking about Hind and comparing her to Judy. Although they were both women, I could find no similarities between them. Hind's life experiences were absolutely minimal. On the other hand, Judy was relaxed, knowledgeable, self-confident, and knew exactly what she wanted from life. She was like a partner, an equal. She was an active participant in her society. I liked that a lot. She matched my developing idea of what a woman really should be.

Of course, neither my parents nor Hind knew that I was spending my free time with an American woman named Judy. They wouldn't believe that we weren't having an affair or hadn't already married. They believed what our religious teachers insisted—that when an unmarried man and woman meet, the devil stands beside them. Being together provokes lustful thoughts and acts and leads them into unrestrained, immoral sex—a virtual whirlpool of sin. In our society, the absolute separation of men and women creates between them an indefinable and ever-present atmosphere of suspicion, mistrust, and fear.

After my first semester in Portland, my father sent a telegram to inform me that Hind had given birth to a girl, and that she wanted to come visit me with our baby. It was impossible for me to say no. Obaid told me that his wife also wanted to visit. Eventually, I came to accept the idea. Maybe living in America for a while would change Hind, although she would certainly never be like Judy.

Obaid and I rented two furnished apartments because families were not allowed in the student residence. On the day of their arrival, we went to the airport together to fetch them. Of course, neither of them knew about Judy or Obaid's girlfriend, Hilary. As they came out into the arrivals area, they were definitely our wives: both of them were veiled in black, and Hind had a black cloth draped over her face. Everyone in the terminal was staring at them. I was overcome by shame and wished I could sink into the floor and disappear. Everywhere, people were greeting their arriving friends and relatives with hugs and kisses; at the very least, handshakes were exchanged. Only our wives averted their heads when they spotted us. Obaid spoke words of greeting to his wife and gathered his five-year-old son up into his arms. Because of her veil, I couldn't judge Hind's reaction to our meeting. Like Obaid, I simply greeted her and took my baby daughter from her to hold. Obaid's wife didn't speak to me, and Hind didn't speak to Obaid. It was like being back in Saudi Arabia. We got into the car. Obaid dropped us off at our place and then continued on to his own.

In our apartment, we first put the baby to bed. Then we sat down facing each other. I asked about the health of my parents and siblings and also inquired about her family members. Her answers were brief and curt.

She asked me only one question: "Do you like America?" Since she didn't fully understand what a university was, she didn't ask me about my studies. She then quietly told me that the passport control officer had coldly instructed her to take off her facial veil. "The pig wanted to see my face. He can do that with his wife, but not with me. Why don't they have a woman there for such a job?" She continued, "I was really so ashamed. . . . I would feel completely naked."

"Well, did you take it off?" I asked, as though appreciative of her so-called traumatic experience.

"Of course not! A female officer came over, and I showed my face to her," Hind replied triumphantly.

"And how did you communicate, since you don't speak any English? That was a problem for you."

"Not speaking English wasn't a problem for me. It was a problem for them, because they couldn't understand my language. Anyhow, a Saudi passenger came over and translated."

I enjoyed Hind's account and our little conversation about it immeasurably; I had finally managed to get her to open her mouth and actually say something. It showed me that a person has to have experiences in life in order to have something to talk about.

Hind was yawning now; she was tired, of course, after her fierce battle against the immoral conduct of the immigration authorities. I tried to reward her for her courageous and stressful international travel with tender caresses, hoping to entice her into our bed, but it was to no avail. She remained passive and uninterested. This made my blood run cold—I suddenly felt anger, and my sexual interest in her plummeted. As these thoughts and emotions raced through my mind, I saw that she had fallen asleep in her chair.

The next day, I went to my classes at the university and met with Judy as usual. She asked me where I had passed the night—she'd looked for me the previous evening in the student dormitory, but I hadn't been in my room. I lied, telling her that I'd spent the night at the apartment of some Saudi friends. She asked me about Obaid. I said that we had been together. Then she asked me if I'd like to go swimming with her. I hesitated for a split second and then replied, "Yes." She wanted to know if Obaid was coming, too. "Probably. I'll ask him," I responded.

Later I called him with Judy's suggestion; he agreed immediately. After all, we would get to swim in a mixed-gender pool, with the women wearing bikinis and the men in swimming briefs. Unfortunately, all I had to wear were my Saudi swimming trunks. They are made of a spongy material and reach down to my knees. I attracted a lot of attention, and everyone was laughing at me. I tried to explain that I'd brought them from Saudi Arabia, where they conformed to religious ideas about male modesty. Obaid and I had a good laugh: After death, everyone at the pool would go to hell, except for me. I would be admitted to paradise because I had worn knee-length swimming trunks made of spongy material. I could take Obaid with me, because he was my friend. There we would meet our two wives. Oh, damn. Change that one! And tomorrow, I'm going to buy an infidel swimsuit . . .

Obaid invited my wife and me to dinner at his place. To make less of a spectacle of my veiled wife on America's streets, I decided that we should leave the apartment after dark. I didn't want Hind to wear her black robes and veil. I told her that it would be dark outside and that nobody in the neighborhood knew us. That meant that other Saudi men didn't live anywhere nearby. "No," she replied. Her parents had taught her to cover her body and her face every time she went outside, no matter where she was. Furthermore, she would feel naked. We reached a compromise. She would go outside without the facial veil but cover her face with her hands.

And that is exactly what happened. She sat in the backseat of the car and kept her hands over her face all the way to Obaid's apartment. As she approached the entrance stairs, already swathed in her billowing black outer robe, she unrolled her black veil and tied it across her nose. Some children who had been playing outside froze and stared at her, mouths agape. "Ghost! Ghost!" they screamed and ran away. That was painful and distressing to me. In Obaid's apartment, we sat in different rooms to eat and chat. Everything was done according to Saudi custom. Nevertheless, Obaid and I spoke about Judy and Hilary—but we were careful to switch over to English. We could hear each other's conversations through the thin walls.

Obaid and I felt uncomfortable and repressed. We now knew what was missing: a chance to communicate with the other gender about their experiences and opinions. It now seemed normal to us to have women attend a social event in the same room. It wasn't our decision to keep our wives segregated and separate. I wanted them to join us, and so did Obaid. But the two women would have been scandalized by the very suggestion; our traditions had wormed into the very marrow of their bones. Saudis who are completely unfamiliar with other cultures believe that they alone know the right way to live. To convince people to give up bad traditions, they have to learn about the alternatives offered elsewhere by the human family. Our wives had no interest in doing that, and no intentions of ever relenting to change.

RAFID

Tribal Honor

Tradition demands obedience, and many people feel an obligation to conform to its demands, as we saw with those involved in Saleh's story. In Saudi Arabia, a person who rejects tradition—for whatever reason—is courting grief. That individual will be mercilessly hounded and, if need be, forced by violence to reaccept the straitjacket of tradition.

This is the story of Rafid al-Otaibi and Nisrin Haq.

Rafid, a Saudi in his early forties, is illiterate. He is a slender, dark-complexioned man of medium height, and he sports a thick moustache, an important sign of masculinity in Saudi Arabia. As a young man of twenty, he had already developed a slightly humped back. The preacher of his village mosque had interpreted it as a sign of humility before God. Rafid is melancholy, pessimistic, sullen, and uncommunicative; he seldom smiles and almost never laughs. He considers life a burden. In his opinion, there is little in the world worth a laugh, but plenty to complain about. Although he prays five times a day, he isn't a fervent Muslim. Despite his melancholy disposition, he is basically childlike and kindhearted. He works as the gate-keeper for a school in Riyadh, and the children like him very much because he cares about them as if they were his own. If he is absent from work, they miss him and become anxious. The teachers also appreciate him because he is helpful and obliging.

Rafid lives modestly. He earns very little: his monthly salary is only four thousand Saudi riyals (one thousand US dollars). In reality, many Saudis don't earn much more and might be feeding a family of eight or ten children on that paltry amount. There are very few rich people in Saudi Arabia, and only the princes possess fabulous wealth. For that reason, many Saudis hold two jobs—perhaps a day job in administration or management and an evening job in sales. Rafid doesn't have an extra job, as he doesn't have anyone else to support. He is a widower, although the very concept of that term is unknown in Saudi Arabia, where a man can always marry again. Rafid's wife died two years ago, and they had no children.

Rafid lives alone in the old district of Riyadh, al-Dira. The houses are already in a pitiful state and are probably left like that with the intention of eventually demolishing them. Erected before the discovery of oil, they were constructed from clay bricks and straw, with roofs thatched with the fronds of palm leaves. An ancient palace built in the same style also awaits demolition in the name of progress; after all, the past is a reminder of suffering and deprivation, of bad times. Better to look at apartment blocks and huge, air-conditioned shopping centers. Speculators have been hard at work in Riyadh for years.

Rafid's place is also rundown and decrepit. It is located in a maze of brick houses built along unplanned lanes and alleyways. Homes and small shops jostle against each other, so the district is filled with chaotic life. The heat of the day is mixed with the dust, stink, and noise emanating from humans and automobiles. Garbage, rotten fruit, and empty carton boxes are strewn everywhere and crushed both underfoot and by the car tires. Rafid's apartment—if it can be described as such—is actually a single room. The walls are blotched and the plaster is flaking off. A tiny window on one of the walls is positioned high up, near the ceiling. The tiny piece of glass that covers it is so dusty that little light enters the room. A metal screen placed over the sheet of glass as protection against mosquitoes is now so filthy that air can't even pass through it. Ventilation is therefore provided by the main door, a piece of raw, dry, untreated wood that has split in several places because of its age. Mosquitoes, dust, and the curious glances of passersby casually enter when the door is left ajar. It hangs aslant on rusty hinges, and a great deal of strength is required to move it.

As for the room, it contains a mattress, a television, and a bolster, since it is the custom in Saudi Arabia and other Gulf states to sit on the floor. In the corner stands a small stove with three small cooking pots on it—one for tea and two for coffee. There are several little drinking glasses. Rafid sleeps, cooks, and watches television in this room. He always prepares the traditional dish: rice with a single piece of bony meat. Because he is a Bedouin, he doesn't eat fruit and vegetables. Since the death of his wife, he lives a very solitary life; his family members live far away and never come to visit him.

One day Rafid was sick, too sick to go to work. He lay rigid and unmoving on his bed, and his face was so pale that only his black hair and moustache distinguished his head from the sheet that covered him. The corner in which he slept was weakly illuminated by a small dusty lamp. That was the situation when Uthman found him. He was an administrative officer at the school and had been sent to track Rafid down after an absence of several days.

"My God, Rafid, why didn't you send news to us that you were so sick? I need to get you to a hospital for treatment," said Uthman with deep concern.

"I need only the help of Allah. He made me sick, and if he wishes, he will heal me. A leaf doesn't fall from any tree without the will of Allah. And anyway, you know that I hate hospitals. I even hate to take medicine," Rafid whispered hoarsely.

"Rafid, you can't go on living like this. You need someone in your life—a woman who will care for you. You must marry again!" Uthman counseled his friend.

Rafid rolled over on the mattress and pulled the sheet over his head.

"Rafid, I want you to know something. I know a woman who's just for you—she's a perfect match and a fine person." Inspired by his sudden inspiration, Uthman said good-bye and hurried out.

After some time, Uthman returned. He stood beside Rafid's bed and called in the direction of the door, "Come in!" A woman stepped timidly across the threshold. Her hands were clasped before her, and her gaze was downcast in abject humility to the floor. She was a Bangladeshi: short, very thin, with dark brown eyes, dark skin, and deep black, shiny hair. She was about twenty years old.

"Rafid, look at what I've brought you!" Uthman said brightly and rather loudly. The sick man moved in his bed. Uthman pulled the sheet away from his face. Rafid risked a lightning-quick glance at the girl and then his head disappeared under the sheet again. A Muslim man must never look into the eyes of a strange woman. By doing so, he shows that he desires her, and, in consequence, she is regarded as a woman with loose morals. Rafid simply didn't know what to do.

"Come on, Rafid. Turn over and listen to what I have to say. This is a fine, competent, young woman. She'll cook for you; she's a very good cook. She'll do your washing and cleaning. Furthermore, she's a good Muslim, and she learned to speak English in Bangladesh. She can teach you to speak English, Rafid. Of course, she speaks Arabic too. Now Rafid, what do you say?"

No response.

Uthman turned to the woman and quietly said, "Nisrin, clean this place up. Do some work."

She immediately went to the kitchen corner and began to put things in order. Meanwhile, Uthman spoke to Rafid: "Her name is Nisrin. She has worked for my wife and me for three years now, so we know her well. You won't regret this. Every month Nisrin sends her earnings as a housemaid home to her family. If you, as her husband, continue these monthly remittances, she'll be the happiest and most obedient wife you could ask for. Say yes. I'll go right away and bring the sheikh to solemnize your marriage."

Nisrin had prepared tea and offered it to the two men on a small tray. Uthman poured it into the glasses and offered one to Rafid. "You've never tasted tea this good. Come, drink. It will help you recover."

Cautiously, slowly, Rafid sat up, silently accepted the hot drink, and carefully took a sip. After a second sip, he smiled to indicate how flavorful it was. Then he glanced around and noticed that his modest room was tidy and organized. He hadn't realized that Nisrin had quietly put things in order for him.

"Well, do you feel better? Don't forget what our prophet Muhammad said—'Women are life's bliss, '" Uthman said with sincerity.

"But my dear friend, Uthman, you know our customs. Sheikh Abdul-rahman, the chief of our tribe, will never condone this. At some point the tribal members will hear about this marriage. Then they will murder both my wife and me. And I can't marry a Saudi, because the dowry will be very expensive. I will never be able to pay it."

"To the devil with your tribe! No one from your tribe ever comes to visit you! How would they even find out that you are married? I'm not going to tell anyone, and neither will my wife. Don't be afraid, Rafid."

In the meantime Nisrin, who had finished cleaning and washing up, had cooked a soup for Rafid. Shyly, she handed him a plate. He refused to look into her face. He ate the soup hungrily and wiped his moustache with his sleeve. Then he said to her, with his eyes still averted, "The soup is good. I would like another plateful."

Uthman interpreted this as a breakthrough. Once again, he asked Rafid if he could bring the sheikh. "If you really think that it's a good idea," Rafid hesitantly replied. Uthman and Nisrin quietly left the room.

One hour later, Uthman was back with Sheikh Ali and two witnesses. Sheikh Ali was the preacher in a small local mosque. He was almost blind, so he wore thick, old, tinted spectacles, and he recited lengthy Qur'anic verses in an extremely loud voice because he also suffered from deafness. Although his white robe reached to the floor, it revealed a corpulent belly and thin legs. The two witnesses were from Upper Egypt; for a little money and a few sweets, they would play witness to anything. Nisrin's presence was not required and her consent would not be sought.

The men entered the room, greeted Rafid, and sat down on the floor. Without any opening niceties and with the dullness of practiced routine, Sheikh Ali opened his Qur'an with a thud, covered his head, chanted a few verses from the Holy Book, and then pulled out a blank form. He passed it

to Uthman to fill in and then pass around for signatures. Rafid, the two witnesses, and the sheikh formally declared their agreement with a fingerprint; although Sheikh Ali knew the Qur'an, he could neither read nor
write. Finally, Uthman stood up. With his face glowing with pride at what
he had accomplished, he brought out a package of sweets, opened it, and
shared them all around. Sheikh Ali and the two witnesses stuffed their
mouths and pockets full while congratulating Rafid and wishing him happiness. Then they said their good-byes and departed.

That's how quickly you can get married in Saudi Arabia. A man can
also arrange his divorce just as fast. In those cases as well, the woman is not
consulted. Sometimes she is informed of her divorce unexpectedly in the
mail. There are no hearings, appeals, or even a court case. In accordance
with the teachings and practices of Islam, if a husband is unhappy with his
wife, the dissolution of the marriage becomes final and irrevocable if he
pronounces the words "I divorce you" three times. After that, he is forbidden to sleep with her. If he does sleep with her, he must wait three full
months before remarriage is allowed.

Rafid perked up and felt much better. He ate the remaining wedding
candies, and his face regained its color. Uthman waited outside in his car
while Rafid, unassisted, slowly washed up and changed into his best
clothes. Finally he got into Uthman's car. They were going to fetch the
bride.

Nisrin was at Uthman's home with his family. According to ancient
Saudi custom, she was dressed in black from head to foot; she was also
completely veiled. Rafid was anxious to keep her hidden from view whenever she stepped out in public—after all, she was a foreigner. He took her
home in a cheap taxi.

Once there, Rafid lay down on his bed, exhausted by the excitement and
activity of the previous hours. Nisrin busied herself with household tasks.
She cleaned the room (taking special care to clean the little window), washed
the bedding and Rafid's clothes, and then cooked rice with meat. She spoke
very little. As a Muslim woman, she had been trained not to take any initiative in conversation unless it was absolutely necessary: "Where is the laundry
soap? Do you like spicy food?" Rafid sank into his thoughts, wondering if he

would be able to keep her ethnic identity a secret from the neighbors and his tribe. He had a gut feeling of dread that eventually, at some unspecified moment, his clan members would find out about this marriage.

Tribe members were allowed to marry within the extended family or with tribes of similar social standing. If, however, in the opinion of family members or chieftains, a man or woman showed contempt for tribal honor through a humiliating marriage alliance, the punishment was banishment from the group or even beheading. The Saudi government refuses to interfere in such "internal family matters." In theory, Islam is against such discrimination, but traditions in Saudi Arabia often come into conflict with the conventionalities of Islam when the religion's leaders are influenced by their native culture and traditions. For instance, the ancient Saudi tradition of the facial veiling of women has nothing to do with the teachings of Islam, but it's culturally reinforced nonetheless.

After eating dinner and drinking a glass of tea, Rafid and his wife went to bed.

Two days later, Rafid was fully recovered and back on the job. Nisrin provided the sparse room with a few further items of furniture and used the household money to buy missing household articles and a curtain to separate the eating and sleeping areas. She stuffed the holes in the split wood of their door with cardboard.

She made some of her purchases in a small shop nearby, which was patronized mainly by men, as few families had a maid in such a poor neighborhood. The owner was surprised that an unaccompanied Saudi woman had come to buy. But when she spoke, he immediately knew from her accent that she wasn't Saudi.

"Why are you veiled? Are you disguising yourself, or are you really too ugly to look at?" he sneered and yanked her veil off her face. Two customers who stood nearby laughed as if they had heard a good joke. Nisrin didn't react. She paid and went home. She was used to being treated roughly and rudely by Saudi men.

The news spread around the neighborhood: Rafid, a single Saudi man, was living with an Indian servant girl. In the house next door, a group of women considered ways to force Nisrin to pack up and leave. "The whore veils her face and struts around like a Saudi. Does she think that we are idiots?" one of them burst out. A few days later, a neighbor observed Nisrin coming down the laneway. She opened her door and threw a pan of dirty water onto the girl. Nisrin didn't say a word. She went into their room and locked herself in.

Nisrin said nothing to Rafid about these incidents. And one evening, three neighborhood men came to speak with Rafid. Since he had very little contact with his neighbors, Rafid wondered what they could want. When they entered his room, Nisrin promptly hid herself behind the curtain that partitioned off the kitchen area. She began to prepare tea for the men and, meanwhile, listened to their conversation. After the customary greetings and social niceties, one of the men began: "We have wanted to visit you for some time now. As you know, our houses stand close together in this neighborhood, but we barely know each other. This is wrong. Our prophet Muhammad declared that Muslim neighbors must care for and support each other. We should visit each other more often."

Another man continued. "Because we don't know you well, we have had to endure a lot of rumors. To tell the truth, it is being said that you are living with a servant girl. We don't believe this, of course, so we have come to you for the truth."

Rafid quickly concocted a lie. "By the will of God! I am a Muslim, a good Muslim, and a good Muslim lives only with his wife. But you must know that my wife is very sick and confined to hospital. The woman you are referring to is the servant of one of my relatives. She is staying with me on loan until my wife recovers and is released."

"Thanks be to Allah! I had hoped that this would be the truth of the matter!" exclaimed one of the neighbors, very much relieved.

From behind the curtain, Nisrin said clearly, "Baba, the tea is ready." The word "baba," used by an Indian servant in Arabic society, is a polite and affectionate term for "master." It suggests a childlike yet subservient dependence on the employer.

Rafid got to his feet, fetched the tray, and served each man a glass of tea.

After the men had left, Nisrin reappeared, with eyes red and glassy from weeping. She had been crying in the kitchen. "Nisrin, I am sorry," Rafid said, "but I had to lie to save us both. Those are cruel men from a heartless society. I always suspected that this would go badly; I even told Uthman."

"Then you also regret having married me?" asked Nisrin, offended and hurt.

"I wouldn't say that . . . but I'm sure that you know our customs, and they are hard and merciless. We have to find a way out of this situation. I hate our customs—I hate our traditions—why can't people leave us in peace?!" Rafid exclaimed in muffled anger.

"Why don't you marry a Saudi? I could stay with you as the housemaid."

"I can't live like that. For me, it's either one woman, or another. And anyway, the bride price of a Saudi woman is very high—I could never afford it."

"Let me go back to Uthman and his family to work. I'll save my maid's salary and give it to you so you can afford to marry," Nisrin suggested with urgent sincerity.

"Out of the question. You're my wife, and I can't allow you to work outside of our home."

"Then let's move somewhere where no one knows us."

"It's not that easy. In the first place, I can't afford it, and second, our new neighbors will want to get to know us. As soon as they see you they will say, 'Imagine that! He's living with a maid!' And you know that is forbidden. So I'll tell them, 'She's my wife!' and they'll say, 'So why didn't you marry a Saudi?' . . . You know, you could have an operation to give you a Saudi face. But I'll never be able to change your voice and your accent," Rafid joked.

Nisrin smiled and replied, "Well, let's move to a place where there are no neighbors!"

"Remember, all Saudis are curious. And when a woman stands in the question, they are even more interested. The honor of our entire nation depends on its women. If a woman is Saudi and she's married, that's fine. If a Saudi man and woman are married to each other, whether they love each other or hate each other, the world is in order," Rafid commented sarcastically.

Rafid lived happily with Nisrin. She did everything possible to make his life pleasant; that was the way she had been raised in Bangladesh. Her life had changed with this marriage. She no longer had to clean and cook for a large family, so the work was easier. But in her heart, she still felt like a housemaid. Not because Rafid treated her like one, but because the society forced her to think of herself as one. All she had to do was show her face or speak a word, and she was labeled as a servant. Even in her own home, Nisrin sat in the kitchen, waiting for Rafid to call her and order something to eat or drink.

Rafid and Nisrin decided that she would no longer go out on shopping trips by herself. They went together, but only to large stores or supermarkets where they would mingle with the crowd and be assured of more anonymity. One afternoon, the two of them, in Rafid's old and barely functioning car, made an excursion to one of Riyadh's largest shopping malls, where both Saudis and foreigners liked to shop. Suddenly Rafid found himself greeted by a man of equal age—a cousin. "Rafid, I am so happy to see you! Where have you been hiding yourself? How are you?" He kissed Rafid and hugged him warmly. Rafid put on a pleasant face and returned the greetings of this individual whom he could barely remember and with whom he felt no connection. In the last twenty years, Rafid had met him possibly two or three times at annual family gatherings, which he had attended from time to time out of courtesy. Rafid's tribe was enormous. He had hundreds of cousins.

The relative inquired about the woman he was accompanying. Rafid stated that she was not his wife. His wife had died, and he had never remarried. "Oh, I know about that, but I thought you would have remarried by now. However, you're a single man, and a busy shopping mall is just the place to indulge in a little woman-hunting, isn't it?" he commented with a crafty look.

"Well, I'm not exactly a spring colt anymore, but I used to do that when I was younger," he replied in a bored tone.

"Well, why don't you remarry? I've got just the match for you. A twelve-year-old girl, the daughter of Uncle Rashid."

"I'll think about it," said Rafid. But his thoughts were elsewhere; he was worried that he might lose Nisrin in the bustle of jostling people. To get rid of his tedious cousin, he acted as though he was in a hurry and moved off quickly. He hoped that Nisrin hadn't lost sight of him.

Normally a Saudi wife walks a few steps behind her husband when they are in public; she is seldom seen in front of him or even at his side. If the husband meets acquaintances on the street, the wife stands off at a distance, or hides behind him. Nisrin had been walking behind Rafid, and she distanced herself when he met his cousin. Rafid had stepped up his pace to appear hurried and then he had veered off into a side passage. Because of this, Rafid and Nisrin lost sight of each other. Rafid plunged into the crowds in search of her, and she tried to find him. Nisrin removed the veil that fully concealed her face so that she could see better and so that he could identify her. It was a huge building. Exhausted after much searching, Nisrin sank onto the bottom of a flight of stairs and began to cry. No one paid any attention to her, even those who passed close by.

After some time a Mutawa chanced upon Nisrin and fixed his lascivious eyes on her. "Why are you here all alone? Where is your master, your baba?" he gruffly demanded. After all, she was an Indian, and therefore a common laborer. Such people were always spoken down to. Also, a Saudi woman would have had a covered face.

Nervous and trembling, Nisrin replied that she couldn't find him.

"Cover your face and come with me. We are going to locate him. Understood?" he said in a heartless and threatening tone.

Foreigners are usually struck by panic attacks if confronted by a

Mutawa, because they are known to be ruthlessly unscrupulous. Nisrin followed the man. Outside the shopping plaza, he pushed her into a car and drove off.

"Where are you going? Where are you going? My baba is still in the store, and I know he is looking for me right now!" Nisrin exclaimed in fear.

"Keep your mouth shut. We're going to find him. What's his name? Where does he live?" he demanded with a ferocious expression on his face.

"I want to go back to the store. Let me out of the car!"

"Shut up! I'm concentrating on my driving!" he ordered, and hit the gas pedal so that the car was flying down the road. Nisrin had no chance of getting out. Soon they were heading toward the open desert, and she was filled with terror.

"Let me out! I know where I live! I'll take a taxi!" she screamed.

The Mutawa slowed the car and paid attention to his steering as he reached behind with his right hand and punched her in the face. Her head was dashed into a side window. Blood streamed down. Gasping, she pulled herself together and surveyed the situation outside the vehicle: desert, no cars, no people. Nothing. She didn't stand a chance.

Finally the Mutawa stopped the car and got out. He opened Nisrin's door. Overcome by panic, she drew her legs up against her chest and braced her arms around her knees. Her jaw was chattering as she begged the Mutawa not to touch her. The policeman raised his floor-length gown to his waist, opened his underwear, and proclaimed, "In the name of God!"

Then he threw himself upon her. Dazed and terrified, with blood still gushing from her head, she couldn't push him away. He ripped her clothing open and violently raped her. Then he fetched a bottle of whisky from the trunk of the car and guzzled it down like water. He got into the front seat of the car, singing and laughing senselessly. Eventually he went silent and fell asleep.

It became dark.

Nisrin attempted to get up, and, after much effort, was finally able to pull herself to her feet. Everything was plunged in inky blackness—no people, no streets, not even a light on the horizon. Without any sense of direction and in her bare feet, she trudged across the desert. Her only point of orientation was the Mutawa's white car. The smaller it became, the safer she felt. She was overwrought and in pain from the rape and her head injury, and her feet slipped in the grainy, sharp sand. Then, suddenly, her feet hit a solid surface. It had to be a road across the desert. Feeling much safer, she walked along it. Wherever it led, it had to take her to people. After about one hour, she made out a tiny light in the distance. She continued to walk.

Nisrin's thoughts wandered back into her past, back to her homeland and her family that had always provided security and solace. This pattern of thinking was at the bequest of her Buddhist ancestors. Buddhist religious teachers, stamped with the influences of Bengal, recommended beautiful memories as a way to cope with pain and resist oppression. So she focused on her family in Bangladesh: her mother, father, five sisters, and four brothers. She considered what each of them was doing at this exact moment. They would also be thinking of her as they sat together outside their home after a hard day of labor, which was their custom every evening. They had been so overjoyed with the small presents that she brought when she went home on leave. And they were also grateful to be provided with the money she had earned in Saudi Arabia, funds that she had regularly wired home to pay off the debts her father had incurred after the flood had devastated their land.

Now that she was married to him, Rafid faithfully gave her some of his salary to wire home to Bangladesh every month. She still had to pay the village moneylender for the cost of her flight to the Gulf. Eventually all her debts would be paid, and, with Rafid's help, she would save up to buy a sewing machine. In the meantime, she was thrilled because her youngest siblings were attending school. They would become doctors and engineers, rich and important people. They would undoubtedly support both Nisrin and Rafid in their old age . . .

A car whizzed by, startling Nisrin out of her daydreams. It didn't stop. Suddenly aware of her ripped clothing and bloodstained body, she decided to sit by the side of the road. She covered her head with remnants of fabric and laid her face down on one knee. Another vehicle approached. It stopped. The driver, a Saudi, asked if she needed help. She nodded and got into the car.

"Where can I take you?" asked the man.

"Home," she replied in a faint voice.

"And where is that, the place where you work?" He turned to look at her, now aware from her voice that she wasn't Saudi. "You're from India, aren't you?"

"Yes," replied Nisrin, who knew that most Saudi housemaids were from India.

"What are you doing alone in the desert? Did your baba kick you out? Problems, huh? The trouble with you people is you don't know how lucky you are to be working here. Back home, all you people starve. You're actually used to it. There are a lot of other Indians who would jump at the chance you got to work in a Saudi household. You get paid, and you get free housing and food. Can you get that anywhere else?"

Nisrin started to cry.

"Stop it. We're almost there. I'm dropping you off at a police station, and they can take you home."

"Please, no! No! Not to the police! Let me out here!" Nightmares attacked her mind at the very word.

"Well, so you don't want to go to the police station, do you? You want to just sneak off? I can't even imagine what you've been up to. Out of the question!" he snapped in response.

His car pulled up in front of a building flying the Saudi flag. A police station.

"Get out."

The driver knew the procedure. He went directly to the on-duty chief, followed by Nisrin. The two men greeted each other with kisses on both cheeks, in accordance with custom; they knew each other well. "What's this? It's past midnight, and you are bringing me your housemaid? Is she creating problems and you want to kick her out?" joked the police chief.

"No, no. She isn't mine. I found her by the side of the road out in the desert. Only God knows what she was up to in her employer's home. I bet they're looking for her right now," said the man.

"No problem. We'll find her sponsor." He turned to Nisrin. "What's your baba's name?"

Nisrin thought quickly. If she told him that she was no longer a housemaid, but had married a Saudi, it might make matters worse.

"His name is Rafid."

"And where does he live?"

"In Riyadh."

"In which district?"

"I don't know."

"Does the family have a telephone at home?"

"No," she replied.

"Do you have your identity papers on you? Do you have your residency card?"

"No."

"Well, how are we supposed to find your home? We're going to have to hold you until your baba wakes up tomorrow morning and comes looking for you."

Nisrin implored the men to let her go. She assured them that she'd find her way home on her own.

"Well, if you don't know where you live, how are you going to find it?" smirked the officer.

"Let me go back to the shopping center. My baba is waiting for me there," begged Nisrin.

"It's the middle of the night; everything is closed. I think this woman isn't completely altogether. We ought to lock her up. Just look at her clothing—she belongs in a madhouse."

Nisrin was fetched by a guard and locked into a holding cell. It had been many hours since she had eaten or drunk. By the next morning, she was begging for a drink. The guard brought her foul-tasting tap water, but she received nothing to eat. Nisrin remained in that cell for nine hours, sitting on the floor in her dirty, ripped, and bloody clothes, her head throbbing with pain from the Mutawa's fierce punch. It was absolute hell. The cell was in the basement. There were no windows and not even bars to peer through—only thick, solid walls and a heavy door. It had been specifically designed for women; it would be improper to observe them, especially while they slept.

Rafid searched everywhere for Nisrin. He repeatedly combed the four floors of the shopping complex, painstakingly approaching any woman with a similar body type. He inquired at the police office, but nothing had been reported. He called Uthman but was told that she wasn't there. He visited a number of police stations in the vicinity. During the night, he lay with eyes wide open and prayed.

The next day he returned to the shopping complex and looked for her again. Then he went back to the police office, gave her name, and described her; he identified Nisrin as his housemaid and said she was urgently needed at home. A policeman who was beginning his shift said he had heard that last night a housemaid had been brought to al-Olaya police station, which was in the vicinity. Apparently she was mentally disturbed, for she had run away from her employer's house. He remembered hearing the woman's name, and he thought it was similar.

Rafid got into his old car and drove out to al-Olaya. When he inquired after a woman named Nisrin, the desk clerk replied, "Yes, we've had her here for quite a while now, but no one came for her. Come with me."

They went down into the cellar. The cell door was unlocked, and there was Nisrin, sitting on the floor. When she saw her husband she cried, "Baba, where have you been? Get me out of here!" She struggled to her feet, hurried to Rafid, and hugged him. "Big love for the housemaid, that's for sure," laconically commented the second-in-command officer. He added, "Is she good in bed?"

Rafid stood speechless and stiff outside the cell.

"Let's go upstairs," said the officer.

Suddenly Rafid burst out in a loud, angry voice, "Why did you lock her up? What law did she break?" The policeman silently led the way into his office, and Rafid followed, with Nisrin clinging to his arm. The policeman sat down, reached for a release form, and asked Rafid for his identity card. Rafid handed it over.

"What? Your name is also al-Otaibi! Imagine that—we're relatives! So, do you have the sponsorship papers?"

"What?"

"The official paper that shows that she's your servant," came the impatient reply.

"No, I don't."

"No problem. I'll get a copy off our computer." He called in an Egyptian clerk and told him to open the program for worker sponsorship and print out the results for Rafid Abdulrahman al-Otaibi.

In the meantime, Rafid was served tea. Nisrin, who was believed to be a housemaid, received nothing.

The papers arrived, and the police officer's face turned fierce as he read them. "*Nisrin is your wife?*" he asked, pointedly hurling out each syllable of the sentence like daggers.

"Yes," Rafid answered sheepishly.

The officer gave a short, shrill laugh and shouted in challenge, "What's this? An al-Otaibi is married to a foreigner—more than that, a housemaid? This is scandalous! Are you trying to ruin the reputation of our tribe? This is intolerable!" He banged his hand onto the desk and made a decision. "The girl is going to be deported."

"That's out of the question! She's my wife! You have no legal right to do that to us!"

"Nasser!" the policeman called to a co-worker. "Take the girl back to the cell!"

"You can't do that! She is my wife! We were properly married in accordance with Islamic procedure. My papers are legal!"

"That is not your wife! That is a whore!"

"Your mother is a whore!"

"Nasser, lock him up, too!"

Rafid resisted arrest and continued to curse the officer. Two more policemen were called in to drag him downstairs and throw him into a cell. Shortly afterward, Nisrin was taken out and paraded before Rafid. "This whore is your wife, isn't that so? Well, I'm going to have her taken out to the desert now and raped by several men. It will help you remember to never marry a housemaid again!"

It was not an idle threat. Nisrin was driven out to the desert again, to a tent where three men were waiting for her. All of them raped her. Then she was taken to a deportation detention center. One week later, she was flown out the country on the grounds that she had illegally taken on extra work in addition to her job as a housemaid. According to Saudi law, the punishment for such actions is immediate deportation.

Rafid was released from jail. He immediately went to the Ministry of the Interior and denounced the second-in-command officer. He outlined the incident from beginning to end. Two weeks later, he was asked to return to the ministry to hear the verdict of the case.

"In the name of Allah. The case registered by complainant Rafid al-Otaibi has been dismissed. The accused Malek al-Otaibi is a respected employee of the Ministry of the Interior and conducted himself correctly in all regards. The complaint against him is an attempt at character defamation. Therefore, Rafid al-Otaibi will receive a punishment of two hundred lashes. This punishment will be carried out in public view." Beneath this was the signature of the minister of the interior.

Saudi Arabia is not a constitutional state. There are no proper courts, no body of public prosecutors, and no attorneys. Theoretically, disputes and crimes are dealt with by Shari'a, the Muslim system of justice. But, in practice, a prince from the ruling al-Saud family makes decisions over what is legal or illegal, right or wrong, in all of the country's regions and provinces.

Rafid, who later traveled to Bangladesh to visit his wife but was barred from bringing her back to Saudi Arabia, personally told me the tragic story of their marriage. And when I double-checked with the second-in-command officer, who at one time had been one of my students, he agreed that it was all true. And he was very proud of himself.

A SON AT ALL COSTS

Rafid and Nisrin's fraught marriage shows just how entrenched in tradition Saudi lifestyles are, from birth to marriage and beyond. For example, even today, all couples in Arab cultures fervently hope to have at least one son. In fact, in the not-so-distant past when most Arabs were tribal nomads, women were openly regarded as a necessary "burden." They could not be involved in wars and expected to fight, and in those days intertribal fighting over pastureland for animals was very common. Captured enemy women were raped, and, against their will and that of their tribe, they became the mothers of their enemies' children. In this way, their own tribe was weakened. Such women faced humiliation, shame, and brutal demoralization. Up to this very day, women in the Arab world are regarded as the weaker half of society because they cannot defend themselves with physical strength and are the usual victims of rape. And if a woman is sexually violated, the honor of her family is tarnished.

In Saudi Arabia, a woman's value comes in part from her ability to bear sons. The following story demonstrates the lengths to which one woman went to provide her husband with a son. Dolari told me this when I was in India.

Princess Hissa is married to one of the sons of Prince Tarek, the brother of an influential Saudi prince. Because she is the mother of five daughters but no sons, her sisters- and brothers-in-law, along with other relatives, subject her to merciless torment. She is spurned and ostracized by everyone. In Saudi Arabia and the Gulf states, a woman who has not given birth to a son is practically worthless. She even risks seeing her husband take a second wife. But Princess Hissa has endured so much contempt from her relatives that she no longer has the emotional energy to endure yet another pregnancy—pregnancy with an uncertain result.

One day Dolari, an Indian maid aged about fifty who had worked for princess Hissa for over ten years, received a letter from her homeland. Dolari was delighted: her daughter had given birth to a boy—her fourth son. The princess noticed that Dolari's face was beaming with joy, although the maid tried to suppress it in the presence of her mistress. The princess demanded to know the reason why, and Dolari quickly fabricated a lame excuse. She knew that Princess Hissa's mother-in-law had recently fired off spiteful and wounding comments, and therefore wanted to avoid any further humiliation of her employer. Curious, the princess asked another servant, a Filipina, the reason for Dolari's behavior and learned the truth from her. Dolari's daughter, a simple peasant, had achieved more respect than a Saudi princess.

Hissa actually liked Dolari; she had often praised her as the best maid in the palace because she was very motherly, kind, hardworking, and eager to help out in any way. She now felt overwhelmed by a need to talk about sons and felt comfortable approaching Dolari about this, as she was herself a mother. So Princess Hissa followed Dolari into the kitchen.

Dolari was astounded and alarmed to see her mistress enter the kitchen, a room she had never condescended to visit before. After all, if anything was needed, it was ordered over a loudspeaker system. Many questions flashed across Dolari's mind: Why is she entering the kitchen now? Is the intercom out of order? Is the princess angry with me? Have I done something wrong?

"Congratulations, Dolari! I have heard that your daughter recently gave birth to her fourth son. Here's a gift from me—five hundred US dollars."

Dolari stood speechless, not sure how to respond. Finally she said,

"Thank you very much, Madam. Yes, I have a new grandson; his name is Farhat. Here—" and she pulled a slightly grubby envelope from a cupboard. "Here is his picture, with my daughter and her husband. Isn't he adorable?" she exclaimed with enthusiasm. The princess gave the photo a long examination. "Yes," she said. "He's adorable." Then she simply walked out of the kitchen.

She went directly to her bedroom, shut the door, and burst into tears. Why had she never conceived a son? The photo of Dolari's grandson and his parents had been burned into her mind—she couldn't stop visualizing it. Then, suddenly, a new idea snaked in as desperate necessity fueled her imagination. Princess Hissa wanted to have a son. She had to have a son. And a diabolical train of thought emerged.

Dolari should fly to India. There, she should seek out a pregnant woman who looked somewhat like the princess. Fortunately, the princess's hair and skin tone was similar to that of many Indians. The pregnant woman should undergo a medical exam to determine the gender of her unborn child. If the fetus was male, Dolari should enter into financial negotiations with her for the purchase of the baby.

Did the princess intend an international adoption? No. The pregnant woman was to enter Saudi Arabia on a housemaid's visa. And it was important that the woman be in the early stages of pregnancy, so her condition would not be noticed at the border.

Princess Hissa would tell the family that she was expecting again. In Saudi Arabia, a husband does not have sexual relations with his wife if she is pregnant. And a pregnant woman who is already the mother of several girls is simply ignored, like an apparently unlucky slot machine in a casino.

Too impatient to wait, Princess Hissa immediately announced that she was pregnant. Fortunately, this ruse was successful: in the ensuing months, her husband, Prince Khaled, took numerous lengthy overseas business trips, and his mother and sisters seldom bothered to pay her a visit.

Then Princess Hissa summoned Dolari to her room and explained the plan to her. The maid was both confused and excited; she unceasingly repeated, "Yes, Madam. . . . Yes, Madam." Dolari was ordered to prepare for her trip. Two days later she received an airline ticket to Mumbai.

Dolari sat in the plane, looked out the window, and wondered. "Will this work? What if I am discovered back in Saudi Arabia? No, I shouldn't think about that. My mistress is a good woman, and it is my duty to try to help her. But is this the right thing to do? What if I get detected in Mumbai?" Then she turned to prayer for the rest of the flight—prayers for success and protection.

After she disembarked, Dolari was overcome by an urge to visit her own family. "They don't live far away; it's only a four-hour trip. My daughter and her sons will be overjoyed to see me. I'll get to see my new grandchild. I have to go!"

Money was not an issue; Princess Hissa had given her plenty. Dolari went into the city to buy gifts so that she wouldn't come home empty-handed. Then she took a rickshaw to the bus station and got on a long-distance bus that made a direct connection to her small town. From there, she took a taxi to her home. She was so happy that she began to sing. It was sunset, and the entire family had assembled on the doorstep to welcome her. Her youngest grandson was the first to notice the taxi, and he ran toward it crying, "Grandmother! Grandmother is here!" Then everyone else rushed to greet her.

Although Dolari was overjoyed to see her family again, her thoughts were often distracted by worry about how she would fulfill Princess Hissa's task. She found herself unconsciously examining the belly of each of her daughters-in-law. Her youngest son, Rajif, had married a few months ago. Dolari wondered if his bride might be pregnant.

Dolari called the young woman to sit with her. "Shisa, come here. Let's chat. Tell me, does my son Rajif treat you well?" Her tone was warm, inviting, and maternal.

"Oh yes, very well." Then she shyly whispered into her mother-in-law's ear, "Especially now that I'm pregnant."

"Congratulations!" replied Dolari.

Should I speak to Rajif about Princess Hissa? Dolari pondered. If so, how should I tell him? No, I'd better not . . . first let me find out if the baby is male or female.

Even in India a son is held in much higher regard than a daughter, especially among country families. Dolari came up with a scheme. The next morning she said to Shisa, "My goodness, you look so pale! Do you feel bad?"

"No, I'm just fine. But sometimes I wake up at night because I get a funny feeling in my tummy."

"I have to take you to see a doctor."

"There's no need. Last week Rajif and I went to a woman healer in Sirwa, the next village."

"That's not good enough, Shisa. We must go to Mumbai. That's where the really qualified doctors are. I need to see you feeling perfectly fine, and I need to know that my grandchild is healthy."

"Mama, please—that would be very expensive."

"Don't concern yourself with that. I have money. You must give birth to a healthy baby," said Dolari in such a firm voice that Shisa didn't dare to disagree.

The next day they traveled to Mumbai. They went to a taxi driver, and Dolari asked if he knew of any modern private medical clinics.

"Yes, Madam. I know one where they even use computers to examine patients. But it's very expensive."

"No problem," replied Dolari. They got into the taxi and were driven to a clinic that was clean and well maintained—at least on the outside.

Shisa and Dolari went in. "Sit on that bench," said Dolari, and she went to the reception. A smiling, friendly nurse greeted her. Dolari explained that she wanted her pregnant daughter-in-law seen by a doctor, and that above all they wanted to know the gender of the baby. The nurse didn't bat an eyelash. She calmly handed over admission forms to be filled in and then conducted them to an examination room.

The doctor concluded that Shisa was in perfect health and that the fetus was male. Dolari was very happy. She hugged her daughter-in-law and didn't let go for a long time.

On the trip home, Dolari began to consider how to explain her mandate from Princess Hissa. She finally decided to speak to Rajif in confidence. Dolari knew she had to move fast. The princess was waiting.

When they arrived at the house, Dolari's oldest son, Shamin, was waiting to greet them. Dolari changed her plan and decided to take him into her confidence first. If he agreed to her idea, Shamin could then influence his younger brother. She asked him to speak with her privately outside.

"Mama, what is it? You look concerned. Is everything all right?"

"Everything is all right. And I am so happy to see all of you children again, even if you are adults now. Shamin, please understand that I truly love all of you. But I have a problem. Actually, I don't have a problem. I have a request. My employer in Saudi Arabia, the princess, needs a child. A son. She has already given birth to five daughters.

"The situation is shameful to her, and she has begged me to help her get a son. How would it be if Shisa gave up her baby to the princess in exchange for money . . . a lot of money?" Dolari was practically in tears.

"Mama! What are you talking about?" Shamin replied in total shock.

"I know, I know . . . it's terribly hard for a mother to give away her child. . . . But the child, my grandchild, would be in safe hands. I would be living in the same house with him. I myself will bring him up. He would lead a wonderful life. He would live the life of a prince. And my employer, Princess Hissa, is truly a wonderful woman. She would care for him so much, she would meet his every need."

"Mama, you know that we are here to fulfill your every wish. But isn't this dangerous? How are you going to smuggle a baby? And what if Shisa gives birth to a girl?"

"It's going to be a boy. The doctor in Mumbai confirmed that."

"Does Shisa know that?"

"No. We only told her that the baby is healthy, and might be a boy. But we were quite hazy about it, so she doesn't have full confidence in that prediction. Shamin, I want to take Shisa back with me to Riyadh. She would give birth in the royal palace, and no one, absolutely no one, will know this secret except for the princess and me."

"Oh, God!" exclaimed Shamin, and then he said nothing more. He sank deep into thought and finally took his mother's hand and gave her a look that seemed to say: I would do anything you ask, even if I'm not convinced of it. Dolari returned his gaze with eyes full of love and overflowing with tears.

Shamin said, "Mama, no one else must know of this. It must remain only between us," and went into the house.

However, the next morning Shamin took his mother aside and startled her when he told her in a low voice, "Mama, I have good news. Rajif and Shisa have agreed to your proposal."

"What?!" she exclaimed.

"I spoke to both of them early this morning, while you were still asleep."

"Where are they now?"

"They are in the field, planting rice together."

"Shisa should not be doing that work—because of the baby."

"Let's go together and speak to them."

Rajif and Shisa were sitting on the edge of the rice paddy, taking a break. When Shisa saw her mother-in-law approaching, she tried to force herself to stop crying.

"Shisa, I know what a difficult decision this is for you. But the child will remain ours. I myself will bring him up. And a wonderful and powerful princess will never forget your generous sacrifice," Dolari assured her.

Two days later, Dolari, Shisa, and Rajif traveled to Mumbai to obtain a passport for Shisa. Dolari phoned Riyadh and spoke personally with the princess. She quickly arranged for the young woman an entry visa for Saudi Arabia, and an airline ticket.

At Mumbai Airport, Shisa and Rajif found their parting very emotionally painful. Shisa cried liked a small child. She clung to Rajif and didn't want to leave his arms. She simply wanted to stay with her husband.

Meanwhile, in Riyadh, Princess Hissa had confided in only one person—her own mother. The princess had also arranged for Dolari and Shisa to be discreetly whisked through immigration and passport control by a palace official, and then they were brought home in a luxury limousine. The only person to greet them was Princess Hissa herself. None of the employees were to know that Shisa was living there. Shisa was given her own private quarters: a bedroom, living room, and bathroom. Princess Hissa gave orders that those rooms were strictly off-limits to the palace's servants, no matter what.

Apart from the princess and Dolari, the only other person to visit Shisa was the princess's mother. She used Dolari as a translator. The princess's mother expressed her hopes that all was going well, and that her daughter would soon become the mother of a son. She hated her daughter's husband. She despised his chauvinistic behavior and felt that he deserved the trick that was being imposed on him. He didn't deserve anything better than this. He wanted a son, and he was going to get one, even if it came from a village in India. And furthermore, this was the only way to buy back his love for her daughter.

The prince hadn't come around in a long time. Actually, he was considering marrying again—a woman who would bare sons. Hissa was hoping and praying that he wouldn't remarry before the baby's birth. Meanwhile, he seemed to be swinging between Europe and America on business trips. From time to time, he would call to ask how his daughters were doing, and how Hissa's pregnancy was progressing. He was anxious to know her due date. The princess deduced that, if the baby was another girl, he would remarry immediately.

She lived in a state of terror—what if he returned in the last days of her so-called pregnancy? "Please, please, don't let him return too soon!" she prayed. Like most Saudi men, the prince didn't like to be around when his wife was screaming in pain as she gave birth or when a newborn was crying at unexpected hours. Therefore, the princess had good reason to hope that he would stay away. Especially if she persistently complained about swollen ankles and a sore back.

Princess Hissa took good care of Shisa. She was under a female doctor's care and received nutritious food because the princess wanted a healthy baby. A nursery was prepared, baby clothes were purchased, and all the baby's needs were on hand. The only thing missing was the actual baby.

As a mother, Hissa understood the terrible bitterness that Shisa was suffering, living each day of her pregnancy in full knowledge that she would be giving up her newborn. Hissa desperately needed a son to make peace with her husband and his family, but she also didn't want to hurt Shisa. She was hopeful that Shisa would return to India and have many more children, including boys, which were just as coveted in India as in Saudi Arabia.

Saudi princesses usually give birth at home. They order in a team of female obstetricians, nurses and nurses' aides from a private clinic, based either in Saudi Arabia or overseas. Male doctors are not allowed.

When Shisa's labor pains began, a medical team was already in place at the palace. The baby was born quickly, and without complications, just after midnight.

Dolari was an experienced and practical woman. She immediately removed the baby from the delivery room and took it to Princess Hissa, who was nervously waiting next door. So that Shisa didn't bond with the child, she was not even allowed to see its face. Dolari hoped that Shisa would be spared nightmares and postpartum depression.

Hissa was delighted with the baby. She took him in her arms and showered him with motherly kisses. Where was her husband? She wanted him to come home immediately, so she could show him their lovely son. Surely he would be overjoyed. From this day forward, he would have no reason to be cross with her. And she would finally be treated by everyone with respect—especially by her husband's mother.

Shisa remained in Riyadh for a few more days and then decided to fly back to Mumbai to go home to her husband. The princess gave her a lot of money. Shisa left with ambivalent feelings: on the one hand, she had been treated well, received a lot of money and many gifts; but on the other hand she was leaving part of her own life behind—her own child. She had never imagined that she would be capable of doing something so heartless.

The princess, with money, had bought a human life and a measure of happiness and social respect for herself and her family. In turn, Shisa used the money earned to buy a house and a plot of land in rural India for her family. But, with all that money, was Shisa also able to buy peace for her troubled soul?

Once again, the rich had won and the poor had lost.

MANSOUR

Like many other Saudis, Mansour employs household help. He has two housemaids from the Philippines. In truth, he doesn't need a maid at all. Unlike Princess Hissa's household, by Saudi standards, Mansour's family is quite small, consisting only of his wife, Khulud, and their seven-year-old son. Khulud is a housewife, but in name only; she doesn't do any work in her own home. Her job is getting herself waited on by the maids. Mansour wants to have more children, but Khulud can't have another pregnancy, so a certain level of emotional tension hangs over their marriage. They frequently argue. Mansour often tells Khulud that, if he could afford it, he would take a second wife.

They live in a small apartment: two bedrooms, a living room, a kitchen, and a bath. This makes them even more inclined to fight. Mansour earns an average salary. He dreams of living in an apartment building where all the other residents would be foreigners, particularly from Lebanon and Syria. In those countries the women don't veil themselves and sex segregation is not practiced. How nice it would be to visit back and forth with the neighbors, to have both men and women together in the same room, socializing and enjoying each other's company. In most Saudi families and neighborhoods anything like that is strictly forbidden.

Mansour has housemaids for two reasons. First of all, as a status symbol.

After all, since the discovery of oil, everyone has them. When guests come to the home, housemaids serve the food and drinks. When the family walks in the street, the housemaids are always a step behind, out of respect. Second, they are cheap and practical. They don't understand Arabic, so household secrets stay under wraps. They sleep on the floor of either the kitchen or the hallway.

Most housemaids are from the Philippines, India, or Ethiopia, because Saudis prefer these nationalities. Mansour's maids earn the equivalent of about fifty US dollars per month, which is a good price because he negotiated for them through an agency. Because he took two, he got a reduction. For Ali, Mansour's seven-year-old, the two maids function as punching bags. Whenever one passes, he hits or kicks her. Mansour's wife doesn't speak English, and the Filipinos don't speak Arabic, so they get by using only the words *tea, coffee, water, meal, faster, go, come,* and two or three others. With such a minimal level of communication, there are many misunderstandings that usually result in anger and confrontation.

The maids don't get any days off, and they are never allowed to leave the house alone. Outside, they have to wear a black abaya, which shrouds them from head to foot; however, they don't cover their faces so that everyone can identify them as servants. According to Saudi Islamic belief, Muslim women must cover their faces, because a woman's face is a sexual organ, and you don't walk around in public with your sexual organs on view. Housemaids, however, are not "respectable" women, so it's not a problem if their faces are exposed.

Mansour is a low-level employee at a branch of the Public Authority. He does little work and comes and goes as he pleases. Khulud is always bored and wants to get out of the apartment every day. Usually she wants to go to expensive boutiques to "window shop." Mansour hates shopping with a passion. Out of annoyance with her husband, Khulud beats the housemaids—often with a stick—until they bleed. The two girls have put up with the abuse for a long time.

Once the brother of one of the maids, Lori, phoned from Manila. Khulud picked up the phone and refused to believe that Lori's brother was on the line. She thought, "No, this must be a stranger—Lori is a common whore!" Khulud beat Lori until she was nearly unconscious. Meanwhile, the other housemaid ran unnoticed out into the street, hailed a taxi, went back to the apartment, forcefully pulled Lori from Khulud's grasp, and then managed to lock the apartment door from the outside. Then the two housemaids fled by taxi to the Philippine Embassy.

After their disappearance, Mansour needed replacements. He needed housemaids. This time, he decided to fly to the Philippines directly to make sure he found good employees. He flew to Manila and entered the offices of an overseas worker placement agency, where he announced: "I've totally had it with getting offered bad housemaids. I want two friendly, smiling girls—the kind who keep smiling even if you spit in their faces."

"Do you want them just for housework, or for bed, too?" asked the grinning agent.

"Both. Maybe I'll want a little variety, or my wife will have her period, or be pregnant, so I'll just grab one of the girls and it's off to bed. Why are you asking, anyway? All Saudis use their maids for housework and for sex."

"I'm asking because we have a shortage of really pretty girls available for bed. A nice-looking girl for housework and bed will cost you one hundred US dollars monthly," explained the agent.

"Prices have really gone up!" groaned Mansour. "I used to have a housemaid who was also for bed at fifty dollars."

"Yes, you're right. Prices are up. And, like I told you, for bed costs more. You Saudis and other Gulf Arabs have really turned the girls off. You're neither good employers nor humane lovers. You guys treat the girls like shit."

"Not in my house. My wife and I have always treated our maids well. We just had the bad luck to always employ bad maids. They just up and left, and we found ourselves with no one to do the work," complained Mansour.

"You yourself know that's not true. A girl doesn't just 'take off' if she's well treated and safe; she runs away because she's treated badly. Didn't you say earlier, 'I want a girl who keeps smiling, even if I spit in her face?'" asked the agent, who was now truly angry.

"Oh, come on, that was just a joke. . . . Tell you what—I'll take two girls and a chauffeur. How much? Will I get a discount?"

"A one-hundred-dollar monthly salary for each of them. And a five-hundred-dollar agency fee."

"Give me a discount!" whined Mansour.

"Okay. Instead of a five-hundred-dollar agency fee, I'll make it four hundred dollars. But not a cent less." And he actually stood his ground.

SERVITUDE THAT ENDS IN STARVATION OR STONING

Throughout the stories that I have related so far, we can track a persistent trend: those who are of inferior status in Saudi Arabia are subject to the most danger at the whims of those in power. This is especially true of those who are in positions of servitude.

Masoud, a forty-year-old Pakistani tailor, came to Saudi Arabia to work. He left seven family members behind in his native village, not far from Karachi. His place of employment was arranged by a labor agency. In order to receive a work permit for Saudi Arabia, he had to prepay a Saudi agent the equivalent of twenty thousand riyals, which is equal to more than five thousand US dollars. For him, this was a horrific fee; he would have had to work for five full years in Pakistan to earn that much money. Not surprisingly, he didn't have that much, so he sold his house and the piece of farmland on which his family relied. His family moved in with his brother's family and became totally dependent on what Masoud would earn in Saudi Arabia. Even after the sale of his property, Masoud still didn't have the required amount, so he took out loans. The entire family hoped for a better future based on Masoud's success in the "golden land."

Masoud had been promised "milk and honey" in Riyadh. Furthermore, as a Muslim, he regarded Saudi Arabia as the center of his religious world. The prophet Muhammad had been born there; his "brothers in Islam" lived there. He was certain that he would be able to depend on their help and human kindness.

His employment agent, Saud, a forty-year-old midlevel manager, picked up Masoud at Riyadh's airport. Saud didn't do this as a gesture of kindness; he did this only because he was obliged to personally sign Masoud's entry papers for the Ministries of the Interior and Exterior. The papers stated that he was "importing labor goods"—that is to say, Masoud.

Masoud's first real introduction to his "golden" life in Saudi Arabia came when they left the airport. The afternoon temperature was over 110 degrees in the shade, and the sun beat down like a hammer. Saud instructed Masoud to jump into the open back of his pick-up truck for the ride into the city. He had asked Masoud if he had friends or contacts in Riyadh. "I do, but I don't know their addresses," he said.

"Don't worry about that—no problem," Saud replied, thinking to himself that Masoud would do just fine sleeping in the back of the tailor's shop.

After a long drive, they stopped at a small store outside the city itself. "Masoud, this is where you will live and work," Saud told him as he tumbled out of the back of the boiling hot pick-up. Masoud was given a key by Saud. He opened the door and went inside. It was a very shabby place and full of dust. Inside was a Singer sewing machine, a table, two chairs, and three shelves. Behind the store was a very small room. In the middle of this back room was a mattress, and in the corner there was a hot plate, a cooking pot, a metal teapot, and two glasses.

Deeply disappointed, Masoud lay down on the mattress and fell asleep.

The next morning, Saud brought him a big order: material was to be sewn into sixteen traditional Saudi gowns of various sizes. "You'll have to get this done quickly," he said before he left. Anxious to make a good impression, Masoud worked fifteen hours a day and sweated more than he ever had in his life because the shop had no air-conditioning. He even worked on Friday, the traditional day of rest for Muslims.

At the end of his first month, Masoud was not paid, and he had already spent the small amount of money he had brought from Pakistan for food and an enormous amount of drinking water. "You'll get paid next month," said Saud. Masoud had no idea what he should do to stay alive. Fortunately, he had met some Pakistanis who worked in the neighborhood, and they sometimes were able to share their food with him.

For "security reasons" Saud held Masoud's passport and his return airline ticket. It is a common practice throughout the Gulf region, whether the employer is operating publicly or privately, to keep all the passports of foreign workers locked up in a safe. But Saud also kept Masoud's work papers and his residency permit. If the police questioned him, Masoud would be expected to produce these papers or face imprisonment. There he would stay for several days until the matter was cleared up, a process that only moved very slowly through the swamp of Saudi bureaucracy. Because he had no papers of any kind, Masoud could leave neither the city nor the country.

Seven months passed, and Masoud had not been paid. He had heard that only the governor of Riyadh could help him. In truth, Prince Salman was the highest authority in the region. There was no legal system in place (in the Western sense), and certainly there were almost no labor laws at all. In any dispute between a local and a foreigner, the governor usually ruled in favor of the Saudi party, and if the dispute was between Saudis, he ruled in favor of the party from the more powerful family. As a rule, individuals with the most connections and influence won the case. If the feuding parties couldn't reach—or didn't want to reach—the governor himself, the matter would be solved by the local police according to the same pattern. That meant that foreigners and citizens from less powerful Saudi families had no chance of getting justice. But Masoud disregarded the facts and went directly to the governor's palace.

And there he was arrested for not carrying his legal papers. After three months behind bars, he received his passport and the return portion of his airline ticket. He was returned to Pakistan, penniless.

Masoud wasn't Saud's only victim; Saud also abused and mistreated his family maid, Viola. She was a young girl from India who lived a hell on earth during the two years she danced attendance on Saud's seventeen family members. She was on call twenty-four hours a day and was treated like a slave. Masoud got off lightly in comparison to Viola.

Viola was stoned to death for a crime she didn't commit.

She had worked in the following situation. Saud lived under one roof with his two wives and fourteen children, who were aged between one and twenty years. The two wives, Budur and Shuruq, hated each other passionately. Jealousy and intrigue were a part of everyday life. They lived, of course, in separate apartments inside the house—each wife had her own living room, kitchen, bathroom, and bedrooms—but they fought incessantly, usually over small matters. Viola was embroiled in a dilemma. She had to eavesdrop on both wives and fulfill all the children's wishes. It was an insoluble conflict of interest.

In two years, Viola didn't get a single day off. She was constantly busy. At bedtime, just after she fell asleep, a family member would often wake her up and demand assistance. During the night, she had to get up several times, either because of the children, the two wives, or Saud, who often came home very late. He usually arrived home at close to two o'clock in the morning and expected a hot meal. Viola had to cook him meat and rice because he refused to eat the warmed-up leftovers from the previous evening. As far as Saud was concerned, a meal that was over an hour old should be thrown out. Viola often found herself doing many tasks at one time: cooking Saud a meal, looking after the children's needs—feeding them, washing them, dressing them—and dealing with the demands of the two wives.

Budur and Shuruq were a bigger problem than the children. Because they were so jealous of each other, when one ordered a cup of tea, the other ordered the same. When Budur ordered orange juice, Shuruq ordered orange juice. Just as Viola would start to clean Shuruq's apartment, Budur would call out, "Viola! You have to clean my side of the house first!"

Shortly afterward, Shuruq would shout, "Viola, where have you disappeared to? Get over here and finish cleaning, damn it all!" This continued day after day, week after week, month after month.

All the family members expected Viola to do what they wanted immediately, and when she wasn't prompt enough, she was hit. They treated her like an unfeeling, soulless machine. Often she wished that she were a machine because when a machine breaks down it is ignored or else taken in for repairs. No one realized that Viola could be sick, feel tired, or want to quit and return to her home.

In the two years of her servitude, Viola never heard the words "please" or "thank you." All she heard were orders: "Come," "Go," "Bring," "Do." No one smiled at her; and despite the family's dependence on her, Viola was treated like an enemy within the household. No one ever talked to her or discussed anything with her. For two solid years, she didn't have a conversation with anybody. She ended up having conversations with herself inside her own head. She wrote to her family, and Saud promised to take her letters to the post office, but instead he tossed them into the trash. She didn't dare to ask him if he had mailed them. She also didn't receive any letters. Her family had indeed written to her, but the letters never reached her. As time passed on with no genuine communication, Viola became downhearted, depressed, and deeply homesick. She degenerated into a spiritual dullness in which she was capable of only one wish: to die.

Viola was a Hindu, and she had begged all the gods of her religion to help her. Just as with her undelivered letters, there had been no response. So she converted to Islam and prayed five times a day like Budur and Shuruq. She hoped that the new religion would help her and that she would be treated with more respect by her employers. She now stood behind one of the two wives at each prayer time and made the same body movements. She didn't know the words of the prayers from the Qur'an, so she substituted Hindu texts. The only profit of her conversion was the five tiny, five-minute-long rest periods that she was now granted each day, when she was allowed to pray. Shuruq and Budur continued to cuff her ears and scream insults at her if she was slow.

The women themselves had nothing to do, but they waited impatiently for Viola to deal with each task. Both of them became fatter and fatter. They barely moved. Each of them sat in her living room with visiting friends and shouted, "Viola, do this . . . Viola, each of my guests needs this . . ."

In contrast to the wives, Viola became petite and fragile, almost reduced to skin and bones. Nevertheless, she continued to work like a horse. She was responsible for providing family support for nineteen family members back in Bihar, India: thirteen sisters and brothers, her parents, and her grandparents. Furthermore, she was expected to pay the equivalent of three thousand US dollars to the village feudal lord, a greedy exploiter who claimed he had brokered her overseas job. If she didn't pay up, her family would be obligated to work his fields for ten years without pay. In the two years she had been working for Saud, Viola had received only two hundred US dollars in pay, and she had sent all of it home.

Viola was often sick but was careful not to show it. One time her illness was very bad. She had sharp pains in her stomach and could barely stand. The two wives, as well as the children, were shouting her name in aggrieved, angry voices, while Viola sat on the kitchen floor, crying, and barely able to get to her feet.

Suddenly Miteb, Saud's nineteen-year-old son, burst into the kitchen. "What are you doing in here, you whore? I've been calling and calling you—why don't you answer?" He kicked her and dragged her to her feet by her hair. She should have brought his dinner to the living room.

"Sir, I'm sick. I can't do anything anymore," she implored in a weak voice and then threw up.

Miteb went to his mother and complained, "The maid is probably sick. She threw up and made a mess in the kitchen. It's most unappetizing."

"Well, then, please take her over to the hospital. She has to get treated quickly because we need her here at home; we don't have a substitute. Your father will be home soon, so I'll have to prepare something for him. Drive her to the hospital as fast as you can."

"Okay, but you tell her to get into the car," mumbled Miteb.

Budur went into the kitchen, stood in front of Viola, and observed: "Well, it looks like you're sick. This is a shitty situation. Who's going to do the housework? Stand up! Miteb will take you to the doctor." Then she left.

Viola pulled together all her strength and, with the help of a stool, got to her feet. Slowly she made her way toward the car. Miteb drove her to the hospital, and she was very glad to see that her doctor was also Indian. He smiled at her and treated her with respect. It had been so long since anyone had smiled at her. He gave her courage and strength. After the examination, he told her, "There's nothing wrong with you except a vitamin deficiency. You need to eat vegetables and fruit, and you also will need a lot of rest. But I know how hard you have to work as a housemaid. That's the way it is, here in the 'promised land.'" Tears rose to Viola's eyes, and she gave the doctor a grateful look, but didn't dare to respond. He put some boxes of medicine into her hands and gave her an Indian farewell. She left the examination room with small, slow steps.

"See?" said Miteb. "It was nothing. You already look better."

"Thank you, sir," said Viola.

In the parking lot, Miteb asked her, "Do you have a husband back in India?"

"No, sir," she replied and got into the backseat.

"Then you've really missed something. There's nothing nicer in the whole world than sleeping with a man. You're sick because you don't have sex." And he leered at her in the rear-view mirror. Viola dropped her head and stared at the floor.

Miteb didn't drive in any direction that would take them to the house. Viola had a strange feeling that he wanted to do something before they went home—maybe buy something or run an errand. But she was afraid to ask to him. Then she noticed that they were already outside of the city. Suddenly overcome with fear, she said, "Sir, we are almost out in the open desert. Have you lost your way? Is there something you need out here?"

"That's for sure!" he laughed in reply, in a loud and malicious voice. "I intend to have some fun with you!"

Viola was so confused and frightened that she didn't get the hint. She wondered if the teen intended to get out of the car and play some kind of game. She looked out of the window and saw nothing but a vast expanse of sand. It was windy. Here and there little whirlwinds of dust rose into the air. Miteb drove the car some distance off the road, parked it, and threw himself on Viola like a wild animal.

She didn't have a chance. She was weak and helpless.

On the way home, Miteb gave Viola her instructions. She was to tell no one about the "incident." Otherwise, he would rape her again or maybe kill her. Anyway, nobody would put the blame on him, and she would be stoned to death. Viola was overcome by panic and fear. Back at home, Miteb coolly informed his family that Viola had just had some kind of little stomachache. So—back to work.

A few weeks later, Viola realized that she was pregnant. She was certain that she would be punished with death. She knew no one would believe that Miteb had raped her. Viola decided to give notice to Saud and return home to India or to flee to the safety of her embassy. When she considered all the money that Saud still owed her and the needs of her family, Viola decided to take her chances and give Saud notice of her decision to leave.

One day when Saud was at home she gently and clearly informed him that she had decided to return to India.

"That's out of the question. What do you need? Money? Here's one hundred dollars. You'll get the rest of your pay in a few days."

"Sir, I'm really very sick. I need to go home to my family and get some rest. When I feel better, I promise that I'll come back."

"That's out of the question," replied Saud, and he left the room.

Viola decided to try it from another angle. Women were usually more sympathetic to other women than men. "Why don't I just tell Budur, Miteb's mother, the truth? Maybe she'll feel sorry for me and find a way to get permission to send me home."

"What's this? What do you want?" demanded Budur as she slurped a tall glass of juice, not even looking at Viola.

"Please, Madam, I'm sick, and I need to take a leave from work. I'll go home to India and come back as soon as I recover. And I'll never forget your kindness."

"Forget it. We don't have another housemaid. Tell you what . . . just work for me and my family. You don't need to have anything to do with Shuruq and her damned kids. Anyway, how many times have I told you this? Can't you figure out that that means less work?"

"Yes, Madam, but Shuruq's family is also Saud's family, and he won't allow that."

"Well, I guess that's your problem."

"Madam," said Viola, and she began to tremble, "I'm pregnant."

"What! You're pregnant? From whom? From Saud?"

"No, Madam; from your son Miteb."

"You whore—how dare you insult my son! You filthy alley cat. Get out of this room. I'm calling the morality police."

Viola threw herself at Budur's feet and begged her not to call the Mutawas. "Please, Madam! This is the truth! Ask your son!"

"I don't need to ask my son. You're a liar."

Budur thought about the situation for a few moments and decided to consult Saud. "Go—get to work. I'll ask Saud what he wants to do."

"Oh, thank you, Madam; thank you, Madam; thank you. I always knew that you have such a kind heart." And Viola kissed Budur's feet.

That evening, Budur spoke to Saud about Viola's pregnancy. In her opinion, Viola should be criminally charged for daring to implicate Miteb, her favorite son. Saud thought differently. He was sure that Miteb had raped Viola, and that the religious police would give their son a hard time. "And furthermore, what will the neighbors say if they see the morality police visiting our home? You know how they talk—especially the women. No—from now on, let's give it out that we intend to let Viola return to India."

During the night, Viola could barely sleep. Her stomach hurt, and the fact that she was pregnant filled her with disgust and fear. She was terrified that Budur would make good on her threats and call the morality police. That would be her end. She knew that illegitimate pregnancies were punished in Saudi Arabia by death.

The next morning, after the men had left the house, she packed a few items of clothing and decided to flee to the safety of her embassy; perhaps they could help her. Budur and Shuruq were still fast asleep. Viola bundled herself into her abaya and swathed her face with her black headscarf so that no one would notice that she wasn't a Saudi. She quietly left the house and got into a taxi. Suddenly she had a shock of panic; she didn't have her passport—Saud kept it locked up. She consoled herself with the hope that her embassy could issue a substitute.

The so-called "diplomatic quarter" of Riyadh looked like a fortress; the Saudi police had checkpoints at every entrance, where they scrutinized everyone's identity papers. Housemaids were strictly controlled because most were attempting to flee to the safety of their embassies. The name and telephone number of a maid's employer was on her identity papers. A policeman would simply dial the number and ask the employer if his maid had created any problems for him and if she had his permission to visit her embassy.

Viola had to show the policeman her identity card. He phoned the house, and Budur picked up. Budur attested that Viola had run away.

Viola was dragged into a police van and taken to the local station. She would have to be retrieved by her employer personally. Viola begged and begged the police to take her home; she promised that she would never try to run away again. They screamed at her to shut up because a soccer match was playing on television.

When Saud came home, Budur was waiting for him, impatient and furious. "Why didn't you listen to me? The whore ran away! She deserves the worst of all possible punishments, Saud!"

"What has happened? Calm down and explain yourself!" he replied.

Budur explained the situation. She told him to pick Viola up from the station and drive her immediately over to the morality police. Saud went to get her, slapped her across the head a couple of times, and did exactly what Budur had requested. He told the Mutawas that she had slept with a strange man and was now pregnant. The station chief took the report and immediately determined that, in accordance with Islamic Shari'a law, Viola should be stoned to death as soon as the baby was born.

Saud was praised for his worthy and responsible actions as a Muslim. They then asked how they could ascertain the identity of the man who had impregnated Viola. Saud said he was sorry, but he had no idea. Viola was then fetched from her cell and asked to identify the father of the baby. She named Miteb, Saud's son. Infuriated, Saud slapped her again on the sides of her head and accused her of lying. The police chief calmed him down and said, "Don't worry—I also believe that she's lying. And anyway, remember that according to Islamic law the testimony of a woman is worth half as much as the testimony of a man."

AWAD

S o far, we have tracked the perilous corruption and harsh religious traditions that can be found in the Saudi education system, on the streets, in employment, and even in the marriage bed. The life story of Awad and his family brings together all of these aspects and shows how even Saudi nationals are subject to these dangers.

The sky is gloomy, tense, covered with menacing, black clouds. The icy wind is as unpredictable as a furious madman—sometimes it blasts from the north, sometimes from the south. But still it doesn't rain. The people below on the huge, infertile, salt-laced plain respond to the weather. They become moody and easily angered but cannot release their emotions with tears. Instead, they wander about, constantly moving in the slow round of their daily tasks, forcing their stiff legs, step by step. Faleh is one of them. Overcome by memories of his lost brother and his family's horrific suffering, he is rendered lame, dumb, wordless, and silent.

Faleh doesn't know if his older brother, Awad, who disappeared five years ago, is alive or dead. Almost everyone believes that he is dead. But because his body was never returned for a proper burial, it is generally believed that his soul is floating above them, unreleased, in torment. Everyone who knew his family claims to feel Awad's disturbed and disturbing presence.

When Awad "disappeared," he was in his early forties and had risen to the rank of officer in the Saudi army. In dictatorial regimes, the "disappearance" of individuals is often "normal procedure." The dictator and his cronies arrange for their "removal" simply because the dictator will not and cannot enter into dialogue with anyone critical of his policies. Saudi Arabia is ruled under a king and a vast network of princes who believe—conveniently—that they rule the country with the full blessing of Allah. Yet the cruelty of the Saudi regime boggles the imagination.

The modern world has known many dictators, from Chile's Pinochet and Uganda's Idi Amin to Iraq's Saddam Hussein. But compared to Saudi Arabia's dictators, these leaders pale into mild-mannered gentlemen. In their countries, Chile, Uganda, and Iraq, foreign correspondents could find ways to file critical press reports. On the other hand, a reporter based in Saudi Arabia is carefully blocked from obtaining or exposing anything negative about the existing regime. And because no information is available to the outside world, the world turns away in disinterest.

One of Awad's close friends and life companions, who first met him when they attended the Qur'an school together as children, told me Awad's story.

Awad wasn't politically active. That doesn't mean, of course, that he was apolitical. But he was not a committed opponent of the regime—otherwise, he never would have been accepted into the military academy. Privately, among muttering and disaffected friends, he would always repeat that it was important for Saudis to have patience with their government. That their country could only be modernized step by step, and democracy would only be achieved in time. Otherwise, everything would implode, like Iran when it faced the radical reforms imposed by its shah.

"Remember," Awad used to say, "our country is only forty years old!" We held him in great respect; he was our idol, our role model. After all, he had learned to read and write. He could actually read books. He could read newspapers. He even came up with his own ideas.

Awad's father, his father's friends, and his grandfather disapproved of his forthright philosophizing. Such discussions filled them with fear. His eighty-year-old grandfather could still vividly recount how the soldiers of the house of al-Saud had put down the popular uprising in Hayel, in northern Saudi Arabia. Anyone who moved had been shot. The survivors had been rendered docile, but they never forgot that brutal attack. Not in a lifetime. But to protect the ignorant and overconfident younger generation, they avoided the subject and sternly advised against any criticism of the regime. The idea of another attack filled the older generation with terror. They never wanted to experience such suffering and loss again.

But, sometimes, unapproachable history found its way to us when we sat around the campfire in the evenings. As I recall, a steaming hot cup of cardamom-flavored coffee was passed from hand to hand, and each man took a small sip. Musa, a fine musician, used to play his rababa—a folk instrument similar to a violin, but with only one string. It was amazing how many melodies and the depth of melancholic feeling that simple instrument could produce. Ah, Musa. He also "disappeared."

When Musa would sing, "O, oppressor, the day of your downfall approaches!" the tears of Awad's grandfather would trickle awkwardly down over the creases of his face and into his grey beard. He would rub them away from his cheeks with his fist and mumble, "I have become an old man." Then he would complain that he had a head cold . . . because desert Arabs don't cry.

Like all Bedouins, Awad was born in his parents' tent. It was pitched in the countryside near Hayel. At that time, the country's oil reserves had just been discovered.

The region around Hayel is forbidding, God-forsaken, and completely ringed by craggy, dead mountains. Grass and a few scattered thistle bushes grow there infrequently, and only in the spring. This is, however, enough to meet the needs of the animals. Over the course of many centuries, sheep, donkeys, and camels have learned to be as frugal as the human beings who live there.

The day before Awad's birth brought wintry weather: a thunderstorm. According to Bedouin beliefs, this was a good omen. Later, Awad's grandfather explained to me: "Our happiness was doubled. God bestowed a boy on us and brought grazing for the livestock. We needed both to survive in such a meager environment."

Like many other Bedouins at that time, Awad's parents lived a nomadic existence, wandering from place to place in search of food for their animals. They owned a herd of sheep and three camels. The camels carried the family's belongings: a tent; a pair of mattresses; pots for cooking and for preparing coffee.

Life was precarious. Proper medical care or even access to midwives was completely unavailable. A sick person would be very lucky if a natural healer happened to be in the vicinity. Every pregnant woman delivered her child assisted only by older women. Awad's mother lost three children at birth. Surviving newborns were dried with sand and swaddled in a sheepskin. Water was needed for drinking; it was much too precious to waste on bathing. Westerners might actually consider the children who didn't make it the lucky ones. Daily survival in such a forbidding natural environment demanded excruciating endurance and endless physical work.

Eventually, Awad's father, Salem, decided they should live in a small settlement called Shaqra. Like most Saudi villages, it had no electricity, no running water, and no medical care—not that Bedouins in that region had ever seen an electric line, a water tap, or a stethoscope. Such places were comfortless, bleak, and inhospitable. They were only reachable by bumpy, horribly neglected roads. The government had little concern for people in rural areas. In contrast, the wealth of the country was concentrated and lavishly displayed in the big cities of Riyadh and Jeddah, where first-rate hospitals were established, fully equipped with the most modern and expensive medical equipment; wide streets were engineered and properly paved; and tons of topsoil were dumped to create parks and green belts, which, in turn, ceaselessly consume millions of gallons of water.

Salem was a small, wiry man who toiled from the break of dawn until late at night with the flocks he shepherded. He was self-confident in acts of generosity, but socially quite shy. Since talking was an effort for him, he deemed it mainly unnecessary. He seldom revealed any emotion.

His wife, Fatima, was a thoughtful and caring person, quite incapable of doing harm to others. Awad spoke about her with great respect. She had to work hard and haul water from long distances. The jar of water and the firewood that she brought home daily after many miles of walking—just like all the other women—weighed more than she did. Her life belonged to her family; she had no concept of personal rights. She had little opportunity to use the word "I." She almost exclusively looked after her husband, her children, the meals, and the milking of the animals. Hard work and self-denial are extolled to this day as special virtues of the Saudi mother. Self-sacrifice is emotionally intertwined with personal honor, so that the more a woman can do for her family, the prouder she becomes. And she is raised to believe that her husband is the unconditional guardian and head of the family.

Fatima also had to look after her father-in-law, who lived with them. He was her uncle and, in her mind, a stepfather, since her own father had died when she was a child. Her mother had remarried a stranger. In any case, like all Bedouin mothers, daughters, and sisters, Fatima was not considered worthy of much notice. Her father-in-law always used to say with a laugh that women were the family treasure—and therefore should be hidden from sight in the back of the tent. One day, Awad shot back sharply, "Treasure is supposed to be cared for, Grandfather, but my mother is worked to the bone."

Awad was the oldest of four brothers and six sisters. He was lively, alert, and curious by nature. At the age of four, he decided that he wanted to be an adult, so he tried to imitate the gait and mannerisms of the old men. Everyone was reduced to laughter by his antics. When wedding feasts were held, he enthusiastically sang and danced for hours. He was a plucky and adventurous child. But, when he was still only a boy, he also felt responsible for his family. He often relieved his father of the supervision of the animals. By the age of ten, he could slaughter sheep and tame camels.

Schools, in the modern sense of the word, did not exist at that time; there were merely Qur'an schools in a few cities. At any rate, shepherds' sons didn't attend Qur'an schools because they were needed for physical labor. School was also out of the question because Bedouins were nomadic. In order to fulfill the obligations of prayer, they learned corrupted verses from the Qur'an, sometimes entirely transposed into Bedouin dialect, from their parents. Becoming literate was considered a waste of time and effort.

After all, a few memorized Qur'anic verses could be used to cure illnesses and solve daily problems. There were no signposts to read in the desert, and a wristwatch was unnecessary: they told time by the position of the sun and learned the four points of the compass from their fathers. There were no borders or property lines to observe, as the desert's scant resources were shared and no one took more than what he needed.

When Awad was ten years old, he accompanied his father for the first time to Hayel, the capital of the region, to sell a few sheep. The transactions went well, and the animals were sold at a good price. The demand for meat had jumped considerably, since many well-heeled government officials were being newly posted to outlying towns to create administration and security systems. Awad and his father often traveled to Hayel to sell sheep. Then his father decided to pitch a tent on a piece of land in the regional capital so he wouldn't have to commute back and forth from Shaqra with his herd. The family continued to live in a larger tent in Shaqra, away from the bustle of Hayel, until Awad's father finally built a concrete block house on the land he had claimed out in Shaqra.

In Hayel, an active and serious market developed. It was a lively place, both day and night, as surprised donkeys, camels, goats, and sheep found themselves facing new owners. The shrill voices of the imams called the faithful to prayer from the minarets of each nearby mosque. A string of small, rundown stalls were erected and displayed the offerings of humble merchants in open sacks and carton boxes: coffee, cardamom seeds, saffron and other spices, rosewater from India. The shouts of the sellers advertising their goods rang out harshly into the square, blending with the bickering of the buyers and sellers negotiating a livestock sale.

In Hayel there were many mosques and also a Qur'an school. Like all Saudi boys, Awad went to a mosque with his father to pray. Books were stacked on a shelf there, but he had no idea what they were: he had never seen one in his entire life.

"What are these things?" he asked his father.

"Books. Copies of the Qur'an, our holy book," explained his father.

"What are these markings?" he asked.

His father answered, "Those are the words we use when we pray."

"Really? And how do you know that?" Awad demanded, incredulous and wide-eyed.

"I'm bigger than you, and I know more," his father replied with a grin.

Awad resolutely decided to decode the "marks," as he called the words and letters. After the evening prayers, he approached the imam and asked him how he could learn to read the Qur'an.

"Here, with me, in the Qur'an school next to this mosque. Actually, we are beginning our lesson just now. Would you like to see?" The imam was pleased to get another student. Awad, full of curiosity and excitement, accompanied the imam into an adjoining room where numerous students, including me, had already gathered. We were sitting on the bare floor before carefully placed open books, reading verses of the Qur'an aloud. It sounded like the buzzing of a beehive. After our lesson, we would neatly stack the holy books on the floor in a spotlessly clean corner.

That was where I first met Awad and got to know him because he happened to sit down next to me. As the days passed, we became friends. Best friends. We played together and had our boyish adventures together.

The room was the entire school: thirteen feet long, ten feet wide, and built from lime and straw. There were two holes in the wall: one for a door, and the other for a window. The imam had asked a carpenter in the town to frame in a window and door for him as a donation. The carpenter had previously paid fees for his son to attend the school, but in his opinion the boy had learned nothing from the imam. So he refused to do the work. The imam had cursed the carpenter and implored Allah to send him to hell.

In the heat of the summer, we enjoyed sitting on the flagstone floor, but during the winter we brought little cushions to keep away the cold. Every evening, over forty pupils sat crammed together, reading by the light of kerosene lamps. And each evening, yet another skinny boy seemed to appear and squeeze out a place for himself. The reason was simple: the governor of Hayel, Prince Miqren, had decreed that every family in Hayel had to send at least one son to the school, and the family had to pay the imam with either money or food. For that reason, the imam's Friday sermon in the mosque always included high praise for the governor's great-heartedness, wisdom, vision, and charitable acts in the community.

Both of our fathers paid the imam with money for his teaching. He stood at the front of the class, declaimed a verse, and had us repeat it. There was one Qur'an for every two students. A lot of the time we didn't understand the meaning of what we were repeating. The most important thing was to be loud, which was a lot of fun; we tried to shout the words at the top of our lungs. A number of boys had already memorized large sections of the Qur'an. We also had lessons in writing, for which we were given small black slates and pieces of chalk. The boys who couldn't pay for these came up with an ingenious solution. They brought a broken piece of black pottery from home and collected a supply of small white pebbles, which were found everywhere around our desert homes. During writing lessons, they copied the letters with the pebbles on the black background.

Even as children, we all wore the floor-length, traditional, woolen, Saudi dress. We were not allowed to let even a fragment of chalk fall onto the ground, and no child was ever to step on a piece of chalk, but it got into the folds of our clothing. At the end of our lesson, we carefully scrambled to our feet with our long gowns gathered in front of us. We toddled over to a specific corner of the room and carefully shook any chalk fragments off onto the floor. Then we had to wash the chalk off our slates and pottery fragments into specific buckets of water. All this was done with great care, because chalk that had been used to copy the words of Allah was blessed and had great power. Before we left for home, the water in the buckets was divided among the pupils. Each one of us had brought a small pot to carry the water home, where it was given to the livestock to drink. We believed that the blessed water would increase their fertility.

During the lessons, the imam sat on a narrow mattress. He kept a long stick in his hand, and any child who made a mistake was hit on the head. From time to time, we took a break because the imam went to a neighboring room. There he would stuff his mouth full with the food that his pupils had brought from home. He was enormously fat, and he usually reappeared from his meal with grains of rice stuck in the corners of his mouth, which he would whisk away with a corner of his headscarf. Once, Awad told him that the small white grains of rice were surely as blessed as the chalk fragments and shouldn't be allowed to fall to the floor. For that impertinence, he got a blessed punishment: one hour in the burning sun with his hands extended over his head.

Every evening after sunset, Awad and I would walk to the Qur'an school together. He was so curious and hardworking that he learned to read and write within three months. He was much cleverer than I was. He seemed to retain everything the first time he learned it. Because he could link ideas and concepts easily, soon he was able to read newspapers. He got them from the local government workers, who were provided with them from Riyadh as part of their isolation benefits. These officials were customers of Awad's father, who regularly sold them a sheep or goat to be slaughtered for dinner. Amused by Awad's interest, they usually appeared to make a livestock purchase with a copy of an old newspaper tucked under one arm. Awad was thrilled to get a paper and read every word of every article, not missing a page.

Reading the Qur'an and the newspapers led Awad to many questions, to issues and ideas he didn't understand. He would always try to get answers, but seldom got a satisfactory reply. Our teacher at the Qur'an school was particularly annoyed because Awad would point out the differences between the expectations for human behavior expressed in the Qur'an and the reality he saw practiced in our daily lives in Hayel. This contrast really disturbed Awad. He also couldn't understand why men and women weren't equal. I was with Awad one day when, standing in the shadow of the mosque on a hot afternoon, he asked the imam if the pupils could bring their sisters to school with them to study the Qur'an. The imam cuffed him on the ear and shouted, "You shouldn't be making such a dumb suggestion. It is sinful."

"Why, esteemed teacher? Allah says in the Qur'an that women should learn to read, too," retorted the boy courageously.

The imam quickly interrupted. "Women should learn the Qur'an at home. Muslim women don't show themselves to men, they keep silence in the presence of men, they never sit with men. Do you understand?"

"I read in a book that women in the time of our prophet Muhammad fought by the side of men and also did business with them face to face," continued Awad.

"That's total garbage. Our women belong in the house, and that's the end of it." The imam then ordered Awad to go out into the sun and stand for two hours on one leg with his hands lifted up. This was, in no way, his first and only punishment.

Our religious teachers were very conservative and dogmatic. They followed traditional modes of thinking and wouldn't modify their thoughts—ever. They didn't approve of questions, and they didn't approve of discussions. The al-Saud regime encourages this rigid approach to religion. For instance, our women were not forced to veil their faces until after the al-Sauds came into power. The religious fanatics the al-Sauds allied themselves with forced all Saudi women to veil themselves.

Two years later, the government built an elementary school. One of the teachers at the new school often bought a sheep from Awad's father. Over time, Awad became friendly with him. The teacher noticed that he was academically bright, so he brought him a set of free elementary school books. Awad was overjoyed.

Independently, with only occasional help from the teacher, Awad mastered the elementary school curriculum, and, within a year, he took the official final exams. Four years later, having worked full-time with his father during the days and without attending a school at all, he successfully wrote his secondary school graduation exams.

Awad wanted to continue his studies; however, there was no university in the region where he lived. Riyadh and Jeddah were too far away, too expensive. His family needed him to remain close by. The only alternative was the military academy in Hayel. He applied and was accepted. Leaving his family to go live in a barracks was very difficult for Awad. His grandfather, who was very attached to him, took his absence very hard.

Only after the initial three months of basic training did Awad return home to Shaqra for his first visit, wearing his sharp, clean, well-pressed uniform and looking very different. His hair was cut short, he was slim and strong, and he carried himself with self-assurance. He brought something his family had never seen: a Polaroid camera. Awad made a snap of his grandfather, and a minute later peeled the developed print from its backing. Awad's grandfather had never seen a photograph, but he had seen himself in a mirror. As Awad held the snapshot up to him, the elderly man began to adjust his headdress, claiming that he looked like an ape. He thought it was a mirror and couldn't understand why the image in the photo didn't change. Awad's sisters demanded to be photographed, but they wanted to be fully veiled. When they viewed the photo a minute later, they burst into laughter. They all looked the same and could be distinguished only by their different shoes.

The whole family was proud of Awad's sharp uniform. The Bedouins like anything military, anything associated with battle. Their traditions include many legends in which victories over their enemies are praised—legends of heroes who fight and die to preserve the honor of their ancestors. Not only his family, but the entire neighborhood as well, received Awad with enthusiasm, song, and dance. A party was organized. Relatives and neighbors came to the feast, and over twenty sheep were slaughtered. At the beginning of the festivities, Awad was made to formally approach his parents' simple house. A sheep had its throat slit on the threshold, and he was obliged to leap back and forth over the pool of gushing blood. The Bedouins believe that this tradition brings good luck.

As the feast drew to a close, Awad's father announced to everyone that a bride had been found for his son: Sainab—one of Awad's first cousins—a sixteen-year-old girl whom the young soldier had never seen. Awad was so shocked that he was left completely speechless.

A Saudi husband and wife meet for the first time on their wedding night, in a state of great anticipation, suspense, and considerable dread. Young Bedouin men are taught to suppress their sexual feelings and desires. Discussing them openly is considered shameful, and sex is only discussed in the context of dirty jokes.

I myself remember well my own wedding. I had no idea how it would go, since I'd never seen a woman in my life, aside from my own mother and sisters. I had met my aunts, but they had been fully veiled. It was hard to even imagine sex with a woman. I didn't even know, in any exactitude, what a woman's body looked like. There I was, in bed with my bride, and I had no clear idea what to do. We didn't even know about kissing. Eventually I was led by my instincts into a totally unfamiliar and unimaginable, biologically driven and emotionally laden life experience. Modern young Saudis get to learn about such things by watching Western television shows. They see the shape of women's bodies and sometimes the actors kiss each other. But we didn't have access to such things.

Awad's wedding was held the following day. In accordance with Saudi tradition, it was another lavish affair for a huge number of guests.

In front of the house, camel hair tents had been pitched to accommodate the guests. One was for women and the other for men. Before their tent, the men performed dances with swords while singing songs of praise honoring Awad. Each man held his weapon aloft and waved it rhythmically while shuffling slowly in a long line. Inside the tents, coffee and dates were continuously served, and, later, an evening meal of mutton and camel meat. The women celebrated with songs and dances on their own. Only the bride's closest female relatives did not take part. They were, indeed, present, but had to pretend to be plunged into deep grief. It was important that they demonstrate that they were only allowing a worthy member of their family to be snatched away with great reluctance. This "theatrical spectacle" was part of Bedouin tradition; anyone who didn't behave according to role would be offending the community's customs, and hence sharply criticized.

According to tradition, it was a perfect wedding. Just before sunset, Awad was led to his bride, who was waiting for him in the women's tent. His closest male relatives and friends accompanied him with dance and song, occasionally jostling and teasing him. Two men danced before him with their swords. Just before reaching the tent, according to tradition, Awad "escaped" his companions and continued toward the tent alone. A woman standing outside the tent lifted the entrance flap and quickly signaled to those inside to veil. When Awad reached her, she handed him a stick about six and a half feet long.

Once in the tent, Awad had to find his bride, who was hiding among the other women. With the tip of his walking stick, Awad poked gently at each veiled woman and asked if she were his bride. The woman was only allowed to respond "Right! Left! Go back!" or "Go forward!" amid much laughter and giggling. The traditional belief behind this game played at weddings in northern Saudi Arabia is that, the longer it takes the groom to find the bride, the more children they will have. When Awad finally found Sainab, she grabbed the other end of his stick with her right hand and didn't let go. He then led her alone into the marriage tent, which stood a few meters away from the women's tent. That was where their sexual union had to be consummated. The sooner it happened, the more potent and masculine was the groom. The men waited outside impatiently, wanting it over in a couple of minutes. Finally, Awad stretched his hand out of the tent to show off a small towel reddened by the blood of the deflowered virgin. It demonstrated that the marriage celebrations had been brought to a successful conclusion. The crowd of men outside the tent was jubilant, and some of them shot their guns off into the air.

After the wedding, Awad and his young wife lived with his parents. Sainab was quickly integrated into the family. She became close friends with one of his sisters and helped his mother with household tasks. The couple got their own room, which his father had previously built onto the concrete block house. Sainab had been raised to fear and respect men—especially her own husband. Awad would spend three days with her and then return to his military barracks. This didn't disturb her in the least. One house was like another to her. As a woman, she accepted that her responsibility was simply to do housework and stay indoors.

Awad had not evolved into a typical Bedouin. He was not authoritarian. He always repeated that, as far as he was concerned, all decent people deserved protection. For him, the family was sacred, and each of its members, even the weakest, merited respect. Unlike other men, Awad spent a lot of time with his wife during those three days, discussing their future, his military service, and his friends in the military. He loved to make plans. He also loved discussion and debate. He kept asking Sainab for her opinions.

After basic training, Awad was entrusted with learning various weapon systems. This schooling lasted nine months and was conducted by officers from Western allied countries, using the help of interpreters. In his spare time, he learned English and soon could forego their help a lot of the time. In contrast to most of his colleagues, who were lazy and unmotivated, Awad found military service interesting, often enthralling. Best of all, after completing the course he would be allowed to go home every weekend.

The graduation ceremonies were held two months after the course ended. The new officers, now experts in various weapon systems, stood at attention in rows on the military parade ground, looking very impressive. Their trainers were very proud. Then the arrival of the minister of defense was announced over the loudspeakers. A band struck up military marches that were quickly drowned out as all the assembled guests rose to their feet to honor him with ceaseless applause until he reached the honorary reviewing stand, which was bedecked with flowers. The minister was conducted to a huge, red armchair that resembled a throne. It sat on a Persian carpet. In front of the chair was a single, well-polished coffee table with an arrangement of fresh flowers on it.

The ceremony was opened with the recitation of Qur'anic verses. Then the band played the national anthem, and the official greetings were given. The chief of the military academy lauded the minister for his personal support of the academy and its members, as well as for his generosity in outfitting the army with the most modern weapons, phrased with so much emotion that it sounded like the minister had paid for it all out of his own pocket. The ceremony was not held to honor the graduates, but the minister of defense himself. Everyone had to express his undying gratitude because the training would not have taken place without his approval. He was repeatedly thanked for finding the time in his busy schedule to attend their humble ceremony, although everybody knew that actually he had a very hazy idea of what he was presiding over. The minister was always distracted by his thoughts about women. He divorced one of his wives every week and then married a new one. Gossip reported that some of those women had driven him insane; he was no longer capable of clear thought—that was the reason why he lurched through his official speeches and made very little sense.

The minister handed out the graduation certificates, which each officer received by bowing and kissing his hand. Finally, he read his official speech. In it, among other topics, the minister said: "Everyone here should be happy that God has given us the gift of Islam. Ours is the best religion to ever exist on earth, and our fortunate country is ruled according to the teachings of Islam and our prophet Muhammad, peace be upon Him. For that reason, we must protect Islam against the decadence of other religions like Christianity and Judaism. Christians and Jews, in fact, are our enemies, and we must fight them."

These passages were not translated into English for the trainers of these troops, who were Westerners from non-Muslim countries. Even the weapons themselves had been manufactured in Christian countries. The minister continued his speech with praise for the bravery and preparedness of the graduating soldiers, who were ready to die for Allah and the king.

Unfortunately, his words were more wishes than reality. Saudi soldiers, as well as their commanding officers, are poorly motivated. They receive promotions according to the whim or mood of the minister, or due to good connections with the ruling clan. For most Saudi soldiers, military service is luxuriously paid unemployment. For many generals, a gold mine. The fact that the Saudi army is quite unprepared for combat was painfully obvious during the Gulf War; the Western military alliance had to simply reject its illogical suggestions for battle strategy. Furthermore, if the Saudi army were to win a war in a neighboring country, it would simply occupy and annex the nation instead of establishing a protectorate or caretaker government.

Awad was now a fully trained officer and received a graduation bonus of ten thousand riyals (over 2,600 US dollars). With this money he bought a modest pick-up truck to help his family transport the sheep. He still lived with his wife in his parents' home and commuted to work each morning— a distance of fifteen and a half miles. Sainab gave birth to their first child, a son. Awad and his family were overjoyed; Sainab was relieved to be the mother of a boy because sons are the pride of every Arabian family, all of whom believe that sons cope better with life's vicissitudes.

Two years later, Awad was transferred to Riyadh to work in the Purchasing Department of the Ministry of Defense. First he made a brief trip to the city to rent an apartment and provide it with basic furnishings for his wife and son. Before the move, he tried to describe the city to Sainab.

"In Riyadh, the houses are built on top of each other."

"What?!" she exclaimed.

"They are called apartment buildings. You reach your own house by walking up a set of stairs that you share with everyone who lives there."

"I don't understand you, Awad."

"All right, all right. I'll let it be a surprise for you. You're going to see buildings with up to twenty stories. And instead of a stall in the *souq* [open-air market], there are these huge air-conditioned halls with high ceilings, filled with every kind of store. You can buy anything there, from a needle to large items of furniture, clothes, food, stuff for the baby—"

Sainab just stared at him. She wondered if Awad had gone mad. The look on her face annoyed him, so he continued.

"You won't be carrying water home on your head. Everything is already in the apartment. You'll open a tap in the kitchen, and water will come out. You'll touch a button on the wall, and the electricity will turn on. By that, I mean lights. Light from small round bulbs in the ceiling. In the kitchen, the gas will be in a big cylinder. You'll have to open the gas to make a fire on the stove when you want to cook."

"I don't understand you!"

"I have to tell you, Sainab, but you'll see it for yourself. You know about cars, we have a few cars and trucks up here. But in Riyadh there are cars all over the streets, constantly coming and going, and you have to be really careful when you cross a road. As for the people, well, they move fast. They're always in a hurry, not like here."

"So, Riyadh is really dangerous."

"Not at all! You'll be fine! And when I get a raise, I'll even get you a maid from India to help with the housework."

"Absolutely not! I don't want a strange woman living with us. If she is pretty, you will marry her."

"That's ridiculous! Marry an Indian housemaid? Anyway, you are the most beautiful woman I have ever met, and you're the mother of my son."

Awad's new job in the Purchasing Department allowed him to develop a bigger picture of both military and civil economic organization. His ever-active curiosity and natural intelligence couldn't let his duties stop with pen-pushing or approving purchase orders. He gradually realized that the Saudi princes had first assumed control of all branches of the economy and then scrupulously manipulated business and trade to maximize their personal advantage. They owned the biggest import firms, ruled the real estate market, and controlled the banking industry with breathtaking nepotism. Unnecessary business deals were made that benefited not only the princes themselves, but also high-ranking ministry officials, who received hidden "commissions." For instance, all the furniture in the Ministry of Defense building was changed almost every year. Unused weapons in mint condition—including tanks, rockets and their fittings—were often left to deteriorate, exposed to the summer desert sun in their original packing for months. Then they were exchanged for more modern systems. For the sons of the minister of defense, the arms industry proved to be extremely lucrative. Prince Ahmed, a son and the co-commander of the armed forces, is said to have personally profited during the Gulf War by more than seven billion dollars.

Prince Truki, a nephew of the king, specialized in the real estate market. In a private capacity, he bought huge tracts of land directly from the Saudi government and then resold them at incredibly inflated prices. He even bought a huge piece of property in northern Saudi Arabia, in Hayel itself, where Awad's father and others like him pastured their sheep and camels. The purchase was made from the state. Later, he sold it to the Minister of Defense for three hundred million dollars. Shortly afterward, the prince bought back the same property for a very low price. These transactions had been agreed upon beforehand by both parties; Prince Turki only wanted to put himself in a position where he could rent the pasture to the shepherds at high monthly rates since the land was now under private ownership. His ultimate goal, of course, was to drive the nomads off the land.

Awad's father and the other shepherds were furious. Animal husbandry had now become a profitless occupation. Competition from Turkey, New Zealand, and Australia was already a threat because another prince from the royal family was undercutting the economic welfare of his own people by importing sheep and camels.

Of course, Awad was also angry that the prince, using questionable methods, had thrown the shepherds' economic existence into a state of complete uncertainty. But his hands were tied. He was only a petty officer with a desk job, not a person who could take on a fight with the royal family. He took a couple of days off work and drove, with Sainab and their son, to Shaqra. While she visited with the family, he sat down to discuss the situation with the shepherds concerned. They met in the house of Awad's father. The older shepherds couldn't see any solution to the problem; they were depressed and discouraged. The idealistic younger men were determined to refuse to pay the exorbitant rental fees and maintain control of the grazing lands by force. Awad sought to placate them: "Come on, we are a modern country, and when problems occur they should be solved peacefully. The time when force was used is now part of the past. You shepherds have no idea how modern Riyadh is. People nowadays have become more civilized." None of those present contradicted him.

Awad decided to collect signatures on a petition. In his opinion, the best course of action was a letter of protest to the Minister of Defense signed by all the shepherds concerned. Over thirty shepherds supported this action. Awad's grandfather was against the idea and offered to visit Prince Miqren himself. "He will respect me and listen to my words, because I am an old man. He will cancel everything, including the rent!"

"Dear Grandfather, this country is no longer run on the basis of respect. We have to approach this in a more modern way," replied Awad impatiently. Then he sat down in a corner and wrote the petition. Then his younger brother, Faleh, wrote down the name of each shepherd. Because they were all illiterate, they "signed" by applying an inked fingerprint to the page.

Awad's father, Salem, was chosen by the shepherds to personally deliver the petition to the minister of defense. He traveled to Riyadh with his son, who had arranged an audience with the minister. Salem would have to enter the room alone, as Awad, an employee of the armed forces, could not risk accompanying him. The minister of defense, however, had more important tasks to attend to. He ordered the petition passed on to the governor of Hayel, Prince Miqren, although not without jotting down the remark that he should do "whatever he deemed necessary." Salem stayed on in Riyadh for two more days to visit with Awad.

He was amazed to find Riyadh full of strange, foreign people. "Who are they? Why are they here? How can we afford to feed them?"

"Father, these are guest workers from other countries. From other Arab lands, from India, from the Phillipines. People in Riyadh are rich now, they have money, and they don't like to work hard. Certainly, we can afford to feed them, Father! But they aren't happy because often they must work for months without getting paid. Sometimes their pay is stolen by their employers."

"That is un-Islamic," replied his father.

When Salem arrived home to Shaqra two days later, he saw a small crowd gathered outside his home: his sons, a few relatives, and neighbors. His youngest son, Ibrahim, ran to him and excitedly announced, "Father! Father! Some policemen have come to visit us. Should I serve them coffee?"

"Yes, of course. Tell them they are welcome, and bring them coffee." The father kissed his son and greeted the crowd. The neighbors whispered and looked concerned, since the presence of police usually signaled trouble. Three armed policemen were already standing at the door.

One of them announced: "His Highness, Prince Miqren, demands to see you." Salem was very happy, thinking that the prince had found a solution to the shepherds' problem. He invited the policemen into the house, but they refused to enter. They put Salem into a police vehicle and drove immediately to Hayel. There, Prince Miqren lived in a palace that was practically a fort and constantly guarded by armed soldiers. The huge courtyard of the castle consisted of lawns and trees that consumed most of the region's water supplies. No one in the area was allowed to build a fountain, in case its operation caused the palace's to run dry. The citizens of Hayel now had to walk long distances out into the countryside to fetch water for their families and livestock. Guest workers from Iraq and Jordan, however, sold water from tanker trucks in the city. Often the men of the older generation would exclaim, "In the past, this was unheard of. Water is a gift from God, and gifts are not for sale."

The palace glittered and shone in every corner. Salem thought he was in paradise. He removed his shoes and carried them under his arm. He felt it would be disrespectful to tread in dusty shoes on the beautiful marble floors and magnificent carpets. He crossed huge marble reception rooms with door handles of gold and sofas upholstered with pure silk. Salem was finally conducted into the audience hall of the prince. Before he entered, he straightened his clothes and his headdress; then he stepped slowly and hesitantly inside. His Highness Prince Miqren sat on a throne like an emperor from Roman times. For a couple of seconds, Salem thought he was seeing Allah in heaven. Smiling and bowing, he greeted the prince. His greeting was not acknowledged. With a severe manner and glowering eyes, the prince stared at Salem. Then his outstretched hand dangled the petition, like something distasteful, in the air before him. Furious, he demanded to know its meaning.

Stunned and shocked, Salem turned red, then took a deep breath. He said, "It is only a request to your Highness to help us who are poor . . ."

"Shut up, you old dog. You and the others who signed this have set yourselves against the authority of the state. You're going to get the experience of your life for this," interrupted the prince threateningly, and then turned to one of his officials. "Get rid of him! I don't want to see him again!"

The prince's reaction to the petition left Salem speechless. He stood motionless, not knowing what to do or say. An official pushed him out of the audience room.

"That was not Allah on his throne," mumbled Salem, wiping tears from the corners of his eyes with a corner of the cloth he wore as a head covering. "But the true Allah will help me. He is merciful."

A few hours later, Salem had still not arrived home. The family and the neighbors were worried. When he didn't return by midnight, two older neighbors and Awad's grandfather went to the police station to inquire. They were merely informed that Salem had made the prince very angry. That puzzled them, because he was a calm man who spoke little and respected Prince Miqren enormously. Awad's grandfather then decided on his original plan and proceeded alone to Prince Miqren's palace. At the gates, the palace guards abruptly repulsed him. The soldiers, who only spoke broken Arabic, were mercenaries from Somalia. Most of the princes employ only mercenaries, who carry out all orders with unquestioning tenacity.

Awad was alerted to the situation by telephone and drove directly to Hayel's police station. He received the same cryptic answer and was not allowed to either see or speak to his father. "What law has he broken, damn it?!" he screamed at the police chief.

"I really don't know," responded the official helplessly, after glancing around nervously.

I was with Awad in the police chief's office and reminded him that he had so often told us to have patience with the al-Sauds. That we were a young country. That it takes time to iron out problems. I forced him to calm down and think logically.

Awad called his boss in Riyadh. This man, a high-ranking officer in the Defense Ministry, really admired and respected his employee, and he promised to help. A short time later, he called back with this information: the prince had given orders that he was not to be disturbed. Anything beyond that could not be discussed on the phone.

Awad could do nothing but wait. So he drove to his parental home with Sainab and their son. There, he waited. Waited for the release of his father. The women assembled in the house—Awad's mother, his sisters, his wife, and various aunts—wept and prayed incessantly. In the meantime, most of the shepherds who had signed the petition gradually gathered there. They kept asking Awad what was happening, and what he was doing to help his father. A number of days passed, and little work was done. The shepherds sent their sons out to graze and protect the flocks.

One afternoon, a police car and a van returned to the small concrete block house. An officer entered the room in which the shepherds had gathered for relief from the heat of the day and asked for a copy of their petition. He noted down the names of those who had signed it and then ordered them to get into the police van: His Highness wished to speak with them. The shepherds were thrown into confusion. All the way to the palace in Hayel, they speculated at length why the prince was requesting this meeting.

There, the men were taken to a bunker on the palace grounds. It was a secret building; only a few people knew of its existence. Many palaces in Saudi Arabia are equipped with similar private jails. There, a prince can lock up anyone he chooses: male servants, housemaids, even attractive women. All the shepherds were forced down a flight of stairs and locked into dark underground cells.

Much later, a palace servant from the Sudan, Safwan, contacted us to share what he knew about the shepherds' experiences. His own brother had been falsely accused of sleeping with one of the prince's wives and put to death in that jail. Safwan had wanted to help them and to contact their families, but he was kept on call around the clock and couldn't get away from his duties without being observed.

At every opportunity, Safwan had brought the men water so they wouldn't die of thirst. Later, he described his encounters with Salem, as well as Salem's eventual meeting with the other jailed men. "Salem was sitting in a dark cell. Whenever he saw me, he would rise to his feet and beg for help. He cried like a small child . . . in my lifetime, I will never forget it. He implored loudly, 'Brother, I beg of you, help me! Get me out of here and home to my family! I don't want any land, I don't want any livestock, and I haven't broken any law. Please help me!' He would reach his hands through the bars, take hold of my arms, and wouldn't want to let go. He was totally despondent. When I gave him a bowl of water, he drank at once, as it was stuffy and humid down there. When the soldier who was guarding him stepped away for a moment, I promised him that I would inform his relatives. Unfortunately, I couldn't get a break from my work to do that. Every day I brought him water and tried to calm him down. During these visits, he repeatedly described his experience in the audience room with Prince Miqren. Every day his condition worsened, and he became both weaker and more resigned. But when the other men were brought into the prison, he gathered up his remaining strength. He stood up to embrace and kiss each of them. One older man wept aloud and shouted in anger, 'May Allah punish the oppressor. Allah will not leave us like this. Allah is great and merciful!' A soldier knocked this old man to the ground with the butt of his rifle, and he began to scream. As Salem bent down to comfort him, he received a kick on the back and on the head."

The princes of the house of al-Saud act quickly and decisively. There are no courts and no trials. When they notice that someone has criticized the regime for any reason or set himself up against their authority, that person is seen as a danger and quickly eliminated. Quick action is intended to terrify the oppressed and consequently make them afraid to question the authority of the state in any way.

In Saudi Arabia, Prince Miqren is well known for his brutality. He realized that Salem and his friends, in organizing a petition against the privatization of pasturelands, were the harbingers of what would become a larger opposition movement. The prince had always been mistrustful of the people who lived in that region. He and the al-Saud clan know that they are hated in the northern regions of their country. The Bedouins who live in the area that borders Iraq and Jordan consider themselves free men, and they regard the Saudis as an occupying force. Their ancestors led a rebellion when the al-Sauds first tried to establish domination over the region. In return, King Abdulaziz, the founder of Saudi Arabia, inflicted a genocidal defeat on the tribes of northern Arabia. The old people of the tribe still recount how soldiers of the house of al-Saud attacked the al-Shimmari tribe: bayoneting or impaling the children on swords, raping women, slashing open the abdomens of pregnant mothers, mutilating men's genitalia, and slaughtering the livestock.

Prince Miqren decided to have Salem publicly beheaded. For the others who had signed the petition, the punishment was to be two hundred lashes. These decisions were not announced. No one was informed.

One Friday morning, Awad drove members of his family and some friends to Hayel's largest mosque to attend the midday service. The mosque was full of men in a depressed mood, for all were aware of the plans to privatize grazing lands and they were well aware of the arrest of the protesting shepherds. The imam curtly informed the worshippers that, after the service, they were not to go directly home, but stay and witness the execution of a lawbreaker on the square before the mosque. Awad and his friends wondered who the criminal was. It had been weeks since the last execution; those put to death were usually foreigners, laborers, or servants accused of stealing, fighting, or sexual affairs.

The men left the mosque and assembled on the square. An official went to the middle of the meeting ground, where a platform was already in place, and removed a piece of paper from his shirt pocket. He scanned what he would have to read aloud. Shortly afterward, an armored police van drove through the crowd, and the condemned man was helped out. He was dressed in black clothes and hooded so that no one could identify him. The executioner, with a sharp, curved sword in his left hand, stepped from the cab of the police van and led the hooded victim to the platform. The man who had to read the sentence aloud demanded silence. As deathly quiet descended, the executioner removed the victim's hood.

A scream rang out over the grounds. Awad was screaming to the heavens with every ounce of his strength: "Father! Father! Father!" He ran toward the platform. Two policemen threw themselves on him, overpowered him, and dragged him away. Friends and relatives of Salem jumped forward out of the crowd onto the platform and sought to free the shepherd. Shots rang out. First the police shot into the air, and then at the men who were helping Salem. Five of them fell to the ground. A voice from a crackly loudspeaker ominously warned the crowd to calm down as extra reserves of police and soldiers pulled into the square. They forced the surge of people back from the platform.

An army doctor confirmed that all five men who had tried to rescue Salem were dead. Their bodies were promptly dragged away. Salem was alive but lay unconscious on the platform, struggling for breath. A police officer drew his gun and shot him in cold blood.

The crowd roared with anger.

Lightning fast, the executioner positioned Salem's head on the execution block and swung with full force at his neck. Salem's head rolled away. The crowd screamed for minutes on end: "Murder! Murder! Down with the house of al-Saud! Down with Prince Miqren!"

A few hours after the execution, policemen pulled up at Salem's house in Shaqra. They quickly barricaded the doors and windows, and then bolted the livestock pens, so that neither the people inside nor the animals could flee. Then they poured petrol over the house and the animals and set everything alight. Inside the house were Awad's wife, his young son, his mother, and five of his sisters and brothers. In the livestock pen were over fifty sheep and ten camels. All that was left was a black heap of ruins and endless corpses stinking of pain.

At that time, Awad's grandfather and two of his grandchildren were in Hayel. When the grandfather saw the burned-down home, he sank wordlessly to the ground, pressed his lips tightly together, and then shuddered. Then he got up again, and, supporting himself on his cane, started to limp away, not wanting anyone to see the emotions written on his face. But then he stopped and began to scream. "Allah will avenge us! Allah will avenge us!" It was a cry of defiance, and the crowd that had assembled before the ruins took it up and repeated it in a huge choir of sound. It rolled like thunder in the heat of the midday. Then the grandfather's voice dropped, and he declaimed in a hollow, lost, wavering voice: "Allah is with us . . ." The crowd echoed this, but loudly and with excitement. "Allah is with us!"

I looked around and saw that soldiers had surrounded us with their weapons in hand. They were standing like wax figures and stared at the sky in embarrassment. Awad's grandfather was brought back to Hayel. Since that time, he sits in the house of one of his sons, staring at a military school graduation portrait of Awad, which he holds in both hands. He talks to that picture all day long.

As for what happened to Awad, no one knows where they took him. No one has ever heard from him. No one knows if he is sitting in jail or if he was killed. No one has dared to inquire about his fate. As for the shepherds who signed the petition and were then imprisoned and sentenced to two hundred lashes—they, too, have never been heard of again.

Saudi Arabia doesn't bother to fill its jails with political prisoners or dissidents. Such people are forced into military aircraft and then pushed out when the plane reaches the enormous and forbidding deserts of the south, the "Empty Quarter." It is an ocean of baking-hot sand devoid of human inhabitants and home to poisonous snakes and vultures. The vultures pick the bones clean, and then drifting sand covers the bones.

Faleh, Awad's younger brother, could not live without seeking revenge on Prince Miqren, even if he died in the process. He gathered the surviving sons and relatives of the imprisoned shepherds and planned an attack on the palace in Hayel. They waited until an afternoon in the fasting month of Ramadan. When they stormed the palace, they were amazed to receive little resistance from the guards. The shepherds disarmed them and locked them into a room. All the servants raised their arms over their heads. They told Faleh that the prince and his family had gone on a pilgrimage to Mecca. They weren't there. In one room, the shepherds discovered a Filipino maid who was scrubbing a floor on her hands and knees. She told them where the palace's secret prison was. Her sister, after becoming pregnant, had been murdered there.

Faleh followed her directions and located a tunnel that led from the palace into the hidden prison. No one was in the cells. But next to the cells, they discovered a large hole in the earth that was covered with soft, loose sand. Suspicious, Faleh and two other men excavated the sand with their bare hands. Then, to their horror, they discovered decomposing bodies. Faleh pressed his hands to the sides of his head as though he needed to prevent angry blood from bursting in his veins. He loudly swore to his fellow palace invaders that he would get vengeance for the murder of his father, his brother, and the other shepherds.

Without pausing to free the guards, Faleh gathered his men together and quickly left the palace.

Afterward, Faleh and most of the shepherds went into hiding, sheltered by friends near Hayel. There they await their time for vengeance. I visit him from time to time.

Every evening, as the sun sinks behind the horizon in Hayel, the sky turns blood red for a few moments. Then it is wiped out by deadly black.

CONCLUSION

After reading this book and learning a bit about the barbaric human rights record of the Saudi regime, it is not enough to passively lament and say to yourself, "The Saudi regime is barbaric." Action must be taken. Every one of us must pressure his or her government to take action against the Saudi regime. With our protest we tell the victims, "We have not forgotten you." We also tell the Saudi regime, "Sooner or later, you will fall; you will disappear. Despotic regimes have never survived forever."

The Saudi regime, backed by Wahhabi Islam, a radical, backward orientation of Islam, has been and is still funding jihad, extremist Muslims, and their fanatic Islamic schools and centers across the globe. These breed suicide and car bombers day in and day out.

The war on terror will never be won unless the West forces Saudi Arabia to STOP funding Islamic fundamentalism and exporting jihad. Wahhabism must be banned, and all those atrocious passages that incite hatred, violence, and discrimination must be removed from the Qur'an and Hadith. For further information on these passages, check out: "Is Islam a Violent Faith?" (http://www.familysecuritymatters.org/publications/id.2287/pub_detail.asp), and "Women in Hadith" (http://www.familysecuritymatters.org/publications/id.2752/pub_detail.asp).

Countless Wahhabi chaplains across the globe, especially in the Muslim world, daily preach in mosques and through the media hatred, violence against followers of other religions, and discrimination against women and non-Muslims—all in the name of Allah, the Muslim god. Young brains are stuffed with a politically incorrect and corrupt ideology.

All this must be stopped. All this has nothing to do with religion and much less with religious freedom.

Hatred, discrimination, and violence are crimes against humanity and must be stopped.

In fact, the Saudi regime uses Wahhabism and terror to survive. The majority of suicide and car bombers in Iraq come from Saudi Arabia and are funded by this regime. Additionally, the Taliban terrorists in Afghanistan and Pakistan are stuffed with hatred and violence in madrassas (schools) funded by the Saudis.

The Saudi regime has discovered in Islamic terror a way to survive and distract from its despotism. A democratic and liberal Saudi Arabia would slowly but steadily imply a demand for accountability for the billions of petrodollars that the princes of the regime spend on building lavish palaces and recruiting prostitutes from all over the world.

Furthermore, the Saudi regime refuses to play a constructive role in combating the destructive climate change that is impacting the earth, caused in significant part by Saudi oil from which the regime is making a fortune. The Saudi regime has rejected calls to pay some of its oil revenues to help combat climate change. This is yet another example of how the horror and ills that are perpetuated within Saudi borders affect not just those within the country but also all of us across the globe.

The Saudis' inaction regarding climate change will cause great destruction, but this is not their only threat. The Saudi princes are parasites and a liability in the fight against terror in the region and worldwide. Innocent soldiers and civilians are dying every day in Afghanistan, Pakistan, and Iraq. Yet the culprits, the Saudis, behind the maiming and killing are defiantly and freely roaming the world.

Increasingly, the West loses credibility because it keeps placing economic and geostrategic interests in the front rows, at the expense of human rights and moral principles. However, in the long run, the West can preserve both economic interests and human rights if it acts honestly and actively pursues the implementation and upholding of human rights everywhere, also in Saudi Arabia.

Supporting a regime like Saudi Arabia's for economic and strategic reasons at the cost of human rights is shortsighted and harmful in the long run. A democratic, free Saudi Arabia that respects human rights and religious freedom is the only guarantee for a stable, peaceful, and prosperous Middle East, and a steadfast custodian of Western interests in the region.